ENDORSEMENTS

Deep inhale. Deep exhale. We are in the future. Recovering Black Storytelling in Qualitative Research: Endarkened Storywork is the book that changes everything. Students and scholars of Black Girlhood Studies must read this book as a necessary Afrofuturist present, centering Black girl narrators with theories, ideas, sources, critiques and interpretations that are matters of fact. Recovering Black Storytelling in Qualitative Research: Endarkened Storywork is a transformative genre-defying practice; certainly an antidote to the violence of Black girlhood in service to disciplinary concept. Thankfully, Toliver makes new questions possible and a bolder praxis of what it means to tell a story like you've given time and attention to Black girls who you wholeheartedly trust to turn it out.

Recovering Black Storytelling in Qualitative Research: Endarkened Storywork provides hope in the form of feeling as there is no way to read this book and not feel as it evolves, give weight to the power of uncertainty, and understand the affirmative histories and contexts that made possible this imaginative path of doing scholarship. Toliver's work transgresses the academy, as a writer in community who reveal themselves as possible because of how she has dared to wonder with so much courage alongside Black girls who are not here for the dress codes, on-going injustices, and horrors of misrepresentation. These are challenging times in part because of the commodification of Black girlhood. Toliver gives us limitless Black girlhood and Black girls with no limits.

I am so here for the weird and unlikely things all happening together in this exquisite text pointing us towards Black girl designed futures implicating Black girl diffraction, Endarkened Aruku, and Black girl photosynthesis. Without Toliver's work, we will not experience justice and beauty in its fullest expressions.

—Ruth Nicole Brown, Inaugural Chair and Professor,
Department of African American and African Studies,
Michigan State University

Using BIPOC framing to center Black storytelling traditions at the forefront of qualitative research, S. R. Toliver provides spirit-guided storytelling for educators hoping for a better way to communicate black girls' sociopolitical experiences. She fully and magnificently demonstrates the endarkened storywork she theorizes in her qualitative study of six black girls attending an Afrofuturist workshop in the deep South. A must have book for educators from kindergarten to graduate school.

—Isiah Lavender III, Sterling Goodman
Professor of English, University of Georgia

Recovering Black Storytelling in Qualitative Research is the kind of methodology text that womanist social scientists will celebrate because it affirms, validates, and explicates womanist knowledge production. Stephanie Toliver has shown us what spiritualized, community and culturally rooted, ecologically situated, co-investigative research methodology looks like and how endarkened storytelling can reshape the world in the direction of justice and inclusion through love-based co-constructive imagination, intuition, and inspiration fueled research methodologies. A great addition to any globally conscious methodology bookshelf!

—Layli Maparyan, Professor and
Chair of Africana Studies, Wellesley College

In Recovering Black Storytelling, Dr. Toliver provides a model for creatively and innovatively writing methods of qualitative research. The Endarkened stories blend and center history, identity and our epistemologies as we strive to (re)cover and (re)member our past to move toward an Afrofuturity.

—Dr. Gholnecsar (Gholdy) Muhammad,
Associate Professor of Language and Literacy,
Georgia State University

Within these pages is the weaving of stories, stories that move beyond the pain, stories that hold Black people, their values, their practices, not as an afterthought or an aside, but as central crafters, shapers, and movers of their own destinies and futurities. Stephanie Toliver asks of us to discover new ways to hold and to share stories, ways that center the amazing ways that Black people have forever adapted, while simultaneously retained that which has been core to their being. And in this call, she has created an action—a book where energies are not spent in the countering or in the resisting, no! The energies felt radiate from stories that are nurturing and healing, uplifting and affirming. They are a truth-telling of, by, and through Black brilliance and joy.

—Timothy San Pedro, Associate Professor of
Multicultural and Equity Studies in Education,
The Ohio State University

Stephanie R. Toliver's Endarkened Storywork is the brilliant harbinger of a new generation of scholarship on Afrofuturism, Black speculative fiction, and Black girl literacies in qualitative research. Resting on the foundations of Cynthia Dillard's endarkened feminist epistemology and Jo-ann Archibald (Q'um Q'um Xiiem)'s Indigenous storywork, Toliver demonstrates the emancipatory potential of liberated imagination — "endarkened and whole" (Audre Lorde) — through her unique autoethnographic novelization of her engagement with Black Southern teen girls in a Black speculative storytelling workshop. Endarkened Storywork is one of the finest critical race counterstories I've ever had the pleasure of reading!

Stellar, groundbreaking, and relevant, Dr. Toliver's award-winning research narrative of speculative Black girl dreaming deserves a place on every qualitative research methods syllabus in the 2020s and beyond. At a time when critical race theory and method is being challenged, Endarkened Storywork represents the exciting critical qualitative research scholarship of the (Afro)future.

—Ebony Elizabeth Thomas, Associate Professor and World Fantasy
Award-winning Author of The Dark Fantastic: Race and the Imagination
from Harry Potter to The Hunger Games

"Recovering Black Storytelling" is a masterful use of African/African Diasporic and Indigenous time travelled storytelling and recovery techniques as academic research and method. Stephanie Toliver's well constructed breakdown captures the art and science of the griot and divine feminine wisdom as both practice and method in interrogating the Black lens and experience. The stardust trail of Afrofuturism in the Endarked Storywork process provides amazing context through which to understand Black lives, Black cultures, and works created by Black creatives. People who've found various western research paradigms to be inadequate in interrogating Black cultures and works will be grateful for this highly integrative process. Others, such as myself, are grateful that she provided a way of codifying the practice of interrogation which highlights the lived experience, discovery, and the magical world of story. I look forward to seeing Toliver's work adopted by students and researchers in the near future.

—Ytasha L. Womack, Author, Afrofuturism:
The World of Black Sci-Fi and Fantasy Culture

RECOVERING BLACK STORYTELLING IN QUALITATIVE RESEARCH

This research-based book foregrounds Black narrative traditions and honors alternative methods of data collection, analysis, and representation. Toliver presents a semi-fictionalized narrative in an alternative science fiction setting, refusing white-centric qualitative methods and honoring the ways of the griots who were the scholars of their African nations.

By utilizing Black storytelling, Afrofuturism, and womanism as an onto-epistemological tool, this book asks readers to elevate Black imaginations, uplift Black dreams, and consider how Afrofuturity is qualitative futurity. By centering Black girls, the book considers the ethical responsibility of researchers to focus upon the words of our participants, not only as a means to better understand our historic and current world, but to better situate inquiry for what the future world and future research could look like. Ultimately, this book decenters traditional, white-centered qualitative methods and utilizes Afrofuturism as an onto-epistemological tool and ethical premise. It asks researchers to consider how we move forward in data collection, data analysis, and data representation by centering how Black girls reclaim and recover the past, counter negative, and elevate positive realities that exist in the present, and create new possibilities for the future.

The semi-fictionalized narrative of the book highlights the intricate methodological and theoretical work that undergirds the story. It will be an important text for both new and seasoned researchers interested in social justice. Informed and anti-racist researchers will find Endarkened storywork a useful tool for educational, cultural, and social critiques now and in the future.

S. R. Toliver is Assistant Professor of Literacy and Secondary Humanities at the University of Colorado, Boulder. Her scholarship centers the freedom dreams of Black youth and honors the historical legacy that Black stories and Black imaginations have had and will have on activism and social change.

Futures of Data Analysis in Qualitative Research
Series Editor: Kakali Bhattacharya
University of Florida

The books in the series *Futures of Data Analysis in Qualitative Research* document the various ways in which qualitative researchers approach data analysis within the context of qualitative inquiry. The series specifically encourages work done from various intersected margins which focus on ways in which a researcher might have had to break rank with traditions, established practices, or privileged, dominant approaches. The books consider multiple aspects including, but not limited to, role of theory, ethics, positionality, processes and their role in generating insights.

While the emphasis of the series is analysis, books in the series could also subvert how analysis is understood and practiced in qualitative inquiry if established discourses are incommensurable for their specific inquiries. Focusing on non-traditional or reconfiguration of the familiar in analysis, the series encourages books written from various interpretive, critical, deconstructive, or other contemporary orientations. The books not only offer narrative details of qualitative data analysis process with examples but also new ontoepistemic, theoretical, methodological, and substantive knowledge.

For more information about the series or to submit a book proposal, please contact Series Editor k.bhattacharya@coe.ufl.edu.

Volumes in this series include:

Intersectional Analysis as a Method to Analyze Popular Culture
Clarity in the Matrix
Erica B. Edwards and Jennifer Esposito

Decolonial Feminist Research
Haunting, Rememory and Mothers
Jeong-eun Rhee

Recovering Black Storytelling in Qualitative Research
Endarkened Storywork
S. R. Toliver

For a full list of titles in this series, please visit: https://www.routledge.com/Futures-of-Data-Analysis-in-Qualitative-Research/book-series/FDAQR

RECOVERING BLACK STORYTELLING IN QUALITATIVE RESEARCH

Endarkened Storywork

S. R. Toliver

Routledge
Taylor & Francis Group

LONDON AND NEW YORK

First published 2022
by Routledge
2 Park Square, Milton Park, Abingdon, Oxon OX14 4RN

and by Routledge
605 Third Avenue, New York, NY 10158

Routledge is an imprint of the Taylor & Francis Group, an informa business

© 2022 S. R. Toliver

British Library Cataloguing-in-Publication Data
A catalogue record for this book is available from the British Library

Library of Congress Cataloging-in-Publication Data
A catalog record has been requested for this book

ISBN: 9780367747305 (hbk)
ISBN: 9780367747336 (pbk)
ISBN: 9781003159285 (ebk)

DOI: 10.4324/9781003159285

Typeset in Bembo
by KnowledgeWorks Global Ltd.

To the Alfredas
To Ashton
To the Endarkened people who dare to dream

CONTENTS

PREFACE

Afrofuturity is qualitative futurity

Long ago, there were no stories in the world. The Sky God, Nyame, owned them all and kept them locked away in a wooden box. Anansi wanted to share these stories with humanity, so he went to Nyame and offered to buy them.

When Anansi reached Nyame, he asked, "What is the price of stories?"

Nyame set a high price, asking Anansi to bring back Onini the Python, Osebo the Leopard, and the Mmboro Hornets. Anansi used his cunning and his wit to capture the great beings and bring them back to Nyame. To capture Onini, he debated aloud whether the python was really longer than a palm branch, as his wife had argued. Overhearing the conversation, the python agreed to help settle the debate, but Onini had trouble keeping his coils straight. Anansi suggested he use his silk to keep Onini fastened to the stick, and so the python was captured.

For Osebo the Leopard, Anansi studied the animal's daily route to the watering hole. Soon, he dug a deep hole, from which the leopard could not escape, directly on Osebo's path. The next morning, Anansi went to the pit, saw the angry leopard, and offered to help him. He got a willow branch and wound his silk around the length of the stick, and when Osebo grabbed it, he was stuck to the branch, stuck to Anansi's sticky web.

The last task was the Mmboro hornets. Anansi walked through the forest until he found the hornet's nest. He took a gourd full of water and poured some on top of the nest. Next, he cut a large leaf from a nearby banana tree and held it up to cover his head. Then, he poured the rest of the water all over himself. While he was dripping, he called to the hornets to warn them about the coming rain and offered his gourd as a hiding place from the downpour. When all the hornets were in the gourd, he wrapped his silk around it, trapping them inside.

When all the tasks were complete, Anansi went back to Nyame to obtain his prize. The Sky God recognized Anansi's work and called upon his nobles to witness the spider-man who was able to do what no others had done before. Loudly, he said, "Anansi, many have tried and failed, but you have done it. From this day onward, all stories belong to you, and whenever a story is told, one must acknowledge that it is an Anansi tale."

When Anansi brought the story box to his home, he and his wife learned each one and eagerly shared them with all who would listen. And so, stories came to Earth because of the great wisdom of Anansi. To Anansi, all stories belong.

This is my story which I have related. If it be sweet, or if it be not sweet, take some elsewhere, and let some come back to me.

Remembering Anansi

My mother was my first storyteller. Through story, I learned about who she was, and I began to understand the deep-rooted communal connections cultivated by my grandmother and grandfather as well as those who came before them. These stories preserved my family history and ensured that I began my life with the foundation of my people. They helped me locate myself amongst the legacy of my family, enhancing my view of self, others, and the world. They helped me bond with my family, those I had met and those I had not. Sometimes, they validated my experiences or provided a level of catharsis when I had a bad day. Other times, stories were an educational tool that helped me learn to read and tell my own stories. Through the masterful storytelling of my mother, I began my storying apprenticeship. However, as I grew older, those stories and my storytelling ability were not a priority, as my K-12 experiences centered argumentative and explanatory writing. We read narratives, but we didn't write them. So, I chose to forget how to engage in the work of story.

Dillard (2006) said, however, that in spiritually guided qualitative research, "we are visited by powerful desires in the course of our work, desires that we can't explain but that almost mysteriously move us to do something we never imagined" (p. 81). When I first came to this project, I couldn't figure out why I was so passionate about storying my research. In some ways, I just knew I *had* to. Now, I realize my spirit was the force pushing me to remember. My ancestors were guiding me back to the work of story. The powerful desire was guided by storying roots intricately entwined with the history of Black people.

Thus, I begin this work with an Anansi story because it's important to start with this history. Storytelling is an essential component of Black existence, a component so integral to life that many African nations had their own storytellers, or griots, who acted as teachers, genealogists, historians, advisers, exhorters, witnesses, and praise-singers (Hale, 1998). The griot was not only central to West African life, responsible for cultivating their verbal artistry, but also in charge of completing various tasks that fostered intergenerational connections and encouraged the remembrance of people's histories, communities, and homelands. By ensuring people's stories were never forgotten, griots engaged in sacred work.

Black storytelling traditions traveled past the door of no return and across oceans to reach the land now called the United States. As Champion (2003) wrote, "despite the horrors of slavery, Africans (now African Americans) still told stories to comfort, teach, and record history in their new home...The storytelling traditions continued from slavery through Jim Crowism, to the Civil Rights movement, and on to present-day America" (p. 3). In other words, my ancestors retained their stories, refusing to let whiteness destroy their connection to the past and to their homelands. Their storytelling traditions were passed from generation to generation despite the horrors of state-sanctioned violence. Their stories continue to teach, to heal, to bring life; therefore, storytelling is not a luxury for Black people, it is vital to our very existence. And yet, our storied lives are often shunned in academia.

Of course, I don't mean storytelling is rejected in the academy. Stories are essential in qualitative research, as scholars consistently gather stories to learn more about the people they are studying. However, researchers are often restricted to gathering stories, not telling them. We are the collectors of tales, charged with the task of stockpiling narratives from our research partners. We don't add our own stories to the work, nor do we tell research stories in different ways, as the structure has already been decided. Still, stories are my lifeblood, the indispensable factor giving me strength and vitality. The stories of my family keep me rooted to my past and present. The stories I hear from Black youth show me possibilities for the future. When I say Black storied lives are ignored in research, I mean the unique storytelling traditions of Black people, those synthesizing Black values and cultural practices, are often disregarded.

Dillard (2000), however, reminds us of the importance of examining culturally indigenous ways of knowing, researching, and writing by calling for the validation of knowledge produced in alternative sites like literature, poetry, and music. She, along with her colleagues Abdur-Rashid and Tyson (2000), further remind us that in Black communities, other genres are used to convey meaning, not just research essays "couched in the traditional communicative pattern of Eurocentrism" (p. 452). That is, Black people have historically used numerous methods to express meaning even if academia tries to restrict us from accessing or using these methods. Thus, it is vital that researchers not only consider new epistemological stances but also new ways of representing research, those that honor the storied traditions of Black people.

To answer this call, I offer the term, *Endarkened storywork*, as a new possibility for qualitative research, one that hinges on Black storytelling traditions and honors alternative ways of thinking about, doing, and writing scholarship. This methodology is built from the confluence of Endarkened feminist epistemologies (Dillard, 2000), Indigenous storywork (ISW) (Archibald, 2008), and Afrofuturism (Womack, 2013), and it allows space for storytelling through fiction, honoring the ways of griots who were the scholars of their African nations. Furthermore, Endarkened storywork is grounded in stories like the Anansi tales. Enslaved Africans "adapted their former home stories to hit the needs of their present home, thereby creating the Anansi stories" (Champion, 2003, p. 3). Similarly, I call upon Endarkened storywork to honor Black storytelling traditions while also adapting the work to the needs of my present home in academia. Endarkened storywork precedes enslavement and predates the existence of a "structured" academic space. So, in this book and in this moment, I reclaim my history, excavating the storied ways of my ancestors to recover and remember what I have been taught to forget. Through this work, I make myself whole, stitching together parts of me that have been ruptured by the consistent need to place standard research documents above my desire to witness, to exhort, to sing praises, to tell stories.

Leaning on my ancestors: theory in the work

Endarkened feminist epistemology (EFE) allows space for alternative ways of knowing, and it also investigates and challenges what is deemed justifiable in research. ISW is a methodology that hinges upon Indigenous storytelling and argues for an expansion of research practices that allows for alternative sites of research and method. Afrofuturism is a cultural aesthetic that honors the speculative thinking of Black people and challenges traditional conceptions of time, place, and being. Although they may seem to begin in different disciplines, they're connected through their commitment to stories and storytelling, to alternative sites of knowledge and being, and to honoring the spiritual within the everyday lives of people whose stories have been discounted in traditional academic settings.

Endarkened feminist epistemology (EFE)

EFE (Dillard, 2000) provides an alternative site of existence in the academy, as it implores researchers to rejoin and reclaim their cultural and historical roots. Dillard (2012) argued that Black women must restore our cultural memories and learn to remember the activities, communal experiences, and spiritual traditions we have been encouraged to forget. In remembering, we return to that which was stolen, that which we have been forced or seduced into ignoring. In remembering, we center our full selves, heal and uplift our communities, and create new worlds in which we might live life more fully. In remembering, we rupture traditional ideologies and standard paradigms to grasp at the roots of who we are and how we've come to know ourselves, others, and the world.

Using the word "Endarkened" instead of "enlightened" was a deliberate and essential choice, as the concept of enlightenment dominating social science research moves against Black cultural ways of being and knowing. Hedge (1998) explained the legacies of enlightenment on qualitative research as:

> (a) the grand rationalistic view of science where truth about reality can be 'positively' established by uncovering causal explanations, (b) reality [as]

an objective structure that can be uncovered and understood, (c) the valorization of objectivity in the research process and the separation of the
researcher and researched, and (d) the view of the subject as a bounded,
autonomous individual.

(pp. 277–278)

The legacy Hedge described limits not only what can be considered research
but also who is considered a researcher and how research should be conducted
and written. However, by rejecting "enlightened," EFE intrinsically discards the
traditional canon of Eurocentric research and chooses to liberate the mind by
allowing space for different truths about reality—truths that refuse objectivity,
require community, and remember responsibility.

A research of responsibility, as Dillard (2006) defined it, demands scholars be
accountable to the people and communities with which we engage. It's an offer
"to become aware of multiple ways of knowing and doing research [and it is]
available to those serious enough to interrogate the epistemological, political,
and ethical level of their work" (Dillard, 2000, p. 663). Interrogation is not
used lightly, for EFE requires us to closely, and sometimes aggressively, examine ourselves (our motives, methods, and reports) and engage deeply with the
community we are studying in ways that are not always valued within traditional research paradigms. In fact, EFE renounces the positivistic, social con-
structionist, critical, and postmodern paradigms that frame qualitative research
and centers a paradigm of spirituality, one in which the researcher's scholarship
serves humanity and the self, seeks creativity and healing, and centers peace and
justice (Dillard, 2006; Okpalaoka & Dillard, 2011). In this way, EFE is not light
work. It requires Black folx and other folx of color to go against traditional ideas
uplifted in higher education. It requires us to return to our roots, to our communities, and to ourselves even when we've been taught to leave our histories at
the academic door of no return.

The politics of refusal EFE demands is essential to Endarkened storywork, as
this methodology rebuffs traditional methods of data representation and allows
space for the creative and cathartic use of fiction as a means to be responsible
to the communities we work with and for. Smitherman (1977) noted that the
Black storytelling tradition is so strong within Black communities it infiltrates
everyday conversation. She further stated that story provides Black people with
a way to condense broad, theoretical observations about life into concrete narratives. These narratives include ghost stories, general human-interest stories, origin
stories, and folk tales, and each retelling "recreates the spiritual reality for others"
(p. 150). Endarkened storywork is emboldened by the spiritual work of EFE and
Black storytelling and attempts to infiltrate the "hegemonic norms of reporting"
(Dillard et al., 2000, p. 452) that currently surround academia. The embeddedness
of storytelling in Black people's lives means researching responsibly would require
storytelling in research, from our data collection to our data representation, especially when working with Black populations.

Ultimately, Endarkened storywork is one way of showing we are serious enough—dedicated enough—to making space for other ways of thinking, knowing, interpreting, and representing our work. It centers community by relying on communal ways of being and knowing rather than committing to becoming the autonomous individual uplifted by the enlightenment. It remembers responsibility by forcing us to interrogate our writing and consider how it aligns with or against methods used by the communities we are blessed to work with. It refuses objectivity by acknowledging that the basic belief system guiding people's worldviews are different based on one's background as well as their social and cultural heritage. It acknowledges spirituality as a conceptual framework by honoring the sacred work of story and storytelling woven into the intricate fabric of Black life. It recognizes that even if these ideals are not integral to the Western ethical framings solidified by the Institutional Review Board (IRB), we must remember that we can't easily bypass subjectivity, responsibility, or spirit because we are beholden to a community much greater than those formed within our institutions.

Indigenous storywork (ISW)

Endarkened storywork builds directly from the labor and legacy of ISW, a term Jo-ann Archibald, Q'um Q'um Xiiem, from the Stó:lō and St'at'imc First Nations created. ISW is a theoretical, methodological, and pedagogical framework that centers the making of stories, the telling of stories, and the cultural understandings necessary to make meaning from stories. To access this framework, it requires us to refuse a focus on Eurocentric knowledge processes and center teachings of respect, reverence, responsibility, reciprocity, holism, interrelatedness, and synergy (Archibald, 2008). According to Archibald and Parent (2019), making and telling stories requires the researcher to do the following: (a) listen deeply to our research partners, ourselves, and our world (respect); (b) attune to our inner beings, to those around us, and to the topic being discussed (reverence); (c) consider the essence of stories and the values and beliefs guiding them (responsibility); and (d) if given the authority, ensure the stories are told to others (reciprocity). Additionally, gaining the cultural and spiritual understandings necessary to make meaning from stories demands that researchers do the following: (a) create space in the mind, heart, body, and spirit to be open to questions and feelings that arise from stories (holism); (b) consider the connections between the storyteller, story listener, and story (synergy); and (c) locate links between the story and listener's personal life experience (synergy). Basically, ISW requires the researcher to put in spiritual-, communal-, and self-work.

The focus on work is essential, as Archibald (2008) recalled that at Stó:lō cultural gatherings, the spokesman alerts guests to the beginning of the activities and calls for them to pay attention by saying, "My dear ones, our work is about to begin" (p. 4). This statement uses the pronoun "our" to note that the storyteller isn't the only one doing work; instead, the collective is engaging in the work of story—the story, the storyteller, and the story listener. Ngāti Awa and Ngāti Porou scholar, Linda Tuhiwai Smith (2012) said, "the story and storyteller both serve to connect the past with the future, one generation with the other, the land with the people, and the people with the story" (p. 146). Anishinaabe writer, Gerald Vizenor (1987), stated that the story listener is vital, as the story cannot work without a participant to actively listen. Thus, all involved in the storying process are responsible for contributing to the futurity of a people, for creating reciprocal relationships that will ensure stories will live through them. By letting listeners know the work is about to begin, the spokesperson is ensuring that people pay attention to the story as they will be involved or impacted by what is said and told (Archibald et al., 2019). In this way, storying is a serious matter, one that requires a great amount of effort on the part of all who are engaged in the work.

In detailing ISW, Archibald (2008) said her goal wasn't to generalize the methodology as one that encompassed the storying methods of all Indigenous peoples, but she believed the principles could "act as a catalyst for examining and developing other storywork theories" (p. 140). To this point, scholars have studied the storywork methods of Indigenous peoples across the globe (Archibald et al., 2019; Windchief & San Pedro, 2019). Still, few scholars have discussed the storywork of Black communities. Coles (2020) coined the term, Black storywork, which deviates from ISW in its focus on how Black people counter society's rejection of Black life. Specifically, he defined Black storywork as "the individual or collective stories, which emerge from the lived experiences of Black people and communities that uses Black knowledge/s as a tool to extend and author oneself beyond the conditions of anti-Blackness" (p. 4). With this framing, Coles specifically named the Black-centric storytelling situated within his research and centered the everyday stories of Black peoples in hopes to counter negative projections surrounding Black life. I agree with Coles about the need for terms highlighting the specific storytelling methods and strategies of Black people, but although Endarkened storywork aligns with Black storywork, there are critical differences guiding the methodology.

Specifically, like ISW, Endarkened storywork is a method of nurturing, not countering. Numerous scholars share that the Black storying tradition is about healing, nurturing, affirming, and truth-telling (Champion, 2003; Gibbs Grey & Harrison, 2020; Hua, 2013). Banks-Wallace (2002) discussed how Black storytelling showcases the enduring commitment of a people to "nurture a unique, spiritually based culture in the midst of an oppressive environment" (p. 413). We nurture in spite of oppression. We experience and cultivate joy despite dystopic realities. Of course, countering negative stories can be a part of the healing process, but Endarkened storywork chooses to "remember the things we've learned to forget, including engagements and dialogues in cross-cultural community that theorize our varying spiritualities, experiences, definitions, and meanings" (Dillard, 2012, p. ix). It chooses to remember our joy, our community, our connection to the land, our traditions. As a radical response to traditional research methods and to anti-Black portrayals of Black existence, Endarkened storywork chooses life, community, nurturing, spirituality, and love. It allows Black people to consider anti-Blackness if they want to, but it doesn't require us to focus upon it.

Endarkened storywork is grounded by ISW through its consideration of the sacred, nurturing ideals of story and storytelling. It requires that we listen to our research partners, ourselves, and our world, considering the connections between the story, storyteller, story listener, cultural traditions, and spiritual relationships even in a field that asks us to view people as bounded, autonomous individuals. It asks us to consider the values and beliefs behind the stories of our research partners and create enough space within ourselves to welcome our feelings and questions about the stories we receive even when traditional approaches ask us to establish objective truths and eschew the subjective nature of feeling and belief. It demands that we locate ourselves within the work and consider the ethical responsibility we have to engage in reciprocity and reverence, to refuse the traditional separation between the researcher and the researched. It uplifts the storied lives of people whose narrative traditions have been ignored in qualitative research. Endarkened storywork signifies the importance of Endarkened stories and reminds readers that our stories are to be taken seriously.

Afrofuturism

The creation and distribution of short stories like "The Goophered Grapevine" (Chesnutt, 1887) and "The Comet" (Dubois, 1920) as well as novels like *Imperium in Imperio* (Griggs, 1899) and *Black No More* (Schuyler, 2011) suggest that Black authors have produced and published speculative fiction for more than a century. Yet, even though Black authors in the early 1900s were writing and publishing speculative fiction, their work wasn't considered as prestigious as the work of realistic fiction authors (Brown, 2014). The late 20th century, however, brought more attention to Black speculative fiction, as Octavia Butler, Charles Saunders, Steve Barnes, and Samuel Delaney assumed prominence. Still, there were few who could claim the same notoriety. The lack of published Black science fiction authors prompted author and cultural critic, Mark Dery (1994), to pose a critical question: "Why do so few African Americans write science fiction, a genre whose close encounters with the Other—the stranger in a strange land—would seem uniquely suited to the concerns of African American novelists?" (pp. 179–180).

Dery's (1994) query prompted him to examine "speculative fiction that treats African-American themes and addresses African-American concerns in the context of the twentieth-century technoculture" (p. 180). This was the definition he used to coin the term, Afrofuturism. To further explain his concept, he provided examples of Afrofuturism through the paintings of Jean-Michel Basquiat, the graffiti of Rammellzee, the comics of Milestone Media, and the music of Sun Ra, Jimi Hendrix, George Clinton, and Herbie Hancock. In addition to these examples, he included interviews with Samuel Delaney, Greg Tate, and Dr. Tricia Rose about race in science fiction writing and fan communities. He used the interviews to further elucidate his notion of Afrofuturism by tying his initial question to the responses of Black scholars and authors. Thus, in coining the term and providing examples and commentary, Dery (1994) defined Afrofuturism and cast his terminology into the public sphere.

Various academics grappled with the concept of Afrofuturism. Some aligned with Dery's (1994) description, but many believed the initial definition wasn't enough to encompass the Afrofuturistic work of Black people. Specifically, Nelson (2000) reasoned that the original explanation was limiting because it centered Black speculative artistry as reactive, rather than creative and constitutive. Lewis (2008) argued that scholars must renegotiate the boundaries between technology and spirituality because "one can easily view Santeria as a kind of technology designed to facilitate communication with higher powers" (p. 142). Anderson (2016) claimed that a focus on Western technology marginalized alternative cultures that believed technology was a combination of earthly and unearthly production. Ytasha Womack (2013) added that Afrofuturism is more than a focus on technoculture, as it values nature, healing, creativity, and mysticism alongside science and technology. Similarly, Lavender (2019) broadened the focus of Afrofuturism by acknowledging that Black people "function as *living* circuits per se when race is understood as a 'labor-based' technology dependent on dehumanization" (p. 6); therefore, Afrofuturism isn't just relegated to Black production, but to Black life as a whole. Essentially, Afrofuturism is hard to define, as many people across public and academic scholarship have attempted to grasp the word's meaning for themselves.

As I consider an operational definition, I describe Afrofuturism as a cultural aesthetic in which Black authors create speculative texts that center Black characters in an effort to reclaim and recover the past, counter negative and elevate positive realities that exist in the present, and create new possibilities for the future. I avoid labeling Afrofuturism as a genre because many Black authors use a hybridization of speculative genres (Hoydis, 2015), so their work does not conform to one specific category. I also categorize Afrofuturism as an aesthetic to centralize the features people use and allow those features to change depending on the context. This ensures that people can focus upon stylistic elements prominent in science fiction (e.g., enhanced technology), fantasy (e.g., magic), African cosmology (e.g., Yoruban deities), history (e.g., Civil Rights Movement), and realism (e.g., popular culture) in examining stories and other speculative texts. Last, classifying Afrofuturism as an aesthetic allows space to view the term as a mode of communication, one that allows us to consider how Black people have used science fiction, fantasy, cosmology, history, and story to communicate the intricacies of Black thought and existence across space and time.

Afrofuturist technologies

Although there is much discussion on how Afrofuturism is presented in books, television shows, architecture, music, and movies, there is limited discussion about the Afrofuturistic realities that exist in the everyday, in the mundane. However, Afrofuturism is a way of grappling and understanding Black realities across time and space, giving us a way to better understand Black freedom dreams, so it is vital to consider how Afrofuturism exists in the everyday lives of Black people. Lavender's (2019) framing of freedom technologies is essential for this reconceptualization of Afrofuturist thought. He argued that:

> any kind of practical knowledge that helps Black people solve problems with their environment and in their society, abetting their escape from physical and psychological bondage and thereby allowing them control of their own actions, qualifies as a freedom technology.
>
> (p. 26)

In this way, literacy, spirituality, language, trickery, coding, communal connection, intergenerational links, dance, hope, imagination, and joy can all be classified as technologies of freedom, as Afrofuturist practices. Reading and writing help preserve and revitalize Black traditions. Spirituality makes space for alternative truths that uplift our connections to the land, our histories, our communities, and ourselves. Linguistic technologies permit the creation of coded messages containing hidden meanings that can only be decoded with secret knowledge. Trickster technologies allow us to use our knowledge to manipulate our environment toward our own benefit. Joyful technologies allow us to fortify our well-being through jubilation, laughter, and happiness even during difficult times. Technology is the application of scientific knowledge for practical purposes, and these freedom technologies showcase the numerous ways Black people employ their knowledge for the practical purpose of freedom.

The Afrofuturist technology of trickery is embedded in the story of Anansi, as the spider-man played upon the python's hubris to tie him to the stick, studied the actions of the great leopard to catch him in the pit, and used his knowledge of the hornets' fear of rain to trap them in the gourd. In each instance, Anansi engaged in trickster technologies to outthink those who were deemed more powerful. Like Anansi, enslaved Africans used these trickster technologies to outwit slave owners. Marshall (2009) wrote that enslaved peoples used the skills of Anansi in their daily lives by feigning stupidity, using deceit, utilizing gossip and rumor, and engaging in scams as a means to outmaneuver the plantation owners. They used these "Anansi Tactics" (Marshall, 2009, p. 128) to lower the owners' expectations, reduce their suspicion and watchfulness, protect their loved ones and themselves, and make their way to freedom. In this way, Anansi tales metamorphosed to meet the needs of enslaved Africans, ensuring that "trickster technologies continue[d] to challenge a white patriarchal and supremacist culture and supply [Black people] with hope through the networked Black consciousness" (Lavender, 2019, p. 103). Anansi stories, then, are sustained through the network of Black tradition, allowing Black peoples to reclaim and recover our past and utilize trickster technologies across generations.

The metamorphic capabilities of Anansi are critical. Marshall (2007) acknowledged that Anansi's fluidity cast doubt on what could be considered true and real by negotiating and uplifting ideals of creative chaos and freedom from oppression. She further exclaimed that the malleability of Anansi and other trickster characters is captivating because:

> they continually change to suit the needs of the people who keep them alive. Embodiments of resistance and opposition, universal archetypes, testers and extenders of boundaries, personifications of liminality and crossroads, they exist in a perpetual stream of transformation...These tricksters of West African origin are symbols of freedom and revolt who will continually be adapted to new circumstances as they can never be fixed, captured, or contained.
>
> (Marshall, 2010, p. 190)

Anansi, like so many Black folk characters, is a medium, a being who exists between the spiritual and the earthly realm. His ephemeral existence allows Black people to continuously transform him to fit our needs. Thus, we use Anansi tales to grasp at impracticality, clutch the currently unreal, and approach different truths. We pass on Anansi stories and Anansi tactics to approach the dangerous zone, the place that moves beyond the bounds of possibility, of custom, of perceived order. Lavender (2019) explained that spiritual technologies produce knowledge by recognizing different truths and applying that knowledge for the purpose of freedom. Like Dillard (2006), Lavender acknowledged how enlightened thinkers discredited the spiritual as scientific, thus removing African scientific thought from Western ideals. However, as Dillard (2012) explained, we must remember what we've been seduced into forgetting and embrace the revelatory and revolutionary aspects of spiritual work that guided our ancestors. Anansi stories create the space for Black people to think otherwise, to imagine beyond the boundaries created for us in life and in research. They ask us to break the confining chains of Eurocentric tradition and revolt against impossibility to create new opportunities for our collective futures.

Naturally, creating new possibilities and dreaming otherwise opens space for dissension and critique, especially when we consider how "good research" is supposed to separate the mind, body, and spirit. However, Anansi stories showcase the intricate work essential to creating, telling, and learning from story, and they present a command of language, thought, and analysis essential to "good research." For instance, Anansi tales were often told in the slave quarters, but sometimes, they were told in the presence of white plantation owners. The public versions of the narrative—the stories white people could hear—often hid the rebellious elements embedded within these stories. Marshall (2009) described how Anansi tales were used to discuss the foundation of greed and discrimination on the plantation while also uplifting defiance and lawbreaking. Stating these aims explicitly was dangerous in mixed company, but storytelling masked the underlying meanings. Black people listening to the story would engage in code-breaking to figure out the hidden message and use that knowledge toward the process of freedom. In this way, Black people used Anansi stories as linguistic technology, where the storyteller could design a story that included intricate coding mechanisms, and the story listener would be called to break the codes by opening their spirits to questions and feelings created by the story and locating connections between the story and their personal lives. In doing so, Black people engaged in scientific processes, where they had to listen, make observations, form connections, and test their newfound knowledge. They engaged in "good research." Lavender (2019) stated that "Afrofuturism *is* a bit like code-breaking in that spoken and written languages can mean very different things in Black America across time. Linguistic coding, or wordplay, becomes a key component that ensures Black survival" (p. 35). Anansi stories use coding technologies to counter negative and uplift positive realities and provide practical survival methods to all story listeners, even when those listeners are generations apart.

I share these technologies of Afrofuturism to show the work of story, storyteller, and story listener, and I connect these technologies to the Anansi tales to engage in cultural memory, to participate in a process of (re)membering that responds to the forced division of mind, body, and spirit. Black people have harnessed Afrofuturist technologies to combat socially constructed realities that converge Black identities with calamity and to contest stories where imaginative spaces associate the persistence of Black lives with a disastrous future (Yaszek, 2006). We've also used these technologies to disrupt modern ideologies that restrict Black imaginations and to provide a space for us to envision the tools necessary to subvert oppressive paradigms and create equitable futures (Eshun, 2003; Hopkinson & Nelson, 2002). Endarkened storywork acknowledges the work of Afrofuturist freedom technologies and considers how Afrofuturism can serve as a medium through which Black scholars can delve into our histories, witness the stories of others, sing the praises of our people, and imagine new ways of building and sustaining our communities now and in the future. It considers what it means to remember the cultural stories that shaped us and use these stories in a process of freedom from traditional research methods. Endarkened storywork is a freedom technology, an Afrofuturist project that allows me to use the technologies of my ancestors to help me escape the academic bondage of Eurocentric writing and make space for the storied, spiritual work essential to Black life in the past, present, and future.

Becoming a story listener

The story within this book includes truths from aspects of my personal life story as well as the stories of six Black girls—Amber, Avenae'J, Bailey, Talyn, Terrah, Victoria—who joined me in an Afrofuturist writing workshop that took place at Deep Center in Savannah, Georgia. The workshop consisted of eight meetings over the course of two months in the summer of 2019. The first six workshops began with a discussion focused on narrative elements like plot, characterization, and conflict. Rather than telling the girls my definitions of these terms, I asked them questions like, "What draws you in to a story's plot?" or "What elements are needed for you to care about the conflict in the story?" In this way, I centered the girls' thinking rather than focusing on how I interpreted the terms. The discussion was followed by the reading of a speculative fiction text, including excerpts from *The Jumbies* (Baptiste, 2015), *Parable of the Sower* (Butler, 1993), *Mother of the Sea* (Elliott, 2017), and "Sera" (Yoon, 2017). We read passages from each text to investigate how these narratives aligned or differed from our earlier conversation about plot elements. After reading, we engaged in a short writing task grounded in exercises from Parker Rhodes' (1999) book on fiction writing for Black authors, focusing explicitly on how we can move from the known world to the imagined. At the end of the workshops, we engaged in collective writing and sharing time, where we took insights from our group discussions, mentor texts, and writing exercises to outline story elements for our speculative short stories.

During these workshops, I engaged in a methodology of surrender (Dillard, 2006) by centering a research process that focused on the synergy between the girls and me. I surrendered the principles of the enlightenment, those that centralized objectivity, disconnectedness, and inequity, and fortified my connection with the girls. We sat down at the writing table together. We talked and wrote together. We listened to each other's aspirations, hopes, and dreams, and we strengthened our relationship across difference in age, geographical location, and class. In rejecting a clear divide between researcher and researched, we were able to develop a more reciprocal and synergistic relationship, one that placed the needs of the group over my personal research agenda. Of course, I was still collecting data to complete the project, but I made space for conversation to flow wherever it needed to go, rather than silencing their voices to collect the data I needed. When they decided it was time to change the subject or move on to a different activity, I listened to them and didn't attempt to "get them back on track." I listened to them talk about their interests and their lives, and I altered my daily plans to better align with what they wanted and needed from our time together. As I listened to them and engaged in conversation, I was transformed. Collectively, we wrote speculative texts that explored possibilities for the present and the future, but individually, I was learning more about myself as a researcher, as a speculative fiction fan, and as a person. In the end, I searched again (re-searched) for what it meant to be a researcher, for what it means to engage with and listen to Black girls.

I audio and video recorded our time together, and I scanned each writing exercise, story outline, and short story. The girls wanted to keep their work and possibly build on it in the future, so I made sure that at the end of the workshop, they had all of their materials in their possession. I had a lot of information to work with and a lot of real-life experience to draw from as I worked to answer my research question which centered how Black girls might use written and oral storytelling to discuss, critique, and subvert experiences with social in/justice. Before I could engage in analysis, I had to become more connected to their stories. I read and reread their written materials to better situate myself in their real and imagined worlds. Rather than just reading the transcript, I continuously listened to the whole of our workshop sessions and our individual interviews while walking, driving, and sitting. I engaged with the realistic stories they told by revisiting news articles and television shows they mentioned. I looked deeper into their stories by investigating the history of Savannah and some of the cultural aspects they discussed. I sat with their speculative fiction stories to try and interpret the evidence of things unseen. This meant I had to align myself not only with the girls but also with the world, with nature, and with Spirit. Once aligned, I was able to make connections between each girl's realistic and fiction stories. I was able to see how they metaphorically positioned real-life events in their speculative fiction stories. I was able to see the linguistic technologies employed to discuss their experiences in the world.

It was at this moment that I ran into a spiritual dilemma. When I initially conducted the study, I thought Western academic resources were required for me to be recognized as a "real" scholar. I slipped away from Black-centered thinking, from the work of story, from myself. I forced my work into the shape of narrative research and thematic analysis even though I was forcing myself to move away from the work of story. A revisit to this work compelled me to break open that methodological cage and seek the methods I tried to forget in order to exist in a white-dominated field. When I chose to remember, to search for the hidden methods created by my foremothers and shunned in the contemporary academic field, I realized that the methods guiding me could be subsumed under the Black historical tradition of quilting.

Jaynes (2005) acknowledged that Black quilters used two techniques: sewing scraps of cloth together (piecing) and stitching small pieces of cloth on top of larger ones (appliqué). To many viewers, there is no apparent pattern resulting from these two methods as there is no uniformity, no cohesive color scheme, and no strict lines or boxes. The rejection of conformity makes it seem like the quilt is haphazardly thrown together, but that's because Black quilts require a deciphering technique. Dobard and Tobin (2000) found that enslaved people used quilts to secretly communicate when they were not afforded the benefit of privacy. In fact, many enslaved people used "quilts and quilt patterns to signal times, locations, and directions along the underground railroad" (Lavender, 2019, p. 38). Black Americans used quilts as a form of resistance (Davis, 1998), as a method of kinship building (Cash, 1995), and as a means to tell the story of their lives (Porter, 1990). In other words, quilts provided coded messages that Black people could decipher to obtain freedom, build community, and tell stories. To break the code, to find the message hidden within the layers of the quilt, it was important to follow the threads, to find the hidden moments that brought the disparate pieces together into a collective whole.

As I considered how Black people used quilting to communicate collective experiences across time and space, I returned to the technologies of Black quilt making and worked to find the seam connecting the girls' stories. Just as each piece of a fabric is disparate but connects and adds to the larger quilt, stories can be about an individual, but they can also connect to an experience larger than the individual. My goal wasn't to find themes across the girls' stories so I could fit them into the lines and boxes required by traditional qualitative methods. Instead, my aim was to consider how the girls' individual experiences were connected to the experiences of the other girls, to my experiences as a former Black girl and current Black woman, and to national experiences of Black women and girls. I needed to engage in methodological piecing to uncover how portions of the girls' stories were stitched to together, adding to the larger quilt of Black life. I needed to follow the thread of story.

Following the threads

To chain piece a quilt, the quilting artist often saves time by not cutting the strings, so I took this idea into my data analysis. When I transported the written data, transcribed interviews, and workshop sessions to Atlas.Ti, I pulled on the threads, unraveling the chain until I discovered the raw edges of the fabric. In pulling on the threads, I hoped the bind of traditional qualitative thinking would come undone, allowing space for me to begin anew at the seam. Of course, the labyrinth of intersecting threads was not always easy to follow, so I had to engage in Black deciphering technologies to make my way through the analytical maze. As Lavender (2019) argued, Black "ingenuity, demonstrated in stitching fabric together in covert patterns within an everyday object like a quilt, sometimes undermined white antebellum power…further building a quite literal and functioning networked black consciousness" (p. 39). For my methodological work, I needed undermine white power structures in traditional qualitative research, tap into the networked consciousness and uncover the covert patterns within the everyday talk and storytelling of Black girls.

Eventually, after reading, rereading, and just sitting with and in the data, I found 60 seams that converged on ideas like police/policing, dreaming/imagination, and gender/sexism. As I considered these points, I realized I wasn't engaging in a rigid practice of constructing and combining codes; instead, I was following the patchwork of a global quilt whose construction began well before the present moment. When I started to understand Black life as a quilt, one without uniform, without strict regulation, and without confinement, I began to decipher the messages hidden underneath seemingly disparate stories and experiences. As Black quilts were used to encode cultural knowledge, I began to see how the threads I followed encoded cultural knowledge and memory through everyday talk and story. I began to realize that every pattern, every intersecting line, and every piece of thread was important in my effort to understand the girls and their stories.

Considering the patches

Once I began to see the importance of piecing, of figuring out how the small strips of cloth worked together, I knew it was time to take a step back, to see the small pieces of cloth the girls were stitching onto the larger fabric of their lives.

In stepping back, I was reminded of Harriet Powers, a Black woman who was born into slavery in Athens, Georgia in 1837. Powers "made storytelling a central part of her quilts" (Urban, 2020, par. 3) and her narration and quilting method were distinctive and respected. She imbued spiritual life into her quilts, and this could be seen through "the individual blocks depicting biblical stories, local events, and celestial occurrences" (par. 2). In remembering this history, I was reminded of the fact that each piece of fabric stitched onto the larger quilt has a story that must be told. In terms of my own research work, I remembered that although it was important for me to follow the threads and understand the larger connections found within and across the girls' stories, it was also critical for me to maintain their individual stories, to see the intricacies of the individual patches, not just how they operate as a part of the larger whole.

It was here where I began to focus on the girls' everyday stories, acknowledge their heterogeneous lived experiences, and consider their locations within a specific time (2019), history (Black people in the South), and place (Savannah, Georgia). To highlight their individual stories, I relied on Parker Rhodes'(1999) book, *Fiction Lessons for Black Authors*. This may seem like an awkward book to consider in a research context, but it helped me to be responsible with the storied lives of my research partners. Specifically, Parker Rhodes (1999) argues that writers must "limber [their] skills of observing, listening, imagining, and assembling portraits of [the] world" (p. 7). To begin this work, she asks readers to engage in journaling exercises that center community events, community storytellers, family tales, and people worth celebrating.

In writing about community events, she asks readers to describe an occurrence and pay attention to detail—"Is it specific? Are there sounds in your description? Are there colors, textures, smells, tastes? What did you fail to observe? What did you leave out?" (p. 8). When centering community storytellers, she asks readers to listen to the storyteller's voice—the rhythms, tone, cadence, and emotion in their speech—and ensure that their voice is centered, not the voice of the writer. For family tales, she asks the reader to focus on specific objects, like pictures or mementos, and identify the stories attached to the objects while also considering what those stories reveal about the Black spirit. To center a person worth celebrating, she asks the reader to consider the depth of representation—"How does your person dress, talk, move? What do they feel? How can you tell? What outward signs best express their personality? How do they react to touch, sight, taste, and sound? What about them are you celebrating?" (p. 9). Each of these exercises were essential to my understanding of the girls' and their stories.

I listened to the audio, watched the video, and read the transcripts to better understand how each research partner added texture, sound, and color to the workshop space. I focused on the specific contributions of each member and made note of my personal observation failures. For instance, I noticed that I often failed to observe how Bailey's silences ebbed and flowed throughout the workshop as she was getting to know a new group of people. As I came back to this work, I saw that I had failed to consider how her silence also added to texture to the space. To center the girls as storytellers, I listened to the audio and attuned myself to the rhythm, cadence, emotion, and tone of their voices. I considered how Avenae'J, whose voice had a low timbre, often elevated the pitch of her voice when she had increased knowledge about a topic and wanted to share what she knew with the group. To consider family tales, I revisited the data and centered the personal stories they attached to their speculative ones while also considering what they revealed about Black girls' spirits. Last, as this project was a celebration of Black girlhood, I searched through the data to ensure that I considered the depth of their representation by noting how they dressed, spoke, and moved. I watched the videos to focus on their mannerisms and reflect on the numerous ways their personalities showed up in speech and action. I reflected on how and why I celebrated each of them.

To become a story listener, I had to recenter Black quilting. It wasn't enough to group ideas into themes and display them as regimented findings. It wasn't enough to identify when their stories occurred, where their stories took place, and who was involved in their stories. Instead, I had to follow the research threads connecting the girls' experiences to the larger quilt that is Black life. I had to make limber my research skills and enhance how I observed, listened to, imagined, and assembled portraits of the girls' worlds. Relying on Black quilting as method made space for me to engage in the Black networked consciousness. Lavender (2019) stated that "each member of the Black networked consciousness represents a figurative circuit that powers the network by transmitting hope across the transhistoric feedback loop, chaining together the cause and effect of Black experience, and influencing our thoughts in real time" (p. 7). That is, the hope and experiences of Black people are transferred across time and space through a connected link that combines Black pasts, presents, and futures. Thus, the methods I needed to analyze this data were not new, as Black people have passed them down from generation to generation. I just needed to reconnect to the transhistoric feedback loop and rely on historical methods to better understand the contemporary stories of Black girls. The quilting methods of my ancestors influenced my data analysis in real time.

(Re)membering the storyteller

As I analyzed the data, I began to engage in the storying process of Endarkened storywork although I didn't know I was beginning this methodological journey. Due to my training and the seduction of forgetfulness, I tried to force the storywork into the confines of traditional narrative and thematic analytic methods, but it just didn't work. The stories wouldn't bend to the will of traditional Western conceptions of data representation. When I realized those methods were ineffective, I tried to connect the storywork to counterstorytelling (Ladson-Billings & Tate, 1995; Martinez, 2013), attempting to showcase how my fictional data representation provided a way to contradict stock narratives about Black girls and Black life. I noticed, though, that although the story could provide a counter to stereotypical narratives, that wasn't the central purpose of the story I created, nor the stories of the Black girls who participated in the workshop. After many attempts and many failures, I realized my problem was that I was trying to force this work into a mold that already existed. I was trying to compel it to follow the rules within a field that had not yet made space for it to exist.

To think and dream otherwise about the possibilities of data representation, I had to consider not just my findings, but the essence of the girls' stories and the values and beliefs that guided them. I had to reopen my mind, heart, and spirit to consider the connections between me (story listener), the girls (storytellers), and their stories, and I had to make room for my personal life experiences and give myself permission to consider how my life synergistically existed alongside theirs. I had to learn to listen deeply, not just for the purposes of a completed research project, but to ensure I was better attuned to the work of story and the embedded meanings within the work. I had to remember Anansi, remember my history, and remember myself. Engaging in these practices was the only way I could ready myself to truly engage with the stories of the Black girls who were willing to share their words with me. Dillard (2000) asked us to consider how academic discourses might differ for Black women and girls. She also asked if those discourses create new possibilities for research. In remembering, I was better able to see the academic discourses embedded within Black girls' stories and use this knowledge to learn from and create a story that mirrored the scholarly rigor of their narratives. It allowed me to see beyond what exists in qualitative research and imagine what can be. It meant I had to remember that story listening wasn't just important for the data collection and analysis phases. It was also essential for my data representation.

Considering the work that had to be done prior to the creation of the story, I asked myself "what were the alignments necessary to engage in this work?" Or, said another way, "how might other researchers make space within themselves to better engage in Endarkened storywork?" I started with the definition. An alignment is an arrangement in which two or more parts are properly adjusted in relation to each other. I began with the term "alignment" rather than tenet because Endarkened storywork does not embrace the rigidity of a fixed set of principles or beliefs. Like the diverse storytelling practices of Indigenous peoples, Black people within the United States and across the African diaspora utilize multiple story formats. Endarkened storywork makes space for all of them, refusing to place the creative, varied, and nuanced storytelling practices of Black folks into a simplistic, monolithic frame. Still, to ready myself for the girls' stories, I had to ensure my mind, body, and spirit were properly adjusted in relation to the minds, bodies, and spirits of the Black girls who were willing to share their stories with me.

Of course, I acknowledge that refusing tenets but providing alignments may seem counterintuitive, as I am still giving a list some will take up as instructions, principles, or guidelines. However, I provide these alignments as a means to explain the adjustments *I* needed to make to engage in Endarkened storywork. I share *my* process to open space for the experiences and knowings of other researchers who wish to engage in this methodological practice. I share aspects of *my* journey in hopes that it will help others begin their own journeys toward Endarkened storywork. EFE asks us to think about what we learn throughout the research process, and through these alignments; I share how *my* views were pushed and strengthened as a story listener. Thus, this book does not provide a step-by-step guide for engaging with Endarkened storywork, but it does provide details about how I committed myself to this work in hopes that others can think about its use in their own research, analysis, and representation.

(Re)centering Anansi

Before I was able to align myself in other ways, I had to recenter Black ancestral, scholarly practices, which meant I had to think about how Eurocentric research methods seduced me into forgetting Anansi. Black people across the Diaspora transform Anansi to meet their needs. Sometimes, the spider–man has a different name or engages with different spiritual and material entities, but he is still Anansi, and that malleability has ensured Anansi stories have endured across generations. Black peoples across time and space have used Anansi stories to "explain, scrutinize, and question the world around them" (Marshall, 2010, p. 178). In this way, Anansi tales provide a critical, ancestral, and intergenerational method of synthesizing and presenting research findings. However, I did not read about Anansi tactics in school, and these practices were not considered important enough to include in traditional qualitative inquiry courses. Qualitative research had ignored Anansi, and so I had forgotten to consider the importance of Anansi to my own work. To remember my cultural roots as well as the possibilities of alternative data representation, however, I had to recenter Anansi. I had to go back to the stories my mother told me—to the stories my ancestors told each other—and recenter these storytelling practices as research possibilities. Anzaldúa (2015) reminds us that we can't use "old critical language to describe, address, or contain [our] new subjectivities" (p. 4), so I had to remember that Anansi was enough, that the storying methods of my ancestors were enough. I had to remember that my storied ways were enough.

(Re)membering the work of story

In recentering Anansi, I began to think about the complexity of Black storytelling. In his introduction to *19 Necromancers from Now*, Reed (1970) said Black literature "is food for a deep, lifetime study, not something to be squeezed into a quarter or semester as a concession to student demands, nor a literature to be approached one-dimensionally" (p. xxvi). Although Reed specifically discussed literature, this quote aligns with all Black storytelling methods. Particularly, this quote reminded me that Black stories are delicate and must be handled with care and respect. It helped me to remember that story listeners must take the time to honor the work required to create and tell these narratives. It pushed me to consider how Black folks breathe life into their words, how each story carries a piece of the storyteller into the larger world. In remembering, I began to reflect on the fact that I, as a story listener, was now a shareholder of storied life, responsible for ensuring these narratives live on even when I no longer exist in a material form. Reflecting on this great responsibility compelled me to engage in a deep study of story and consider the multiple ways in which history, community, and self are imbued within Black narratives. I had to sit with the girls' stories, practice patience, and embrace ambiguity. I had to remember that my ancestors put in work both as storytellers and story listeners, and it was my job to commit myself to this work as seriously as they did.

(Re)covering Afrofuturist technologies

Lavender (2019) centered the importance of locating "science-fictional elements in non-science fiction texts at the level of language, imagery, and metaphor" (p. 17). In other words, he considered the speculative elements that exist alongside Black people's everyday existences. Recovering Afrofuturist technologies meant I was responsible for studying the language, imagery, and metaphor located within the stories of Black girls' everyday experiences. It meant I had to reconsider the "what" of scientific knowledge and the "how" of technology. It meant I had to reclaim the technologies Black peoples have used across space and time. As I explain above, a freedom technology can be described as any practical knowledge that helps Black people solve problems, escape oppression, and reclaim control. As I engaged with their personal narratives, I noticed how the girls used trickster technologies to outmaneuver oppressive authority figures within and outside of their schools. I learned how they consistently used coding technologies throughout their story retellings to ensure only those with the ability to decipher meaning could understand the multiple implications of their words. I saw how they used spiritual technologies to create space for alternative and imaginative truths about their lives. Seeking the freedom technologies embedded within their real-life stories helped me to better understand the intricate coding mechanisms they employed to engage in a practice of imaginative freedom even in a society that attempts to confine Black imaginations (Thomas, 2019). By reconfiguring traditional conceptions of technology and scientific knowledge through an analysis of their everyday stories, I was better able to see how their speculative stories were literacy technologies in which they imagined responses to their problems, provided ways to escape oppression, and reclaimed control of their futures and imaginations. In learning this, I was better able to represent Afrofuturist technologies in my own storied text.

(Re)visioning who the work is for

This book is published by a traditional publisher, so I understand how this section might be confusing to some readers, but before this book reached the hands of traditional academics, it was read and critiqued by three Black middle school girls. After the workshop, I asked each girl if they would be willing to be paid consultants, and three of the six girls (Amber, Avenae'J, and Bailey) agreed. I created a Google Drive folder, and I uploaded chapters as soon as the section was completed. The girls read and commented on the document, and I used their suggestions and questions to assist me during my revision process. By engaging in this method, the girls were able to read and evaluate the story before anyone else was able to see it. Of course, this work wasn't easy. I had to surrender my storied creation to the wisdom of young Black girls in a society that still refuses to believe in the intellectual expansiveness of Black girlhood. Still, I realized that I wasn't writing this book for traditional academics or an ignorant society. I was writing this book for young Black girls. I was writing to ensure their voices were intwined with my analytical and representational methods. The discourses they employed to review, critique, and suggest differed "from what is traditionally know or spoken of as 'academic'," (Dillard, 2000) but they pushed to me to think more deeply about their stories and about the story I was creating. They demanded a deep understanding of their work and helped me to sit, learn, and grow. Black girls know, and they deserve research that speaks to them, not just about them. As the storyteller, I needed to treat Black girls' stories with care and that meant foregrounding their ideas, their knowledge, their dreams, and their lives.

(Re)integrating joy in data representation

Recentering, remembering, recovering, and revisioning were never-ending processes as I was consistently at war with my traditional qualitative training. I do not use the word war lightly. I was regularly in a state of conflict between different ideologies—those I'd learned within the confines of the academy and those I'd experienced by listening to the stories of my mother and other community members. I wasn't sure I was prepared to win this battle because there were always small voices reminding me of the strict nature of academic research. They reminded me that some traditional academics reject scholarly work that doesn't follow the guidelines laid out by the "real" scholars who construct articles and books using the standards praised within Eurocentric circles. I realized the unyielding criteria constrained my work, especially since the work of story can be cyclical, traversing space, time, and spirit. Stories don't always fit within tight spaces and guiding frameworks.

After fighting myself and my storied work, I began to see the resistance of story, how it consistently pushed back when I attempted to force it into the confines of traditional academic work. Specifically, I remember discussing with a colleague how each chapter aligned with a traditional section of an academic text, but when I tried to clearly delineate each segment, I realized that the sections were blurred. I had an introduction that presented the problem, but the overarching conflict in the story was based on threads I followed across the data.

In this way, I was already showcasing some of my data analysis before I reached the "methods" or "findings sections." After multiple attempts at trying to constrain the story, I just let the story go where it needed to go. I stopped fighting it, and I stopped fighting myself. Once I let go, I was able to experience joy. Dillard (2019) said that Black womanists and feminists experience joy when we feel visible and heard, when we feel respected, and when we feel whole. I felt seen when I allowed space in the story for personal details about my life and experiences. I felt whole because I was able to consider the history of storytelling across Black communities and utilize these methods as a means to present the whole of a research endeavor. I felt joy because I let go of traditional qualitative research methods that no longer served me and the work I was doing. In letting go, I opened space for new possibilities and new methods better aligned with the work I was trying to do.

EFE asked me to consider alternative sites of research, analysis, and representation, and ISW asked me to put in spiritual, communal, and self-work. My spiritual work began with Anansi and the work of Black storytelling. My communal work is located in a rededication to the centering of Black girls, a commitment to understanding the Afrofuturist technologies embedded within the everyday practices of Black peoples, and an excavation of the links created through the Black networked consciousness. My self-work is represented by the continuous state of becoming needed to keep my mind, heart, body, and spirit aligned to the work of story. These alignments and ways of knowing form an epistemological basis for Endarkened storywork and make space for alternative representations of data that are better attuned to the storytelling practices of Black people.

How to read this book

In sharing this book with new readers, my goal is three-fold:

1. Endarkened storywork is built within Black and Indigenous frameworks, and it asks scholars to consider what is lost, forgotten, and erased when we refuse to dream otherwise in qualitative research. So, I hope this book encourages readers to consider alternative ways of knowing, those that are often restricted or rejected in academe.
2. I also hope readers will engage in the work required of a story listener. This means readers must create space in the mind, heart, body, and spirit to be open to questions and feelings that arise; consider the connections between the storyteller (me and the girls), story listener (the reader), and story (the fiction); and locate connections between the story and their personal lives.
3. Last, this book is centered around my idea of Afrofuturism, but readers will notice that even though it is set in the future, the Afrofuturistic elements are represented within the everyday thought and ideas of the characters. This was intentional, as I believe the technoculture of Black folx exists beyond the confines of Eurocentric constructions of technology. I hope readers locate

and analyze the Afrofuturist technologies represented through the characters and consider the technological work that occurs in Black communities throughout the world.

In traditional academic books, there is a general outline of each chapter which details what the reader will find in the text. That's difficult to do in a text constructed as a fictional story because I don't want to give any spoilers. However, I will provide a succinct description of each chapter to assist readers in understanding the general flow of the book. Chapter 1 is an introduction that provides an overview of the worldbuilding extrapolated from the current world. Chapter 2 further explores the theoretical background that guides the text and introduces several characters who metaphorically represent Black womanist/feminist ideals. Chapter 3 contains a lot of information-dumping, as it expands upon the theory and incorporates the literature review. Chapters 4–10 focus on the girls and their stories. Their speculative stories are included, and the words they say within those chapters are those they said during the workshop. The final chapter acts as a discussion section, centralizing my thoughts about the content of the girls' stories, but also a reflection on what we need to do to ensure we no longer asphyxiate Black girls' dreams.

To help the reader better understand how I infused the empirical work of the workshop, the research literature, the real world, and my personal life into each chapter, I have written companion chapters to accompany the fictional ones. Individual companion chapters are included for Chapters 1–3 and 11, and a collective companion chapter is included for Chapters 4–10 to showcase the collectivity of thought across the girls' stories. The companion chapters do not include every detail or thought that went into the creation of the story, but they are meant to assuage those who are less interested in the "what" of story and wish to focus on the "how" and to assist those who struggle to understand some of the linguistic technologies embedded within the text. Ultimately, this book begins with this preface, moves to the fictional text, and ends with explanation chapters for those who want to know more about the story's construction. Because this book is designed in a way that differs from traditional research texts, I offer several possible ways to read it.

- **Read the Fiction; Skip the Companions:** The fictional story comprises the majority of this book. It is Endarkened storywork in action. The companions help to contextualize the chapters, but they are not necessary to create personal or academic meaning from the story.
- **Read the Fiction; Skip Some Companions:** There may be chapters where you want to learn more about the information embedded within the fiction, but there may be other chapters where you are able to locate the connections more easily. Read the companion sections you deem most necessary and don't read the others.
- **Read the Fiction Then Read the Companions:** Endarkened storywork centers the connections created between the storyteller, story listener, and story. With this in mind, one way to read the book is to read the fiction first

and then read the companion chapters. This way, you're not influenced by what I say about the text. Instead, you make space for your own meanings and use the companion sections to build connections between my meanings and yours.

- **Read the Companions Then Read the Fiction:** Because this text is also an academic work, I understand the desire to situate the book within the context of traditional research categories. Reading the companion sections first will allow you to see what elements influenced the whole of the text before you read it.

There are multiple ways to enter into this work, some I listed above and some you will create as you read. However, there is no wrong way to read this book as long as you read the fictional part of the work because that's where the Endarkened storywork thrives. The ability to enter through multiple doors, engage in multiple meaning-making practices, and align the self with the work of story is essential to Endarkened storywork. I have shared my journey and my writing with you, but you must make your own journey through this work. I only hope this preface serves as a guide.

Conclusion

Throughout this preface, I noted how Eurocentric research methods thwarted the creative process that led to this work. I discussed how Black storytelling traditions have been shunned by traditional qualitative methods, how I, as a Black female researcher, have been shunned by traditional qualitative methods. I mentioned the inner war that ignited as I tried to represent the data in a way that honored the girls, my community, and myself. I centered ISW and EFE, methodological frameworks and epistemological stances that exist on the margins of theory and paradigm, and I showcased how this work doesn't exist without them. To do the work, I had to decenter that which has always been centered. I had to recenter Black people and Black histories. I had to recenter Anansi.

Remembering Anansi taught me that although Black storytelling is not a formal part of the qualitative canon, Black storied traditions have and will always persist. Anansi tales are past, present, and future. They have traveled across oceans and through generations to influence the minds of Black people throughout time and space. We have read, told, and learned from these stories, and even though we may not know their history, we do know of their importance. In this way, Anansi tales are part of the Black networked consciousness. We hack the codes embedded within the tales to learn about our past, to consider our present, and to dream of our future. We modify the code to meet our needs and pass on the decoding mechanisms to ensure the hidden meanings are not lost on future generations. We use our freedom technologies to unlock themes of liberation, freedom, and rebellion and use these ideas to fight for freedom in the present in hopes of a better, anti-oppressionist future. The persistence of Anansi tales and tactics across time suggests that Afrofuturity is qualitative futurity. These stories, specifically, and Black storied traditions, generally, have existed and will exist well into the future. Black folx been engaging in this work; qualitative research just needs to catch up.

The Endarkened storywork represented in this book highlights the socio-political concerns of Black girls while simultaneously featuring Black girls as researchers whose stories utilize the past and present to theorize possibilities for the future. It considers the ethical responsibility of researchers to focus upon the storied lives of our research partners and engage with them as story listeners, not only to complete a research endeavor but also to better understand our historic and current world and better situate inquiry for what the future world and future research could look like. Furthermore, this book decenters traditional, white-centered qualitative methods and utilizes Afrofuturism as an onto-epistemological tool and ethical premise that asks researchers to consider how we move forward in data collection, data analysis, and data representation by centering how Black girls reclaim and recover the past, counter negative and elevate positive realities that exist in the present, and create new possibilities for the future. It asks us to consider the technologies Black girls use to create Anansi tales of their own.

References

Anderson, R. (2016). Introduction: The rise of astro-Blackness. In R. Anderson & C. Jones (Eds.), *Afrofuturism 2.0: The rise of astro-Blackness* (pp. vii–xviii). Lexington Books.

Anzaldúa, G. (2015). *Light in the dark/Luz en lo oscuro: Rewriting identity, spirituality, reality.* Duke University Press.

Archibald, J. (2008). *Indigenous storywork: Educating the heart, mind, body, and spirit.* UBC.

Archibald, J., Lee-Morgan, J. B. J., & De Santolo, J. (2019). *Decolonizing research: Indigenous storywork as methodology.* Zed Books.

Archibald, J., & Parent, A. (2019). Hands back, hands forward for Indigenous storywork as methodology. In S. Windchief & T. San Pedro (Eds.), *Applying Indigenous research methods: Storying with peoples and communities.* Routledge.

Banks-Wallace, J. (2002). Talk that talk: Storytelling and analysis rooted in African American oral tradition. *Qualitative Health Research, 12*(3), 410–426.

Baptiste, T. (2015). *The Jumbies.* Algonquin Young Readers.

Brown, K. N. (2014). *Writing the Black revolutionary diva: Women's subjectivity and the decolonizing text.* Indiana University Press.

Butler, O. (1993). *Parable of the sower.* Grand Central Publishing.

Cash, F. B. (1995). Kinship and quilting: An examination of an African American tradition. *The Journal of Negro History, 80*(1), 30–41.

Champion, T. (2003). *Understanding storytelling among African American children: A journey from Africa to America.* Routledge.

Chesnutt, C. (1887). *The Goophered Grapevine: A short story.* The Atlantic. https://www.theatlantic.com/magazine/archive/1887/08/the-goophered-grapevine/306656/.

Coles, J. A. (2020). A BlackCrit re/Imagining of urban schooling social education through Black youth enactments of Black storywork. *Urban Education.* https://doi.org/10.1177/0042085920908919.

Davis, O. (1998). The rhetoric of quilts: Creating identity in African American children's literature. *African American Review, 32*(1), 67–76.

Dery, M. (1994). Black to the future: Interviews with Samuel R. Delany, Greg Tate, and Tricia Rose. In M. Dery (Ed.), *Flame wars: The discourse of cyberculture* (pp. 179–222). Duke UP.

Dillard, C. B. (2000). The substance of things hoped for, the evidence of things not seen: Examining an endarkened feminist epistemology in educational research and leadership. *International Journal of Qualitative Studies in Education, 13*(6), 661–681.

Dillard, C. B. (2006). *On spiritual strivings: Transforming an African American woman's academic life.* State University of New York Press.

Dillard, C. B. (2012). *Learning to (re)member the things we've learned to forget: Endarkened feminisms, spirituality, & the sacred nature of research and teaching.* Peter Lang.

Dillard, C. B. (2019). To experience joy: Musings on endarkened feminisms, friendship, and scholarship. *International Journal of Qualitative Studies in Education, 32*(2), 112–117.

Dillard, C. B., Abdur-Rashid, D., & Tyson, C. A. (2000). My soul is a witness: Affirming pedagogies of the spirit. *International Journal of Qualitative Studies in Education, 13*(5), 447–462.

Dobard, R., & Tobin, J. (2000). *Hidden in plain view: A secret story of quilts and the underground railroad.* First Anchor Books.

Dubois, W. E. B. (1920). *The Comet.* Hachette Book Group.

Elliott, Z. (2017). *Mother of the sea.* Rosetta Press.

Eshun, K. (2003). Further considerations on Afrofuturism. *The New Centennial Review, 3*(2), 287–302.

Gibbs Grey, T. M. D., & Harrison, L. M. (2020). Call me worthy: Utilizing storytelling to reclaim narratives about Black middle school girls experiencing inequitable school discipline. *Equity and Excellence in Education, 53*(3), 1–17.

Griggs, S. (1899). *Imperium in imperio: A study of the negro race problem.* Project Gutenberg. http://www.gutenberg.org/cache/epub/15454/pg15454.html.

Hale, T. (1998). *Griots and griottes: Masters of words and music.* Indiana University Press.

Hedge, R. (1998). A view from elsewhere: Locating difference and the politics of representation from a transnational feminist perspective. *Communication Theory, 8*(3), 271–297.

Hopkinson, N., & Nelson, A. (2002). "Making the impossible possible": An interview with Nalo Hopkinson. *Social Text, 20*(2), 97–113.

Hoydis, J. (2015). Fantastically hybrid: Race, gender, and genre in Black female speculative fiction. *Aglistik: International Journal of English Studies, 26*(2), 71–88.

Hua, A. (2013). Black diaspora feminism and writing: Memories, storytelling, and the narrative world as sites of resistance. *African and Black Diaspora, 6*(1), 30–42.

Jaynes, G. D. (2005). Quilting. In *Encyclopedia of African American Society* (Vol. 1, pp. 672–673). SAGE Publications, Inc.

Ladson-Billings, G., & Tate IV, W. (1995). Toward a critical race theory of education. *Teachers College Record, 97*(1), 47–68.

Lavender, I. (2019). *Afrofuturism rising: The literary prehistory of a movement.* The Ohio State University Press.

Lewis, G. E. (2008). Foreword: After Afrofuturism. *Journal of the Society for American Music, 2*(2), 139–153.

Marshall, E. Z. (2007). Liminal Anansi: Symbol of order and chaos an exploration of Anansi's roots amongst the Asante of Ghana. *Caribbean Quarterly, 53*(3), 30–40.

Marshall, E. Z. (2009). Anansi tactics in plantation Jamaica: Matthew Lewis's record of trickery. *Wadabageri, 12*(3), 126–150.

Marshall, E. Z. (2010). Anansi, Eshu, and Legba. Resistance and the West African trickster. In R. Hoermann & G. Mackenthun (Eds.), *Bonded labour in the cultural contact zone: Transdisciplinary perspectives on slavery and its discourses.* Waxmann.

Martinez, A. (2013). Critical Race theory counterstory as allegory: A rhetorical trope to raise awareness about Arizona's ban on ethnic studies. *The WAC Clearinghouse, 10*(3), 6–7.

Nelson, A. (2000). Afrofuturism: Past future visions. *Color Lines (Spring)*, 34–37.

Okpalaoka, C. L., & Dillard, C. B. (2011). Our healing is next to the wound: Endarkened feminisms, spirituality, and wisdom for teaching, learning, and research. *New Directions for Adult & Continuing Education, 131*, 65–74.

Parker Rhodes, J. (1999). *Free within ourselves: Fiction lessons for Black authors*. Doubelday.

Porter, E. (1990, 05). Faith Ringgold: Every quilt tells a story. *Essence, 21*, 78.

Reed, I. (1970). *19 necromancers from now*. Doubleday.

Schuyler, G. S. (2011). *Black no more*. Dover Publications.

Smith, L. T. (2012). *Decolonizing methodologies: Research and Indigenous peoples*. Zed Books.

Smitherman, G. (1977). *Talking and testifyin: The language of Black America*. Wayne State University Press.

Thomas, E. E. (2019). *The dark fantastic: Race and the imagination from Harry Potter to the Hunger Games*. NYU Press.

Urban, K. (2020). Harriet Powers: A Black female folk artist who regained her glory. Daily Art Magazine.

Vizenor, G. (1987). Follow the trickroutes: An interview with Gerald Vizenor. In J. Bruchac (Ed.), *Survival this way: Interviews with American Indian poets*. University of Arizona Press.

Windchief, S., & San Pedro, T. (2019). *Applying Indigenous research methods: Storying with peoples and communities*. Routledge.

Womack, Y. (2013). *Afrofuturism: The world of Black sci-fi and fantasy culture*. Lawrence Hill Books.

Yaszek, L. (2006). Afrofuturism, science fiction, and the history of the future. *Socialism and Democracy, 20*(3), 41–60.

Yoon, N. (2017). Sera. In Amerie (Ed.), *Because you love to hate me: 13 tales of villainy*. Bloomsbury.

1

INTRODUCTION

My name is Jane and this is my world

May 1, 2085

The bluer the eyes, the more successful the programming. That's what they tell us anyway. The Dreamers' eyes are brown, amber, green, gray, or hazel. My eyes and the eyes of all the Endarkened are different shades of blue, some as piercing as the color of LED lights and others as bright as the sky on a sunny day. I sometimes wonder if the brightness of our eyes is what stops us from dreaming. Darkness is the space of dreams; it's the place where imagination can grow; it serves as the backdrop for the magical. But I think the piercing blueness of my eyes punctures the darkness, keeps the darkness at bay. I long for the days when I'll be able to close my eyes and see blackness. But to dream is to imagine something better, to envision a reality that's different from this one. That's why we're not allowed to dream. The Dreamers haven't allowed us to do that for a long time.

In history, we learned that in the early 2000s—2019 to be exact—the experiments started. They'd been experimenting on us for centuries, but that was the first year they started the dream extractions. They used Black women first due to the procedure's scientific infancy. Black women were prime specimens, proud mules ready to bear the burden of scientific progress for the betterment of society. Well, better for the Dreamers anyway. A lot of Black women died in childbirth. Too many. The extractors never took an accurate count because they didn't care how many of us died as long as they reached their scientific goals. And they did.

An old government entity, the CDC, said Black women died at higher rates, but at the time, the scientists didn't know what was really happening in the hospital's maternity wards. Later, some activists discovered that the deaths were due to procedure rejection, and they posted their findings for all to see. Many people thought this information would lead to revolution, but it didn't. Instead,

DOI: 10.4324/9781003159285-1

it made it easier for the public relations teams to change the narrative and blame the deaths on divisiveness. They said that Black women refusing or fighting against the extraction was a disruptive tactic to tear America apart. Endarkened rights weren't being infringed upon; we were infringing upon the world's right to scientific innovation. Now, if one of us dies, people just say survival of the fittest is doing its magic, weeding out those who lessen the greatness of this country. I sometimes wonder how many chose to die knowing they'd be defamed upon their deaths. I wonder how many chose to jump off the operation table to save themselves and their future children.

Girey Cuviems, INC., otherwise known as GC, funded the first procedures, financing our deaths long before other large industries followed suit. Because they controlled the experiments, a practice many Dreamers supported, they gained power over time. GC controls the procedure, so they control the government and the majority of the nation's people. Because more than half of the country's population is Endarkened, we now have a society filled with Endarkened children who can't dream and Endarkened adults who don't remember the dreams of their youth. We have a society filled with people like me.

We all have similar names: Jane, Jill, John, or Jack followed by our birth number. It's an easy way to keep track of us, I guess. The numbers started after the first successful extraction, June 2030. Now, 55 years later, there are so many of us that we all have long numbers after our names. Those with unique names have either died or had their names forcefully removed.

The good thing is that no one mispronounces our names anymore. They get it right within four tries. My name is Jane–9675214. I'm the 9,675,214th Jane in GC's United States.

I decided to start writing about my history and who I am because I'm hoping it will help me remember. I'm not sure what I hope to remember, but I do know that recounting my past gives me courage to do what I have to do. A few days ago, after writing down what I know about this country, I decided to try something. It would require me to go against everything I know, but I'm out of options. I can't keep pretending like everything is ok, like this world is an Endarkened utopia. I can't keep acting like the removal of Endarkened dreams creates unity. I have to do something, and I chose to do the only thing I could think of. It may sound courageous or even a little daunting, but I decided to steal a book.

The library enforcers are always on high alert during the morning shift. When they log off, and the afternoon workers arrive, there's a little more freedom because the librarians are allowed to enter, taking away some of the enforcers' authority. Libraries were *technically* defunded over two decades ago, but GC thought they should leave them open to alleviate political unrest. People get mad when you take their books. GC funds the enforcers, and outside donations cover the librarians. I know they don't get paid much, but the librarians come in every day to sneak books to those of us who are brave enough to take them. They're on the front lines of change.

People used to be able to checkout whatever they wanted as long as they brought the book back, but now, most of the library is "restricted." The sign doesn't say who is restricted, but we know. I heard John–1 had his hand chopped off and one of his eyes gouged for reading a restricted book. They left one eye and one hand to remind him that they could take the other just as easily. Of course, that's all hearsay, but none of us want to test our luck. In this society, the loss of a hand, an eye, or both mean you can't get a good job. If you can't work, you're nothing. GC has made that pretty clear. In fact, "if you can't work, you're nothing" is on several posters and billboards, so we don't forget.

I sat at the library all morning, waiting for the afternoon group to arrive. As I waited and watched, I kept looking at the ominous bookcases and wondered if I should risk it. After all, a lot of people thought Jane–12 was mentally unstable when she started talking about reading restricted books. People kept their distance, knowing she could cause trouble for them. I mean, she started calling herself Harriet–2 and openly talking about deserting GC. No one understood why she'd name herself when the government gave us names. No one understood why she'd want to leave when there was nowhere to go. Nevertheless, there was something intriguing about her words. Something hidden beneath her ramblings.

"Find the butler. Find the map. Find your dreams," Jane–12 said as GC took her away again. She was constantly taken back to the First of two institutions that Help the Omnipotent Manufacture Efficiency (FirstHOME) for an injection. Somehow, she kept passing their release exams, but then she would say some nonsense to get her sent back. I didn't understand it. In fact, when she first said, "find the butler," I was confused. Butler was no longer an occupation. Once Amazon started shipping Alexa 10s through same-hour delivery, it was only a matter of time before the job became obsolete. Either way, I didn't understand what she meant until I remembered a message from one of my SecondHOME observers before she was taken by GC for inciting thought.

Lori Jackson wasn't like me. She had a real name. Lori was a short woman with dark auburn hair and white skin, and she was one of the nicest observers I had during my transition years in SecondHOME. She was one of the only ones who actually *saw* me if that makes any sense. Every so often, she'd randomly repeat this string of words, and no one knew why. Hopkinson, Lorde, Butler, Due, Hurston, Morrow, Forna—every few months or so. We'd ask her what she was talking about, and she would just say, "remember my name." That was it. I'll never forget those words, though, because they were the last words she said to us before she was taken away for good.

"Jane! Jane–9675214!" I heard an enforcer say.

They don't like when you sit too long. Staring into the distance looks like daydreaming, and they can't have that. The good thing is that I was prepared.

"Jane! Jane–9675214!" The enforcer said again, a little too close to my ear.

"Yes?" I replied.

"Jane, you have been occupying this seat for 37 minutes. You have the King James version of the history text in front of you, but you have not been reading this book. You appear to be engaging in daydreams."

"No, sir," I said as I plastered the sweetest smile I could muster on my face. "I work for Altered Truth, and I was trying to use our history to figure out the best way to tell the truth about what happened earlier today with Jane–12. The history guides us to the truth. Without it, we know nothing. So, I was letting it guide me."

I put it on a little thick at the end, but I couldn't take any chances. One injection, and I'd be reset, not forgetting my task but losing my will to do anything but what I'm told to do. The injections are GC's way of making sure we're consistently compliant. They can't perform dream extraction surgeries too often because they're expensive. Plus, the surgeons found out that repeated operations destroyed a person's mental functions to the point where they were no longer able to work. They couldn't afford to lose their unpaid labor, so they came up with the injections. They're safer, and they can use them more often.

"Very well," he said in a huff. "Please finish your duties expeditiously."

I know that tone. My job in GC's Altered Truth division means I'm a "good one," uppity and privy to government secrets even he doesn't have clearance for. He hates me for the knowledge I hold. I hate him for the dreams he's wasted on hating people like me.

With one last scowl in my direction, he moved to his next victim. "John! John–47563! You have been occupying this seat for 34 minutes …"

When the enforcer was out of earshot, I noticed John–762940 walk in. He's like Harriet–2 because he changed his name to Elonnie–2, but instead of outwardly defying GC, he's been helping us from the inside. He's the one who helped me understand Harriet–2's riddle, and he's also the one who told me the words Ms. Jackson repeated were names. I guess I would've figure it out eventually since Ms. Jackson gave us a hint, but I'm glad Elonnie–2 was there to help.

"Jane, I see that you're finished with this book. Shall I put it back for you?" Elonnie asked.

I knew my response to this question was my last chance to go back to my sedated life. I could've said no. I could've backed out and continued pretending to look through the history book. If I said yes, though, I was telling him I was ready, ready to find the map and learn to dream—or at least to try and dream. When I walked to the library this afternoon, I already knew my answer. I wasn't turning back.

"Sure, John. Thanks for your help."

"Of course. There's a book that fell over there," he said, pointing to a book in front of the restricted section. "Can you grab it for me, so I can put it away?"

"Sure," I said, my eyes darting to the illegal book on the ground. The cover had been removed and replaced with a shiny, black hardcover casing. I couldn't figure out what it was, which was good because if I didn't know, I doubt the enforcers could figure it out at first glance. I walked over to the spot and picked up the book. I flipped through several pages, careful not to linger on any one for more than a second.

"John, I think I can use this in my most recent PR case," I said a little too loudly and a little too quickly. "Can I check this out?"

"Hard, black binding means it's on its way to be burned, so I don't see why not. Just make sure you bring it back before the incineration date stamped on the cover," he replied with a slight smirk on his face. Once a book was stamped for incineration, no one would be looking for it.

I stuffed the book in my bag and hurriedly walked toward the door. I didn't know what was in it, but it must be important for it to be classified as restricted, for Harriet–2 to go through so much to get this book in someone's hands, and for Elonnie to risk his life. It's important enough for me to risk my position. My life. I thanked Elonnie and left the library before I could change my mind.

May 2, 2085

As I walked back to my dorm, I kept looking behind me to see if an enforcer was on my trail. I outranked the enforcers in terms of occupation, but my credentials didn't mean much when they were looking for someone to make an example out of. Enforcers aren't friendly neighborhood protectors, charged with upholding the law. They are there to enforce the will of GC by any means necessary. "By any means" often meant one of us was killed to "preserve the peace." Enforcers were never charged for murder, never held accountable for the deaths of my people. But then again, why would they be? Most of the Dreamers don't see us as people anyway. It's almost as if they don't consider us to be human, like we're zombies walking among the living, always hungry for dreams and humanity.

When I finally closed the door to my dorm room, I felt the heavy load of stress and fear. Once I opened the book, life could change for me. I mean, my current life isn't so bad. I have a pretty decent home, consistent access to food pills, and a well-paying job. I may not be able to dream, but I am able to mold the truth in creative ways. Last week, I constructed a campaign that explained why the Georgia Annex was getting smaller. The real reason is climate change and how GC refuses to implement laws to protect the Earth. The true answer is GC ignored aid requests when natural disasters struck the former state of Florida and the smaller island territories below it. Due to their negligence and an influx of Category 5 hurricanes, most of the state is now underwater. Now, there's not enough left of Florida to call it a state, so GC renamed it. Now, it's the Georgia Annex. My job was to twist the story and ensure GC was never implicated.

The Florida Weight Campaign is probably what I'm best known for at work. Through it, I showed how the Annexer's reliance on straws and their refusal to recycle and compost added increased weight to the state, thereby causing Florida to sink. For good measure, I added that there was no empirical evidence show-ing humans have any influence on climate; subsequently, blaming GC and large corporations for the failures of individual people is scapegoating, at best, and dis-crimination against corporations, at worst. How dare GC residents blame their employers for problems that individual people created. It's ridiculous, I know, but if you say something nonsensical loud and long enough, people start to believe it, and it's my job to twist the narratives so people can't help but believe.

Although I'm allowed access to climate campaigns and some involving the education given at FirstHOME, I am not involved in acquittal campaigns for the enforcers. Those spots are often reserved for Dreamers, although some Endarkened are allowed to sit in for photo ops. It's always great to have a photo that makes people assume everyone is on board with a campaign, no matter how discriminatory it is. The most successful campaign to ever arise from that PR team is the "fear codes," a list of statements now posted in the enforcer handbook that allows them to be acquitted for murder:

> I was scared to death.
> I thought I was going to die.
> I had no other choice.
> I perceived a threat.
> I feared for my life.

These five statements, taught to enforcers throughout the country during their 2 months of training, sign multiple Endarkened death warrants. They also sign freedom papers for enforcement officers. They can't be murderers if they fear for their life. It doesn't matter if they charge into our houses and kill us while we're sleeping. We apparently look menacing in our sleep. Each officer is only allowed to use one fear card per year, but that's enough. I guess, the only good thing about the extraction is that we don't have nightmares anymore. We're no longer able to dream ourselves into the positions of murdered Endarkened people.

There used to be protests, outrage-filled people marching through the streets to bring awareness to injustice, but that was long ago. They happened before the Change Rooms were created and before the dream extractions were fully tested. The Change Rooms destroy people, alter their brains in ways I'll never understand. The dream extractions make sure that once people are broken, their future generations will never fight back again. Anyway, there aren't any declassified documents left from that time in history, but I've heard stories from Harriet–2. She's told me everything I know about the past, things I'd have never learned otherwise because GC edits the history books. To write down the history Harriet–2 tells would be to preserve an account that differs from the altered truth. To write it down and have that writing discovered could result in death.

I think that's why I was so afraid to open the book. Bound in thick black leather, the lightweight text seemed as ordinary as any of the required books included in each dorm room. But it's also a restricted book, a book I'm not supposed to read. What would happen if there were security traps in the book? What would I do if the enforcers decided to engage in random inspections? What could happen if I figured out what made the book so blasphemous that it landed in the restricted section? What might happen if my fingerprints can't be erased from the pages, and I am taken back to FirstHOME for reprogramming? Or worse, what if I'm taken to the Change Room? All these thoughts bombarded and overwhelmed me, but I had to know. I opened my bag and felt the cold book in my hands. I turned to the title page. It said: Octavia E. Butler. Parable of the Sower. I dropped the book.

In FirstHOME, we learned about this parable. The King Trence version of the Bible tells the story of a farmer who sowed seeds indiscriminately. Some seeds drifted to places with no soil at all, some fell on rocky ground with very little soil, and some fell on soil that was filled with thorns. These seeds yielded no crops. However, some seeds fell into good soil, producing crops that could feed multitudes. Our observers said most of us were one of the first three, which is why they couldn't trust us with dreams or knowledge because, just like the crops, we didn't have enough fertile soil. We were destined to misuse the knowledge, and they were protecting the world from our knowledge abuses. That's why we were sent to FirstHOME, an educational system best suited to our intellectual levels. Dreamers, however, were more capable of producing good crops. This is why they never even enter FirstHOME … unless they decide to do Endarkened missionary work and become teachers.

I turned the page, and the number at the top said 2024. That was sixty-one years ago. I moved to the next page, and I saw a date: Saturday, July 20, 2024. I skimmed some more, and I saw the last entry was Sunday, October 10, 2027. I think it's a history book, one of those epistolary accounts of the times. Based on the day, it was written before the first successful dream extraction. Based on its place in the restricted section, I know she's probably Endarkened like me. As I turned it over and over in my hands, I was mesmerized by the potential content of the book. I knew there was something more here, that there was a reason why this book was placed in the restricted section and why Harriet–2 kept talking about it. I just had to figure out what that reason was.

I've never read anything like this before, so I want to immerse myself in the text before I attempt to figure out why it's classified. I'll read and reread until I break the code and find the key—find the map to my dreams. Hopefully, I'll be able to figure out not only why this book is confidential, but also why Ms. Jackson included Butler in her list of names.

I opened the book and read the first several lines:

> All that you touch
> You Change.
> All that you Change
> Changes you.

July 21, 2085

So, Butler's book is definitely a history book. It took me a while to get to this idea, but after reading the book a few times, I noticed several things kept resurfacing. Once I saw them, I had to read the book again, just to see if I could follow the threads throughout the book. I guess, the easiest way to build up my reasoning is to start by outlining the historical events in Butler's book. I think writing this down will help me outline my thoughts, help me find my truth in Butler's words.

Butler was frustrated that there was so much money wasted on a space program when people couldn't pay for food, water, or shelter. In the years before GC came to power, space trips happened every so often, and astronauts explored the great unknown, but the National Aeronautics and Space Administration was eventually disbanded in 2063 to divert more funds to the Space Force, a military organization who was charged with organizing, training, and equipping forces to be ready for possible space attacks. No one really knew what the Space Force was supposed to do, but many people wondered why new government branches dedicated to protecting interests in space were being formed when money wasn't being allocated to ensure people on Earth were protected. Butler also said the Secretary of Astronautics didn't have to know about science as long as they knew about politics, and that was true then, just as much as it's true now. Our newest Space Force commander used to be the favorite cook of GC CEO, Donny Cuviems. I'm not sure what a cook knows about commanding a space force, but as long as you have a friend in the government, you have a job whether you're qualified for it or not.

There was so much the former government could've done to protect every person on Earth, but I guess certain people were always safe, so they didn't bother to look at those whose existences were always in danger. Butler showed a good example of this when she talked about all the poor people who couldn't read and didn't have jobs or homes. She even talks about how polluted the water was. I'm thinking that she was talking about the former city of Flint, Michigan. We're not allowed to talk about it because if the truth got out, there would be more unrest, and GC likes civility.

I don't know much, but what I do know is Flint used to be a thriving city, home to a major plant, although I don't remember what they were manufacturing there. Then, a pipeline was built that outsourced water from the local river to the homes of residents. Dangerous levels of lead polluted those waters, and people complained, filed lawsuits, and protested. After years of activism, nothing changed. After five years of fighting, prosecutors dropped all pending criminal charges because they wanted to start their investigation from scratch. The cycle kept happening—prosecutors would file charges, drop them, and start over.

Fifty years passed, and Flint's water was still as dirty as ever. They couldn't boil the harmful elements out of the water, and many of the residents died because they couldn't afford the exorbitant doctor's fees, especially since insurance companies deemed living in Flint a precondition not covered by their plans. Flint residents tried to show the world what they were going through, but Altered Truth had more reach. By the time the PR department was through with the situation, Flint's residents were being sued for poisoning the water and faking illness. Eventually, the people became jobless and homeless, and they lived without decent, unpolluted water. Now, Flint is the state landfill, and sometimes, I think that's what they wanted it to be in the first place.

Although Butler's comments on space force and water pollution resembled some historical events, her focus on the pre-GC enforcers was what led me to believe this text was historical. Before GC took over, there was a different group of enforcers. Most people called them police officers, although there were various other names people used. Butler said these officers solved cases by somehow discovering the evidence they needed to convict. When people called for help, they wouldn't come, and when they did, they made the situation worse.

I once heard Harriet–2 talking about police with some of the other Janes and Jills. She described how police planted evidence, resulting in undeserved prison time for many Endarkened people. I don't remember every instance of official misconduct she mentioned, but I do remember an officer named Wester, who she said pulled people over for minor traffic violations, planted drugs in their vehicles, and arrested them. Over 100 people had to be exonerated in cases tied to his efforts to "clean up the streets." He was caught, but I'm sure there are many others who falsified arrest documents and turned off body cameras. They've mostly transitioned from the police of history to the enforcers of contemporary times.

Once I saw Butler was trying to embed historical content into her book, I also started to see how she was anticipating our current predicament. She saw GC coming. She mentions a president named Donner who plans to produce more jobs by suspending minimum wage requirements as well as environmental and worker protection laws. He believed that by doing so, companies would be willing to support employees by providing them with training as well as room and board. Reducing labor laws enabled several companies to build what Butler called Company Towns. She talks about a company called Kagimoto, Stamm, Frampton, and Company that had taken over a small coastal city. The town was bought out and privatized, and the people who lived there worked to earn their place in the city. However, new hires had a hard time living on the offered salary and were in insurmountable debt to the company. By page 129, Butler anticipated that eventually, the country would be divided and distributed amongst several groups.

I'm not sure how Butler saw this coming, but she was right, more or less. The only difference is that instead of various companies buying towns, GC bought the country, then divided states and communities among the organization's brother corporations. Amazon, Facebook, Microsoft, Apple, Berkshire Hathaway, Oracle—they all own at least four states each. GC kept the rest to use as a way to build alliances with other countries. It's kind of like GC owns America but allows its friends to manage other states so its load is reduced. The Endarkened work for the organizations to earn our room and board. It's also what warrants our nationality. We live in a precarious state of citizenship that can be revoked at any time, but as long as we continue to be productive, we are allowed to remain on US soil.

To earn a spot in the company towns, the people in Butler's novel had to apply. We, on the other hand, take entrance exams. The tests occur sometime before graduation from FirstHOME. It doesn't make sense to test us for our future occupations at this graduation because we leave FirstHOME when we're 13. I guess GC figures it's best to use our SecondHOME years as trainees. They use FirstHOME to teach us the basics, like how to read, write, and comply. Then, they use SecondHOME to make sure that as soon as we leave, we are ready to be productive members of society, working in places like Altered Truth, operating the various machines in the factories, or joining one of the military branches.

The entrance exams consist of 14 hours of physical testing and eight hours of knowledge testing. The physical part is easy but traumatic all the same. They test our will and see how long it takes to break us. The longer we can withstand their attacks, the higher our placement. This is not a physical attack in the general sense. Instead, they test our mental capacity. For hours, they show us videos of violence against Endarkened people. We see lynching demonstrations, whippings of enslaved people, the forced removal of Endarkened from their native lands, and concentration camps filled with Endarkened children. We are allowed to blink, but we aren't allowed to look away for longer than four seconds. If we can withstand the physical test, our chance of obtaining a GC position is almost guaranteed. The test is easy because FirstHOME prepares us for this task throughout our schooling, and GC offers movie events to desensitize us. By the time we get to the physical test, most of us are more than capable of passing. Sometimes, we just choose not to.

The knowledge test is more arbitrary because they've already decided our scores before we enter the exam room. Every Endarkened child is born and taken directly to a FirstHOME. At five, we leave the nursery wing and are welcomed into the traditional school building. During that first year, multiple observers watch carefully, analyzing our future occupational prospects. At the end of the year, the observers meet and classify each child. We are labeled gifted, honors, general, or skills. Once tracked, it's hard to move across categories. Our knowledge scores are essentially decided based on whatever level we occupy before the transition, at least that's what they tell those of us who were accepted into the gifted and honors levels. I'm not sure what they told the kids in the general and skills sections. All I know is that they always seemed less prepared, as if the observers assumed that the level decided upon years ago was all they could ever be.

I also know that those who were tracked into the lower levels got the worst jobs, and they were less likely to obtain jobs where they could live relatively debt free. All the companies use company dollars rather than money that could be used anywhere. But only GC dollars can be used across the United States. So, once the general and skills kids were hired by non-GC companies, they couldn't move to a different place. They were stuck. Sadly, most of their children were stuck, too. Once they were taken from their parents, they were sent to a HOME in another state owned by their company and placed on the same track. It's like they've created an intergenerational class of lower level workers. Every so often, they "find" a good one and allow them to be in higher classes, but that doesn't happen too often, and it usually only happens so GC can say they don't discriminate.

The idea of workers paid in company dollars was also something that Butler talked about, and interestingly, this is the part that let me know she knew what was going to happen even if she didn't know it would just happen to Endarkened people. She talked about wages being paid in company scrip, not cash. Workers shopped at company stores and paid for everything in company dollars. Even rent was paid with company money. Of course, their wages weren't enough to cover everything, so they went into debt, and there were laws that prohibited people from leaving employers to whom they owed money. So, in the end, a cycle was created where people got company jobs, went into debt, and were forced to work off their debt as indentured servants or convicts. If they refused, they'd be arrested, jailed, and given back to their employers.

Real life is just like Butler's book. We can only spend money in stores owned by the companies we work for, ensuring that the little money we make always goes back to the company itself. Because we are paid little, we can never afford to leave. If we refuse to be enslaved by our companies, we're jailed for some arbitrary reason, and the employer has to bail us out. It's interesting how the pipeline works, forcing the Endarkened into jail-like schools, then asking us to work in jail-like conditions, and then putting us in an actual jail when we ask for an acknowledgment of our humanity. How did Butler know so much?

July 22, 2085

Yesterday, I was so caught up in the history of Butler's novel that I forgot the most important aspect of the work. The book is a map to a sacred place where Endarkened people can thrive. In the book, Lauren, the main character, takes a journey to seek a place called Acorn, a place where Earthseed, her community, can thrive. The story takes place somewhere in California, and the characters all journey north to find their new home, a place the oppressive world can't infiltrate. Living in the Georgia Annex, I'm far from California and the actual Acorn Lauren found, but I think it's a metaphor. I think it's a way to find liberatory spaces created and nurtured by Endarkened women like Lauren, a place to challenge the racialized policing of GC's United States. The reader just needs to figure out the location using clues within the text. That has to be the map Harriet–2 was talking about.

Lauren says people were always moving to the north and her plan was to start walking in that direction in hopes that she'd find a good place. She also says that even though she planned on going up toward Canada, she knew she may not be able to get that far. To me, this means Acorn is north. I'm not sure how far north, but I'm thinking that because she remained in the same state throughout the book, Acorn can be in any state, just not in the southernmost parts of the state. She also talked about being on the coast within sight of the ocean. I'm pretty sure this means Acorn will need access to a water source. I know of a few cities on the eastern coast that have been abandoned by GC, so I'm sure that Earthseed could hide in one of those places. Based on this, I'm thinking maybe

Savannah or Tybee Island could be Georgia Proper's Acorn. It's on the eastern coast, and although it's not completely north, it is located at a point where Georgia meets the ocean right before turning into the North Carolina Annex, the former South Carolina.

If I try to go there, I know there's a possibility that I'll find nothing, but I have to try, especially since Butler's descriptions of this community are so inviting. Lauren says the world is falling apart and she wants to build something constructive with the help of her community, a community of survivors. She says that to survive, the community fights together against enemies and helps if any one of them is in need; they educate their community members and themselves; and they contribute to the fulfillment of their destinies. Basically, they learn to live outside the system, fending for themselves rather than relying on the oppressors to save them.

I want to be a part of something like that, but I'm scared. I'm not like Harriet–2. I can't keep getting sent back to FirstHOME, and I don't want to lose my life in the Change Room. Still, something is drawing me to this place. I've felt it ever since Ms. Lori tried to teach us to dream so many years ago. I've needed it ever since I first saw Harriet–2 get taken away for spreading lies against GC. I've sensed it from the moment I opened Octavia E. Butler's book.

Of course, I can ignore it and choose to live out my life happily. I am one of the "good ones" after all. I can live the rest of my life without agitating the balance, without risking everything I have ever known. But what kind of life would that be, choosing to be docile just because I don't experience the same hardship as other Endarkened people? Choosing silence means choosing the life I have now, a life of servitude, lies, and isolation. Choosing silence means ignoring the suffering of my Endarkened siblings. I don't want this life anymore. I want something different. I want to find Acorn and join Earthseed. I'm leaving tomorrow.

July 26, 2085

Ok, so leaving was harder than I thought it would be. The book gave me motivation to find Acorn, but it also made me hyperaware of how I'd be considered a criminal if GC ever found the illegal book in my possession. Most Dreamers see us as criminals even if we don't consider ourselves to be one. The general consensus is that we're nothing but trouble, and most believe Endarkened women are the worst of all, so I'm consistently aware of the added risk. Endarkened women's troublemaking is one of the reasons dream extractions were instituted.

Before the extraction and the formation of the FirstHOMEs, the Endarkened were sent to public schools. I would've been called Black back then. Black girls like me were less likely to graduate on time or earn a college degree. We were more likely to be suspended than any other racial group. When we did achieve a bit of success, our accomplishments were belittled, as the observers focused more on how we acted in class, rather than acknowledging our academic success.

FirstHOME was created to help us, to teach us how to adopt standards of race-lessness so we could blend and be a part of the melting pot. In some ways, they succeeded. We used to be Black, Latinx, Indigenous, Asian, Middle Eastern, and combinations of these. That's what Ms. Jackson had told us, at least. Now, we're Endarkened; we don't have individual racial identities anymore because the Dreamers said individual identities caused division.

Maybe that's why it's so hard for me to think of a way out of all of this. We've lost so much of our history and culture as GC strategically eliminates our indi-viduality. I can reminisce on my past and try to think of ways my Endarkened ancestors searched for freedom, but I will never know for sure. The written words we have access to don't really help, and those who know our history and are brave enough to share it are detained, maimed, or killed. Once they're dealt with, Altered Truth erases their history and their words. Look at Harriet–2. No one really knows her story anymore. It's all rumor, hearsay, and altered truth. What's funny to me is that's actually how the term, Dreamers, came to be. Harriet–2 told me all about it.

There was once an Endarkened man, a Black man, named Martin Luther King Jr. He had this speech where he talked about dreams. He talked about wanting a world filled with equality. He said he wanted his children to live in a world where they wouldn't be judged by the color of their skin but by the con-tent of their character, a world where people could work together to transform the clanging discord of our nation into a beautiful symphony of brotherhood. At the end, he shouts, "Free at last! Free at last! Thank God Almighty, we are free at last!" Harriet–2 said he meant for Endarkened people to be free to make our own decisions, to be released from the wake of enslavement and Jim Crow. Dreamers took it to mean that cultures needed to just melt together, to erase race entirely since that was the reason for the discord. They took up the mantle for this altered form of equality and called themselves the Dreamers. Then, they forced their beliefs on us, using the Altered Truth division to spread their idea. It's funny how the only race that didn't deserve erasure was their own.

July 27, 2085

Harriet–2 is dead. She died of pneumonia while waiting to be released from her latest bout of reprogramming. They decided to have a party at my job to cele-brate. People even made speeches. Some were ecstatic because they wouldn't be forced to alter her stories anymore. The senior manager even gave a speech about her death. He wanted to congratulate us on all of our hard work, on all the lies we've created to hide parts of Harriet–2's story. He said that during questioning, she kept saying, "I go to prepare a place for you." He thought that was hilarious. He couldn't imagine that Harriet–2 was now free, preparing a place for someone else. He doesn't think Endarkened people are capable of doing anything but taking orders. The cake had her state name on it, Jane–12. She would've hated that. I hate it, too.

August 6, 2085

I'm sure Harriet–2's final words weren't meant for me, but something about those words helped me figure out how to escape the Dreamers' grasp without bringing too much attention to myself. I'm going to use Harriet–2's history to help me escape. I mean, the Dreamers, generally, and the Altered Truth division, specifically, have had to deal with her antics for decades. She would pass the tests required to show she had been reprogrammed, then she would disappear for a while, staying out of sight until her presence was forgotten. Then, once GC believed she'd finally changed her ways, she'd be found telling stories to any Endarkened who would listen. She would talk about dreams, ancestors, and our collective history. She'd be taken away, and the cycle would occur all over again. The weird thing is that right before she was taken back to FirstHOME or the Change Room, a small group of Endarkened would disappear.

There are rumors in the department that Harriet–2 convinced the Endarkened to leave their homes to find a better life elsewhere, but there was never any proof. She was always interrogated, and she would never say a word. With no new information, they'd complete the dream extraction and send her on her way. Too many people knew about her existence to execute her. Better to appease the masses by letting her live. No one in GC could understand how she kept resisting the extractions. She had undergone the procedure numerous times, more than any other Endarkened I knew. But she always found a way to fight back, and GC wanted to understand how she was able to continuously break the hold of the serum. I'm hoping their ignorance and drive to stop future Harriets will help me get out of here.

My plan is to convince them to let me work undercover. I can tell them that I'd like the opportunity to bring down Harriet–2 and her ilk once and for all. I can promise to bring back information, detailing the whereabouts of the Endarkened who have deserted. I can guarantee that I will find their leader, helping GC to silence all resistance. I think they'll go for it. After all, Dreamers have a history of destroying the joy and successes of the Endarkened. For example, over 100 years ago, an Endarkened enclave in the city of Tulsa, Oklahoma was destroyed. The alleged circumstances that resulted in the riot mirrored numerous other conflicts between Dreamer women and Endarkened men, but that was mostly an excuse. They would've used any reason to promote the destruction of a self-sufficient community of Endarkened people.

In the end, thousands of Endarkened lost their homes and their lives, and even though fighting happened between both Dreamers and Endarkened, enforcers ignored due process, and only the Endarkened were imprisoned. Even though numerous accounts show that most Endarkened people were victims of the event, local media reframed the narrative to portray the riot as an uprising lead by Endarkened people armed with weaponry. They said the push for equality had festered in the Endarkened community, causing us to collect guns and ammunition and prepare for a fight. We were the issue. Demanding equality was the problem. We were responsible for our own demise, and Dreamers had nothing to do with it.

Since thriving Endarkened communities scare them so much, then it makes sense to suggest the razing of whatever community brought about the existence of Harriet–2. If Endarkened resistance against the hold of the dream extraction is a major GC concern, then it makes sense to use someone with knowledge of GC to infiltrate the enemy camp and provide the information necessary to remove the obstacle. In fact, having an Altered Truth employee work as a spy makes it easier for GC to alter the story of the community's downfall. An Endarkened woman working against her own people would give them the tools they need to suggest that there are some Endarkened who understand the benefits of the melting pot, the benefits of racelessness. It would provide them with a story of acceptance, a token that proves equality has been reached.

I'll let them believe these things. It's what they want to believe anyway, so it won't require much effort on my part. It sucks to have my intelligence consistently undermined because they think less of me, but sometimes I make it work to my advantage. All I have to do is set the idea in motion by making it seem like it's their idea. It won't be hard. It happens in meetings all the time. I'll say something. They'll ignore me. Then, a male Dreamer will say the exact same thing, claim it as his own innovative idea, and the whole room will applaud. I'll do the same thing this time, and once he is celebrated for his idea, the group will beg me to be their spy. They'll ask me to leave, and they might even tell me to take as long as I need to bring them the information they seek. I'll use that to my advantage. I'll take the time I need. I'll find Acorn, and I'll never come back.

August 10, 2085

The Friday morning meeting started off in the usual way. The director praised the Dreamers for their hard work at keeping America great. She commended their strong efforts despite the various ways in which the Endarkened attempt to spread lies and half-truths to the masses. She recounted the various Altered Truth projects completed within the last week, celebrating the hard labor of Dreamer workers who surpassed all odds to complete their tasks. She didn't mention our work. She never does. We're invisible to all who work there, and we're not allowed to talk to each other. It makes for a very lonely work environment, a very lonely life.

After singing the praises of her staff, the director reviewed the agenda for the meeting: the discussion of new projects; the planning of a celebration for another record month of acquittal cases; and the reading of an update from the head of GC. As far as meetings go, this was standard.

"Charles, great work last week," the director said. "I don't know if you all know about the work that Charles has done, but it was a masterclass in truth telling. We all know Enforcer Shelbi was acquitted of all charges because she feared for her life. She was a first-time fear code user, so she was going to get off anyway, but the Endarkened were furious. Charles, here, knew they'd be upset. They're always upset about something. So, he goes and works with the judge to get it expunged from her record and works with the other state leaders to remove all history of the incident from the Internet. Now, if any Endarkened things have something to say, there's no record of the event. Gone. Poof! A master … class!" she shouted.

Everyone applauded … everyone except the six Endarkened employees. We don't clap for anything. They don't expect us to. In fact, I think they make us come to these meetings to prove they see us as diversity hires, subhuman entities existing only to prove GC is benevolent enough to hire Endarkened workers. The director's use of the phrase, Endarkened things, solidifies my point. Things. The word leapt from her lips without the slightest hesitation, as if she was using the word to describe a lamp or a pencil.

"I bring up Charles and his amazing accomplishments because we have a slew of new cases coming in," the director continued. "Enforcers Yanez, Salamoni, Lake, Loehmann, Wilson, Pantaleo, Dean, Atkins, Brelo, James, Daniels, Campbell, Dupra, and Servin have all invoked the fear codes, and their cases need to be handled. Charles provided the model we should all aspire to, but I know we can't all be as efficient in our work as he is. But we can work to get these good folks acquitted, transfer them to a new enforcement unit, and alter the story to fit the narrative. Dodge and deflect."

She listed a few more names, but I tuned her out. There are always at least five names each week, but this week the number is larger. Fear codes can only be used sparingly, but what happens when multiple enforcers use codes simultaneously? What happens when every week, hundreds of enforcers enact the codes to cover their murders? If every enforcer uses the codes sparingly, then the number can't be small. It's a system-wide get-out-of-jail free card that transforms the murder of the Endarkened into a normalized business practice.

If the listing of the names wasn't bad enough, the next item on the agenda was for a celebration of the acquittals. The director thinks a party will add to company morale. Once again, I sat silently as my Dreamer coworkers decided on a party theme, determined who was bringing which foods, and agreed on an appropriate time for the event to begin. I wanted to yell, to scream out at them for planning a celebration right after reading an obituary column. I wanted to throw something, make a scene, and curse out loud because they, once again, ignored the increased levels of trauma that occurred each time we are forced to sit in a room while they celebrate our deaths. I wanted to do a lot of things, but I knew I couldn't. If I want to do more than survive in this world, I have to get out and find Acorn.

With the planning complete, the director moved to the last element of business, an update from the head of GC. We don't get messages directly from the top too often, but I'm always wary of the information they hold. It's never anything good. Charles, due to his "amazing" job last week, got to read the letter to the rest of the room.

Greetings Altered Truth Division,

First, let me commend you on a job well done. I have heard great things about your skill, dedication, and loyalty, and I want to ensure you that your efforts have not gone unnoticed. Your success in the last few months is the reason why this letter has been sent to your division, rather than to the director of enforcement. As Altered Truth employees, it is your job to spread truth throughout the land, squelching the numerous lies continuously spread by the Endarkened. It is your job to uphold the King James version of history and ensure that its truths are unquestioned. Recently, however, there was an Endarkened who, somehow, continuously undermined these truths. Even with multiple attempts at reprogramming and frequent dream extractions, this thing continued to resist. It called itself Harriet–2, but its name was Jane–12.

Now, don't be alarmed. It's true that it is dead and can no longer spread its lies. Still, we fear it has started something, given information to other Endarkened across the country, although we have not been able to figure out how. More and more of them are disappearing, leaving their jobs in the middle of the night. We have sent our best enforcers to track them, but their efforts are always thwarted. For instance, we chased an Endarkened all the way to the Canadian border, but as we were about to close in, all we saw was a barren wasteland. The Endarkened deserter seemed to literally disappear. Another time, we chased an Endarkened to the coast, close to the burned city of Savannah, Georgia. The enforcers followed it through the debris of the forgotten city all the way to the water's edge, but when they reached the shore, the Endarkened was gone. Once again, these unintelligent things eluded our grasp.

Based on these failed attempts, we realize the enforcers are never going to catch the deserters. We also recognize someone is helping them escape. At first, we believed Jane–12 to be the only one, but now we know there are more, and they are everywhere. There are deserters in several states, and the oddest part is most never cross state lines. At least, we don't think they do because they never reach the state borders. Still, we cannot find them. Thus, we have decided to use mental strength, and our best and brightest minds work for this division.

We are tasking the division with infiltrating the Endarkened deserter strongholds. You will have freedom in how you choose to do this, mainly because you are our last hope in crushing this resistance before it becomes too great. Historically, the Endarkened peacefully and sometimes violently protested, but there weren't as many of them, and they did not always work together. This new resistance has started with a small group but branched out to other Endarkened communities across the land. If their strength grows, there is no telling what the outcomes could be.

We have faith you will infiltrate the resistance, spread the truth, and kill their lies in the name of GC. This must be done to ensure this country continues to reign in its infinite glory. We are Dreamers, tasked with fulfilling the American Dream of life, liberty, and the pursuit of happiness. We can't let the Endarkened take that away from us. Without our dreams, the world falls to divisiveness. You can't let that happen.

Thank you for all you do to make this country great.

Girey Cuviems, INC.

"Thank you, Charles," the director said. "Now, everyone, we've been tasked with a great mission, one that could uplift this department exponentially. Yes, we already carry great favor with the heads of GC, but if we achieve success in this assignment, all of us gain prominence. We might even be moved from this division to a state or country-level position!"

The gleam in her eyes betrayed her motives. She didn't care if the people in the room were rewarded for their efforts. She wanted to be moved from the director of Altered Truth to some higher position. She wanted to be in a place of dominance that surpassed the privileged place she currently had. I'm pretty sure she's had a conversation about space before, so maybe GC will make her the secretary of space force.

"Charles, since you're our star employee, what do you think about taking the lead on this?" the director asked.

Charles beamed at the idea. "It would be my honor, director, though I believe a team would be better than one person. If the enforcers couldn't catch the deserters, I know that one man can't do it by himself."

"Agreed. How many people do you need?"

"I'm thinking five should work. I'll take the best Dreamers we've got."

"I think we can do that. The acquittal cases can be handled by our second-tier workers. We surely have enough of them to go around."

I knew if I let them finish their conversation without speaking up, I'd never leave GC and find Acorn, so I took advantage of the moment. I whispered to Jack–67402762 and made sure the whisper was loud enough for Charles to hear. I knew he'd notice because we're not allowed to talk to one another, and I never say anything in these meetings.

"It would probably be easier to infiltrate the Endarkened groups by using an Endarkened spy. Why would the resistance trust a random Dreamer?" I murmured.

Charles heard my comment because his eyes widened, and a sly smile crossed his pinched red face. He waited a moment, looking as if he were deep in thought. He put his finger up, and then back down, shaking his head vigorously. Next, he opened his mouth and made a small sound, and then he shut it just as quickly. His acting skills are superb. I almost believed he was really thinking of some extraordinary plan.

"Is something wrong, Charles?" the director asked.

"This idea might sound far-fetched, but I had to share just in case. Hear me out before you say no." The director eyed him warily, but Charles continued, "What if we add an Endarkened to the team? I mean, if the goal is to infiltrate and spread truths within the Endarkened resistance, what better way to do so than to have one of their own betray them? They'll never see it coming, and we may be able to have an inside member we can use in the future if all goes well. Why would the resistance trust a random Dreamer anyway? Plus, we've had an Endarkened helping in the Jane–12 case, so she would know more about Jane–12 than others would."

I could tell the director didn't want to do it. She doesn't trust Endarkened people. She doesn't even consider us to be people. Why would she trust us to handle a job that could elevate her career? But Charles' plan was appealing—my plan was appealing. She wanted to be in the good graces of GC, and what better way to do that than to succeed in this mission? Additionally, if they send one of us and the plan works, the Altered Truth division and GC will have another Endarkened poster child to tokenize as the face of GC support. She may not like us, but it was her best option.

"What a brilliant plan!", the director exclaimed. "This is why you're our number one employee. Now, I believe Jane–9675214 was the Endarkened on this case. Jane has been with us for about five years, but do you trust her to carry out this mission? I mean, this mission has been handed down directly from GC, so we want to make sure all goes well. Any errors could mean the loss of our current positions within GC hierarchy."

"Trust?" Charles began. "With all due respect, director, I'd never trust an Endarkened, but I believe she is capable of completing the task. We'll just have to map everything out for her, so she doesn't have to think too hard. You know they lack some of the intelligence necessary to carry out tasks requiring more than rote memorization. We'll also need to send her in for an enhanced dream extraction to make sure she doesn't get any ideas of her own. We wouldn't want her to desert GC. You know how easily influenced they are."

Charles gave me a distrustful glare, but he had to know it was a better idea than anything he could have come up with. Every time he's gotten praise from the director or GC, it was on the backs of others. I'm not sure he's ever come up with a good idea on his own. He finds ways to take credit for other's ideas because he wants to be the Director of Altered Truth someday. If the director gets what she wants, then Charles is next in line for the position. It's not official, but we all know it. He's been eyeing the job for years, sucking up every chance he gets. Plus, he's a male Dreamer. That automatically pushes his application to the top. It's weird how much I know about company business. You learn a lot when you're invisible to those around you. It's kind of like I only appear when they need something. Poof! Your Endarkened girl is here to do your bidding, oh Mighty Ones!

It's also funny how much he belittled my intelligence. They know we're intelligent and capable of doing things they never dreamed of doing, but because of the color of our skin, they refuse to acknowledge us, choosing to pass off our ideas as their own and then telling everyone how unintelligent we are. I don't get the logic behind it. I know the goal is to make themselves appear more intelligent than we are, but there's no point in sneering at us when we know where their ideas come from. I guess it's just to make them feel better about themselves.

"That works for me," the director responded, interrupting my thoughts once again. "I'll need to speak with her before she begins to work with your team, however. There are some things we need to discuss. Jane, head to my office now. Endarkened, you're dismissed. Dreamers, stay a moment so Charles can select his team. I'm sure ..." I left before she finished her sentence.

After 18 minutes of waiting, the director finally walked into her office. She was calm, almost stoic as she sauntered to her oversized mahogany desk. She sat, but she ignored me at first. I waited, looking up at her. I'm pretty sure she had the visitor chairs lowered, so she could tower over whoever dared enter her business lair. After checking her "perfectly curled" blonde hair and fixing the makeup covering her blotched overly tanned skin, she turned to me with a smirk on her face. She relished in my anxiety.

"So, Jane ... I see you're looking to ... increase your ... station?" she spoke slowly, choosing each word carefully. I sat quietly and waited for her to continue. I couldn't agree with her because I wasn't trying to increase my "station." An Endarkened person increasing their place in GC hierarchy is only superficial at best. Accolades, awards, and friendships only provide the impression of high status. If you're Endarkened, you're only safe until a Dreamer finds you or your confidence threatening. Once that happens, your honors and friends disappear. I also couldn't disagree with her because she already suspected I was up to something. I noticed her skeptical stare when Charles made his statement.

She continued, "I've known a few Endarkened who were ambitious, self-centered, conspirators. I don't think you're like that, though. You don't seem to have the same ... drive. You've been here for about five years, came straight from job training at SecondHOME to this division, a good Endarkened who showed signs of intelligence that just aren't found in most of your kind. Still, I can't be too cautious. Sending you out on a mission of this magnitude requires a level of astuteness I'm not sure you possess, no matter what your test scores may imply. So, I brought you here because I think it's important for you to know a few things."

I wasn't sure I wanted to know what she had to say, but she kept talking anyway. "Jane–12 is ... one of many," she began. "We've known about an underground movement for quite some time, but we have not been able to catch their leaders, their spies. They range in age, location, gender, and ability so it's been difficult to get a profile. We also have reason to believe there are Dreamers who assist them, although I can't figure out why they'd betray their own interests." I thought about Ms. Jackson as she said this, wondering if she had ties to the underground movement, wondering whether she knew Harriet–2.

"We've always altered their stories, making sure those who have challenged their station through social action are effectively muted. We hide their efforts, dodge, and deflect any event that could thwart GC's efforts to create a true melting pot. We distorted their stories to quell their need to promote divisiveness." She paused to look at her nails before she continued. "For example, we learned that Endarkened writers were attempting to reshape societal discourse. Using pseudonyms, like Octavia, Toni, Alice, Nalo, Cherie, Gloria, etc., they wrote stories that challenged the life GC created for them. They tried to write of dreams, hopes, and experiences. They tried to spread lies about GC oppression. They tried to promote a conversation about equity and justice for the Endarkened without realizing how good they already had it. The Dreamers carry the burden of dreaming, so the Endarkened don't need to worry about such things. But they fought and continued writing. This is why we have the restricted section in the libraries. We are protecting good Endarkened things like you from yearning for something that will only bring you sadness."

"This disease was not just present in the adults, however. There was a 15-year-old girl named Jill–7801 who called herself Claudette. She tried to challenge the transportation laws, so we hid her protest. For a while, no one knew she existed. Then, there was 16-year-old Jane–89447, a well-known traitor who joined an Endarkened movement called the Black Panther Party. Calling herself Tarika, she tried to lure Endarkened workers away with her lies disguised as goodwill programs and safety measures, but we were eventually able to erase her efforts from the historical records and position her little group as a terrorist organization. The youngest one I remember was 11-year-old Jane–191350, who attempted to speak out against gun violence. She was … compelling, amassing a lot of attention. People started using her altered name, Naomi. So, we created a media intervention that focused on her age as the reason why she could never speak about such things. What do children know anyway, especially Endarkened ones?"

She paused as she let her words sink in, and she waited for a reaction. I gave her nothing. I just looked at her and waited. Still, my mind was racing. I didn't know why she was telling me this information. Yes, I knew there were more leaders throughout the country. Harriet–2 couldn't do everything on her own. I also knew that our division was responsible for hiding the truth. Her speech, however, let me know how little I knew about my own history, how much knowledge the Altered Truth division and GC had hidden from the Endarkened. The King James version of history leaves out Endarkened protests. It also erases any mention of Endarkened people dreaming, unless it is talking about events before the dream extractions came to be. So much Endarkened history is edited out of our history books.

"I tell you this information for two reasons," she yawned and twisted in her seat. "First, I need you to know the Altered Truth division is one of the best. There is no doubt I shared information you were unaware of. Your ignorance is a result of our alterations and our well-constructed schooling system. If you cross us, your existence can be erased just as easily as we have erased the efforts of so many others. Second, I need you to understand the burden of dreaming when no good can come of it. If you have read any available fiction about the future, you will see that Endarkened people are not present. There is a reason for this: the future belongs to the Dreamers. Your job is to minimize yourself and become part of our dream. If you refuse, you are more than welcome to go to the Change Room. I'm sure you'll agree once they're through with you."

She smiled wide, a menacing grin showing a set of yellowing teeth. I shuddered. The director didn't know about my book or my journal, but I could tell she suspected I was up to something even if that truth contradicted her belief that Endarkened people are incapable of sustained thought. Why else would she issue this threat? They already send Endarkened people to the Change Room for disobedience. It's mostly used for extreme cases, but it's a consistent threat hanging over our heads. I've never been there, but I've heard stories. I hear they torture us into confession, using inhumane tactics that used to be outlawed in the United States. Once we give them the information they seek, they continue to torture and maim until they have broken us. Once broken, they provide the serum that alters the chemicals in our brains. We become automatons, completely different beings who only wish to serve GC. We lose all sense of identity. I don't wish to learn if those rumors are true.

The director turned to leave her office without saying another word to me. I guess she was done with her speech, believing me to be effectively cowed. Then, she turned back around and looked at me. "I do hope you consider our conversation as you begin this mission. You're one of the good ones, one of the best Endarkened workers we've had in a while. I'd hate to lose such productivity over something so … trivial. Still, I think it would be best to have you undergo a bit of reprogramming before you go. I'll fill out the paperwork today, and you are to report to the hospital for an updated dream extraction surgery in the morning. How long has it been since your last update?"

"It's been five years," I replied, "Right after my release from SecondHOME."

"Yes. I think it would be best if you were to have it done before you go. It hasn't been too long, but your eyes are looking a little less blue these days. We wouldn't want the serum to wear off when you're in the middle of such an important task."

With that, she turned to leave the office, heels clicking across the floor as she walked through the doorway and down the hall. I was expecting this, but I also know how the surgeries make me feel. I lose my drive, my will to think about the future or to imagine something better. I lose my desire to accomplish goals for myself. Even with the surgery looming over me, all I could think about was my eyes. I haven't looked at myself in the mirror in days. There was no need. The last time I checked, my eyes were still an electric shade of blue. But if the director says that my eyes were losing their sharp hue, then that meant the effects of the dream extraction were wearing off. But why?

August 20, 2085

I've only had the surgery twice—once before birth and once at my graduation from SecondHOME. I don't remember how I felt the first time, of course, but I know how I felt the second time, and I definitely know how I feel now. It's a feeling of emptiness, an impression that parts of my brain are being blocked by some unknown, outside force. The brain is still functioning, but there are parts I can't access. It's been sealed within some impenetrable stronghold, and a haze overcomes my mind each time I try to break through the fortress.

It took a full week for me to remember my plan, and if it weren't for my journal, I'm not sure I'd have ever remembered what I had set out to do before the surgery. When I was released from the hospital, I went home and walked around aimlessly. I knew there was something I needed to do, but I couldn't remember what it was. Whenever I feel lost, though, I busy myself with menial tasks—washing dishes, vacuuming the living room, making my bed, and doing laundry. It was my desire to remain active that helped me find Butler's book and my journal again, tucked away in the darkest recesses of my closet underneath a full laundry basket. I must have placed it there knowing this would happen, knowing I'd want to remember everything I learned in the past several weeks. Still, I wonder what would've happened to me and my plan if I didn't hide these items in a place I'd happen upon naturally. I wonder what could've happened if I lost my map to Acorn.

August 22, 2085

My orders from Charles say I'm supposed to come up with a plan for how to approach this situation. It took him over a week to think of his plan, and his plan is for me to make a plan and for him to take credit for it. Classic Charles. Part of me wants to live up to the director's expectations and fail to create a strategy because that would get both the director and Charles in trouble with GC. The other part of me knows if I want to find Acorn, I need to create something that would allow me to get away from the committee. I need to be strategic and use their ignorance to my advantage.

The plan I came up with is simple. I'll tell Charles that I need to go to Savannah alone because Endarkened people may be watching my movement and having Dreamer escorts will make them wary of my presence. I'll let him know I need at least 6 months to gather information because I need time to gain their trust. An Endarkened proverb is "all skinfolk aren't kinfolk," so I need to make sure they believe I'm one of them, a deserter. Once there, I'll send communication to Charles once every 2 months to make sure he doesn't come after me. These messages will be coded to ensure that no suspicion arises.

My real plan is to learn how Harriet–2 was able to consistently fight reprogramming and to learn about Earthseed—how it was created and how it thrives. I'd also like to learn more about these maps. Six months isn't enough time to learn everything, but I can learn what I can. Once I'm away from GC, I'm not sure if I will actually return. If I stay, I can be a member of Acorn until I die, learning and dreaming alongside others who have defeated GC socialization and dream injections. I could be happy there, living with those who made it to freedom.

If I come back, I can be like Harriet–2 and Elonnie, helping others to find the maps they need to leave this place. Six months may not be enough time to learn everything I need to learn, but I'm sure it's enough time to make my decision. It's a tough one, and both have their benefits. Whatever I choose, I don't have to think about it right now.

Charles loves my plan. After I outlined the details, he took my report to the director and claimed my idea just like I knew he would. I don't care, though. I want him to think he's in charge so I can do what's necessary. I don't know what will happen on this journey, but I know I must go. I know I must find Acorn. I just hope I'll be welcomed once I get there.

2

EXPLORING WOMANISM

Finding the Othermothers, entering the harbor

August 27, 2085

Today, I traveled over 300 miles away from Altered Truth. It took about 6 hours for the bus to get me close to Savannah. The bus only goes to Pooler since Savannah is too dangerous for large vehicles. The fire of 2063 destroyed over 500 buildings and over 300 residential homes, and the timeworn picturesque city never recovered. Over time, the debris in the air made it hard for people to breathe. To make matters worse, parts of destroyed buildings were always at risk of falling onto some unsuspecting traveler. The companies, deciding it would cost too much to fix the damage, let the city burn. It had an unusually high Endarkened population, so I guess they figured it was a way to force the Endarkened into more controlled areas. Or maybe they hoped Savannah would plunge into the ocean and the Endarkened residents would drown with it. It's still standing, though. The city refuses to give up on itself even though it is withered, beaten, burned, and forgotten, and if that isn't a metaphor for Endarkened people, I don't know what is.

Since Pooler was as far as Altered Truth could take me, they gave me a bike and told me it was the best they could do. After riding for more than an hour, I finally arrived in Savannah, but what I found was disheartening. Blackened bark and rotted trunks commemorated what was once lush foliage. The air was ashen, with tiny molecules of dust and debris blanketing the ground and sky. It was bright and sunny in Pooler, but the golden sun that sat in the sky 10 miles away didn't exist in Savannah. Nothing did. No animals scampered through that wasteland. No people walked about. It was forsaken and reeked of decay, stale and stagnant. I breathed in and tasted the surrounding death, and my lungs choked as they struggled to find clean air. I picked up some dirt, and it crumbled immediately, all nutrients that once saturated the rich soil were gone.

DOI: 10.4324/9781003159285-2

I don't know what I expected to find when I got here, but I hoped I'd come upon this place and just see Acorn. I wanted to immediately find an Endarkened stronghold surrounded by lush trees, sunlight, and warmth. I hoped I'd be welcomed by an Endarkened rebel leader who would help me leave GC's world behind forever. Although farfetched, I hoped the original Lauren would be here, waiting for new people to show up. Lauren and her crew had trials in Butler's book, but it seemed to end when they got to Acorn. Technically, the book ended, but I imagine all was well after that.

September 3, 2085

There are no homes or hotels in Savannah, so I've been staying at an Endarkened-friendly hotel in Pooler. It's been 6 days, and life is so monotonous. It kind of reminds me of my work schedule in Altered Truth. After eating my daily meal supplement pill, I'd go to work in the morning and leave a little after dusk. During the workday, I would walk around conducting research for my assignments and write Altered Truth media posts. At the end of the day, I would return to the safety of my home in the Endarkened dormitory, and I'd write or think about writing in my journal. My days are similar, here. I wake up, eat a meal pill, ride my bike to Savannah, walk around searching for Acorn, head back to Pooler, and write in my journal. I've got 6 months, so even if I don't find anything, I'm not going to rush back to GC. I'll go to Savannah every day and search just because I can. Who knows? Maybe I'll find something on my 135th day.

Since I've been here, I've given myself a lot of time to write. My journal is a part of me now. I never bring it with me when I go to Savannah, though. If I did, the soot might cover the pages and hide my words behind the ashes. I'm writing to remember, to think things through, to create myself in a world that tries to confine me to a small, rigid box. Within the lines of my journal, I shape and mold myself, untouched by GC and its methods of surveillance. My writing is my own. My pages share my story, my history, my hopes, and my fears. My narrative challenges the stories GC creates and Altered Truth maintains. I want to preserve it because maybe one day it can help another Jane find Savannah, or maybe it can tell her to avoid the area since I haven't found anything. If I bring it to Savannah, I risk losing these possibilities. It could get wet; the wind could blow the pages away; the dust could forever cover my writing. I don't want this to happen.

I go back to Savannah each day, leaving a piece of my identity in a safe place, and when I return to Pooler empty handed each night, I know my journal is waiting for me. I like coming back to it because it reminds me that no matter what happens to me, I will be kept alive through these words. If I bring it to Savannah, and something happens to me, no one will know I existed. No one besides GC knows I'm here. My journal knows, though. It's the evidence proving I exist, no matter what GC alters.

September 17, 2085

I've been wondering if going back and forth between Savannah and Pooler is why I haven't seen anyone yet. Right now, I am both insider and outsider because I'm an Endarkened person, but I'm not from here. To make matters worse, I only have my GC-issued clothing, so that might make them think I'm a traitor. I leave Savannah because Pooler safer, but if I keep leaving and refusing to stay, how will I shift from stranger to friend, from GC ally to Endarkened accomplice? Of course, I might be overthinking everything, and there might not be anyone here for me to be a stranger to, but my spirit tells me I'm here for a reason. It's saying I'm in the right place, and the Endarkened people who are here—wherever they are—are waiting for me to stay. So, I've decided to stay in Savannah, at least for a day or two. If I want to learn more about the Endarkened people who live here, I have to stop running from them each night. I need to become a part of their story because I want them to become a part of mine.

Finding shelter wasn't easy, but after searching for a while, I found a building with three solid walls. There's no ceiling, but it should protect me well enough. I'll just have to remain alert to guard myself from the front. My safety has never been guaranteed, so sleeping in this dismal city without protection should be nothing new. And yet, it is. I'm too anxious to sleep, too scared of closing my eyes in an eery and unguarded place because all my life, I've been caged. I've existed on a linear path, a narrow hallway where the walls are constructed through lenses of grit, zest, and compliance. The ceiling is low, and it pushed itself toward the ground until my dreams turned to dust. Of course, there were a few who pushed through the ceiling's cracks, but those who reached the other side often sat on the ledge with their feet dangling, as they were never fully able to stand on the side of privilege, never fully able to escape the cage, just sit on top of it. They may have reached the other side, but they are still Endarkened. They and their future generations still have the ability to fall back down with the rest of us.

I felt safe in the cage because I was blocked on all sides from the unknown. I've always known my path. I've pretty much always followed the rules. I never had to worry about the possibility of things not seen. But now, there's an opening—three walls, no ceiling. It's a freedom I'm not sure what to do with it. When the structures that raised you refuse to prepare you for a life beyond subservience, what can you do? How can you imagine something different when the people in power collectively work to confine and destroy your dreams? What happens when I'm set free? What if I don't know how to be free?

The building blocks most of the ocean breeze, but some cold air still seeps through. There's a gentleness I don't know what to do with, an unfamiliar placidness. In the darkness, I can more clearly see the beauty of Savannah's history—lost beneath the ashes, but preserved in the waves and carried upon the air and in the heart of this place. I can feel the peacefulness of an Endarkened city left to thrive on its own. The ashes feel like they contain the remnants of forced confinement joined with the ugliness of corporate greed and governmental neglect, but the wind represents how we continue to push back and reclaim our lives. The wind carries the past and present as it pushes us toward the future. The wind ensures this pallid land can hope for better. It seems like Savannah knows who it is, and knows where it comes from, but I don't think I know myself in the same way.

I've loved the idea of dreaming my entire life. There was something freeing about envisioning a future wrought with undiscovered possibilities; understanding the universe beyond the immediate realm of my real-life experience; and imagining innovations that could impact how the current world shifts and changes. However, even though I loved the idea of it, I didn't talk about my love for it because, according to most of the people I knew, Endarkened people were never supposed to dream. Our ancestors had dreams once but only because the Dreamers hadn't discovered how to free us of our ailment. According to GC, dreaming wasn't meant for the Endarkened because it caused us to want for things we could never have. Dreamers "saved" us from our dreams by removing them before we could ever know what dreams were. We're Endarkened. It's a term that not only describes the pigment of our skin, but also our inability to dream. We are Endarkened; our dreams are forever obscured.

Even though I know this, I still want to dream. I never gave GC permission to wrest my dreams away from me. In fact, Endarkened women were forced to be test subjects for Dreamer experiments. Once GC perfected their technique, there was nothing we could do. They were in power and signed laws stripping what few rights we had. So many Endarkened children accepted an inability to dream because we were never given access to the mechanics of dreaming. We were never taught what it looked, felt, or sounded like to dream. We were stripped from our parents, so they couldn't pass down their methods. Even if we did happen to dream, we couldn't be sure. We were never given books about dreaming written by Endarkened authors. The books we did see were always written by and about Dreamers.

We were constantly bombarded with visuals of Dreamers who were imagining, and our only role in the dreamscape was to exist as the monster, the hunted, the Other. I didn't like being the evil one, the antagonist, the scary thing, so I always thought that was why they saved us from our dreams. They knew we'd dream ourselves monstrous. But, how could they know dreaming wasn't for the Endarkened when the Endarkened were never allowed to write these stories and Endarkened people weren't included in existing stories? Instead of attempting to answer this question, I kept my preferences to myself. After all, I didn't want to be reprogrammed.

As an adult, I wonder how my childhood could've been different if I knew Butler existed. I wonder what dreams I may have had, and I wonder what stories my Endarkened community and I could tell. I wonder what those stories would allow us to do. In fact, if Endarkened girls had access to Butler's writing, I wonder if they'd be influenced by Butler's style of writing and infuse their stories with historical and current events like she did. I wonder how they might talk about or criticize some of the things happening in the United States. I wonder how they would bring in their own experiences or how they would talk about the obstacles in their way. I wonder myself to sleep.

September 18, 2085

When I woke up, two questions were written in the ash on the wall next to me:

> WHO ARE YOU?
> WHAT IS YOUR PURPOSE?

I looked around trying to figure out how and when someone was able to write a note. I see nothing but decay and ocean. It must've been written recently because the ash swirling in the air would've covered it otherwise. No matter how or when it got there, I'm not sure how to respond. I don't have enough space to explain my life story on this wall, and I'm not sure how to explain my reason for coming here. I know I want to find Acorn and be a part of Earthseed, but I don't know if the person who left this note read Butler's book. If they haven't, how will they know what I mean?

Also, the blueness of my eyes proves I'm an Endarkened who's had a dream extraction recently. How will I be able to explain I'm working for GC as a way to work for myself? How will they know I'm not a spy who's attempting to infiltrate their ranks and turn them all in so they can be reprogrammed? I don't even know how best to answer these questions. Do I say my name is Jane–9675214, and I've worked for GC for the past several years? Who am I outside of GC? Do they care? Even if they did, could I answer that question right now? I've never thought about who I am beyond being Jane–9675214, beyond being an Altered Truth employee, beyond being Endarkened.

Here's what I know: If I'd the chance to pick my own name, I'd choose Lauren. I don't know many other names, but I think Lauren is a name I can live up to. In Butler's story, Lauren was a survivor, someone who knew fighting for existence in her world meant finding community and working together with that community for the betterment of herself and her friends. I could do that. I could be someone who works with others to build a thriving community. In fact, I think that will be my new name. I will be Lauren Jane. I know it's weird, but it feels powerful to take the name GC gave me and move it to secondary status. Jane is who I've always been, the name GC given to me, but I have the power to reclaim my name, pushing it to the back, but never forgetting my history, no matter how harsh. Maybe I'll drop it at some point, but not yet.

I also know I'm a writer, maybe even a storyteller. I wasn't before, but since I've been writing in this journal, I realize how much I enjoy this. I like telling my story, and even though I don't think anyone will read it, I appreciate the process of putting my pen to paper and writing about what's happening in my life.

I wrote a lot before starting my journal entries, but it was never writing for me. I wrote because the observers in the HOMEs said I had to write well in order to be a top-level Endarkened student. I wrote because Altered Truth said I needed to write the truth in order to keep my job. I wrote because GC told me if I didn't comply, I could be sent to another corporate state. Within the pages of this journal, though, I write for myself.

I want to be a *dreamer*. I don't mean I want to take the position of the Dreamers and resituate myself as an authoritarian being in this world. I want to actually dream, to see what it's like to harness the dreamscape and imagine something different. I want to be able to see darkness when I close my eyes, rather than the whiteness I currently see. I want to know what it feels like to be an Endarkened *dreamer*, someone who can use their imagination to put Endarkened people into dream spaces. I want to know what it feels like to see myself in spaces beyond this reality. So, I'm Lauren Jane. I'm a writer and a person who wants to be a dreamer. I don't know much else, but I know these things to be true.

I look at the ash-covered wall. The two messages are now hidden beneath a fresh layer of soot, so I begin to write my answer: *I am Lauren Jane, a writer and want-to-be dreamer. I wish to find Acorn, my homeplace. I wish to find Earthseed, my community.* I don't know if this message will last until the message writer returns, but I hope it does. If it doesn't, I decide to do the one thing I've been scared of doing since I got here. I leave my journal out in the open on top of a pile of rubble. I don't know if they'll read it, but I think reading my writing is the best way to answer their questions. I stare at my heart laid bare on top of the wreckage, and I pray my words are enough.

September 19, 2085

When I woke up this morning, eight brown eyes were staring down at me. They belonged to four of the most beautiful Endarkened women I've ever seen. Their skin was a patchwork quilt of darkness—carob, umber, cedar, copper, obsidian, bronze, hickory, tan, and wood all working together to decorate the skin covering the length of their bodies. Their skin was a colorful assemblage that seemed to commemorate the collection of Endarkened people across time and space. I'd never seen such an array of brown within one body, but more importantly, I'd never seen an Endarkened person with brown eyes. Every Endarkened person I know has blue eyes, and although the hues of our irises might be different shades, they're still blue. These women, however, have deep brown eyes that pierced my soul each time I looked too closely. And yet, I continued to stare.

I opened my mouth and attempted to speak, but the eldest of them spoke before I could muster a sound. "Wait," she said, her voice a deep, soulful tone that commanded respect. I listened, closing my mouth tightly. Another woman picked up my journal and showed it to the elder. She carefully took it and began reading through the pages. I sat and watched for about an hour as she repeatedly read excerpts and looked at me. She had a countenance of indifference, and I didn't know what to make of it. Once she finished her first skim, she started over again. This time, she shared pages with the three other women. I have no idea which passages they read, but I do know they all kept reading and then looking at me. I was being judged.

"Who wrote this?" one of the younger women finally said after at least an hour of agonizing silence.

"I did. I was told to find the Butler, and then I didn't know what that meant, and then I went to the library to find out, and then I stole a book, and then ..."

"Please," the elder's wrinkly finger pointed upward. "We see your journey through the pages of this book. Who has seen this? And, which term aligns with who you are?"

"Term?" I asked.

"I mean your familial term. GC does not allow variation outside of the binary, but we would like to acknowledge who you are. Many people go by sib, sister, or brother, but there are other terms. Do you identify with sister, brother, or sib? Is there another term that works best for you?"

"Sister ... I think. And ... only I have seen the journal ... and now the four of you. I've kept it hidden ever since I started writing."

"Follow us," another woman said. Then, they all turned around and started walking.

We walked for about an hour in silence. I live on my own and never have people to talk to, so I am used to silence, but I had so many questions. I decided to break the silence with the most pressing question I had. Using the most bashful voice I've ever heard come out of my mouth, I said, "Um ... excuse me, but who are you?"

The elder continued walking, but she answered my question. "I am Layli Jane Walker, founder of the Savannah Harbor. My accomplices are Venus Jill Collins, Gholdy Jill Winn, and Ebony Jane Womack. These are our chosen names, and we have elected to keep our Endarkened names as a reminder of who we work to protect. We are known as the Othermothers because we are the leaders of the Harbor. As you probably know, Endarkened children are taken from their mothers upon their birth, so many of the residents don't know where they come from. We step in and take on that role, as do many others. Of course, we also have wide networks across the country, so we have been able to reunite families even after GC and their ilk have tried to keep them apart. It's difficult, but it can be done. Does this answer your question?"

My mouth hung open as I processed this information. Somehow, I found a way to respond. "Yes," I stammered. Like me, these women had chosen to keep their Endarkened names even if they kept their names for different reasons. I wonder why they chose those names, though. I wonder if there were books with characters named Layli, Walker, Venus, Collins, Gholdy, Winn, Ebony, and Womack. I wonder if they were writing to help others find Earthseed and Acorn and that's why these women, the Othermothers, chose to keep those names as their own. I wonder if the Harbor is their name for Acorn. I guess that does kind of sound better, especially since it's located in Savannah near the ocean.

I also wonder how vast their networks are. GC keeps children locked away from their parents and siblings. There's no easily accessible familial database to keep track of one's family tree. I know GC must have one because they want to ensure the production of certain types of Endarkened people, but I have no clue where it would be. Plus, how could the Othermothers have access to it? I have to give them credit for being able to operate even in the face of all of these obstacles. Somehow, they were reconnecting families, creating spaces of safety, and rescuing people like me. My curiosity got to me, and I asked another question. "Um ... sorry to bother you again ... but ... um ... can you tell me about this place we're walking to?" I wanted to assure them my words are not normally this clumsy, but I chose silence and waited for their response.

"We're going to the Harbor," the one named Venus stated. "It's a secret space we've cultivated to provide a safe place for Endarkened people to solve problems that affect us and to affirm our identities as Endarkened people. In many ways, it's a site of resistance where we engage in conversations and actions banned by GC. In fact, this resistance is more meaningful because we're often hiding in plain sight. They know we're here in Savannah, and they can do nothing about it. Within our Harbor, we plot, scheme, and plan, and we do it without GC's gaze. All the while, we're watching them. We've found a way to maintain, rescript, and reauthorize Endarkened values even when GC and the enforcers attempt to silence us. Once we've learned to better understand our history and our current place in society, we are better situated to enact change for the future. All of their little tricks and attempts to divide us can't deter us when we have a strong, albeit hidden community."

"Exactly," Gholdy said, her black curly hair flowing in the breeze as she walked. "We work as a community, doing different jobs to help us move forward. You've probably noticed more and more Endarkened people have gone missing recently. You may have also noticed more and more Endarkened are fighting against the dream extractions. We help with that. My job is to work with Endarkened children. I try to help them see how Endarkened people, specifically Endarkened women, have historically engaged in reading and writing to record and make sense of their lives. I try to help them engage in reading and writing in an effort to seek justice in this world. It's kind of like what you're doing in that journal of yours."

"Since we're talking about our jobs now, I work with dreams," Ebony said proudly. The breeze lifted her red hair, but I noticed it was a style I'd never seen before—there were small, interlocked sections of hair seemingly fused together, thicker than individual hair strands, but thinner than a collection of ponytails. It was beautiful. "Most of the people who come to us have never dreamed before, so it's my job to show them how to access them. The dream extraction does a number on the brain, and the lack of dream examples y'all get as you grow up makes it harder the older you are, but I can usually get them to find their dreams.

You're older, so it's probably going to take you a little longer, but then again, you did read Butler, and if you were able to read her work and make it here, you might not have as hard a time with it. It's easier to help children dream, because they're able to access their dreams quickly. The barrier isn't as hardened, but it's not impossible for adults to learn. It just takes courage to reject what you know and make space for the unfamiliar. My question is … are you brave enough to imagine? Are you willing to do the hard work of sculpting a new reality from your dreams?" Ebony turned and looked at me questioningly, waiting for my answer.

"Yes?" I didn't sound confident, but how could I be? I didn't know if I was brave enough to imagine. I've never done it before. And the way she said it made me feel like it was a difficult process. According to Ebony, it's easier for children, probably because they haven't completed their training in FirstHOME, and probably because they haven't been socialized into GC's ideals for as long as adults have. Gholdy's words put me at ease, though, because she helped me see I'm at least doing something people do in the Harbor. I don't know if they are writing in journals, or if they're writing books or something, but I suspect they're writing about themselves. I can at least do that.

As we continued walking, I noticed something I should've observed the moment I saw them staring at me: the Othermothers were breathing this ashen air as if nothing was wrong. But, when I walked around Savannah, I had to cover my face to stop the coughing. "I know I've been asking a lot of questions, but I'm really curious about something. How are you able to breathe with so much ash in the air?"

Layli chuckled a bit and stopped walking. "That is what your senses tell you?"

"Yes," I replied sheepishly, feeling as though I asked a stupid question.

"I was wondering what this place would feel like to you," Layli said. "I think I can best explain it to you by first saying we have designed this place in a particular way to ensure those who mean us harm will always struggle to see. By altering what they see, we remain the unseen. We can see them because our eyes are not clouded by the world. We exist in community with the world and see it as what it can be, what it wants to be, not what it is."

I know she meant for that to be helpful, but it wasn't. How do you design a place that stops people from seeing what you don't want them to see? How can you alter what someone sees? How do you see what a place can be when what is actually there is a ruined mess of a city? Moreover, why do I see, taste, and feel ash when they are walking around seeing the unseen with no problems?

"We exist in a commonweal," Layli continued, sensing my discomfort, "a state of collective well-being that includes the Endarkened and all living kind, from humans to animals to plants to microorganisms. It even includes inanimate parts of the Earth, the myriad universes beyond the Earth, the spiritual worlds, and the transcendental realms. This principle of a commonweal binds us, as we have built relationships among Endarkened groups, between the Endarkened and the environment, and between the Endarkened and the spiritual. Because of these relationships, we are able to see things those outside of the commonweal cannot. The Othermothers seek to heal the wounds resulting from the imbalance, but because you have not yet learned to find the balance, you will not see the unseen."

Although Layli talks in riddles, I understand her point … I think. Somehow, the Othermothers built a connection between themselves and the world around them. Because of this connection, they can see things those without the connection won't be able to see. I don't have that connection, so I see the world as it is, not how it wants to be. I kind of wonder if this is how I see other Endarkened people, too, since I don't exist as part of this commonweal thing yet. I wonder if having balance in the world helps people to see each other more clearly.

"So, this place is not filled with ash?" I asked.

"Yes … and no," Layli responded without turning around.

"It's like this," Ebony jumped in. "You haven't learned to find the balance, so you see a world imbalanced. GC ensured your world was dismal. They focus on building wealth to the detriment of the environment. They refuse to acknowledge the spiritual and transcendental realms existing alongside the real one. They focus on uplifting the Dreamers and keeping the Endarkened in a place of stagnancy. This throws off the balance. Because you're socialized into GC's unbalanced system, you, too, are removed from the commonweal. Of course, you can work toward the commonweal, but you're still too tied to GC to really reach it. Some people come here from other company states and see different things, but it's always a bleak picture—ash, unending fires, never-ending darkness, shadow monsters. It's always interesting to know what others see since we don't have the same vision of the world."

I was right. I don't have the connection they have. I think what hurts most, though, is that I can't see the unseen because GC's hold is still too strong. I thought I was moving away from them because I was reading and writing. I thought I was distancing myself because I'd chosen to leave the Annex and find Acorn. I guess that's my fault for thinking undoing all of GC's work would be a simple task. I know better. Reading one book and doing a little writing isn't enough to completely change my worldview. Doing work for a few weeks isn't enough to help me see the world differently. It takes a long time to see the world as it wants to be seen.

After at least 2 hours of walking, we paused in front of an old, rundown building. It had a good frame even if parts of it were missing. I could see inside from where we stood, and I noticed there were metal bookshelves leaning against the walls that were still standing. This was probably a library at some point, but GC let the books burn along with everything else. I wonder what the Othermothers saw. I wonder if their sense of time was similar to mine. Maybe they saw the library as it wanted to be seen, as it could be seen in a future world. Maybe they saw shelves of restricted books waiting to be borrowed by curious readers. Maybe the walk that felt like 2 hours for me was only 15 minutes for them. Nothing makes sense to me right now.

"We're here," Gholdy said.

"Where's here?" I asked, noticing "here" looked very much like nowhere.

"One of the tunnel entrances," Ebony answered. "The Harbor is underground, and this entrance is the most accessible. There are a few other entrances—beneath an old eatery, underneath the Pirate's House, below the First African Baptist Church, and even under Savannah's former law school. The tunnels go all around Savannah, so we're able to move about pretty freely. The best thing is the Dreamers don't come down here because they believe the tunnels are blocked. Their books tell them there's nothing down here, and they believe it. It's funny because in their attempt to erase Endarkened history, they've lost access to important information that would've led them to our hideouts."

Layli began walking toward one of the leaning bookshelves and pushed it aside. It seemed much lighter than it looked, or Layli was much stronger than she appeared. Underneath the shelf was a hidden door. Venus, Gholdy, and Ebony each handed Layli a key, and she inserted and turned them one by one. Nothing happened until the final key was rotated. A deep groaning sound erupted from beneath the floorboards, and the door creaked open.

"After you," Layli waved her hand toward the door.

I cautiously looked into the dark hole, knowing this choice would determine if I was brave enough to imagine. I could turn back, but my curiosity was pulling me forward. I found the ladder rungs and inched my way down toward the darkness.

September 19, 2085 (continued)

The main hub of the Harbor is the most beautiful place I've ever seen. Even though the tunnels are far underground, a brightness remains. Electricity surged through the tunnel's veins to bring light to the body of the concealed Endarkened city. Endarkened people, most of them Black, roamed about the open space, gathering what they needed from vendor stands located around the hub. There were no sellers, though, just unattended shops where people seemed to just take what they needed. They didn't leave payment or anything, but I did see some people taking items from the shelves and leaving different items in their place. It's a fascinating trade system where people refuse to horde goods for themselves.

The people were dressed in vibrant colors with no color dominating any one item of clothing. They wore black, blue, and green pants, multicolored shirts and vests, mismatched shoes, piecemeal headwear, and rainbow-colored dresses. It seemed like everyone's clothing was made from a collection of various materials, as if they threw all of their old belongings together and made new clothing from it. Above ground, I couldn't see the Othermothers' clothes because they wore black and gray coverings which, I guess, was used as camouflage. As they removed their outer layers, I noticed they, too, had vivid colors infused into their clothing. The clothing was as diverse as their skin.

As I looked around, I was fascinated by the children playing along the corridor. One girl zoomed by in her wheelchair, followed by several kids running in the same direction to avoid being tagged by the Endarkened child running after them. Another child sat in the corner painting a scene of the hub, paying close attention to passersby. Further down, I saw a group of children standing on a platform talking to any person who agreed to stop and listen. I couldn't hear everything they were saying, but they seemed to be attempting to persuade people to start an intergenerational debate team.

As we walked through the center of the hub, I expected people to part ways, stepping aside to let the Othermothers through, but everyone just kept going about their day. Some nodded and waved hello, some walked right up to them and gave them hugs and high fives, and others just minded their business. I was confused. The Othermothers seemed to hold a place of prominence in this enclave, but there was no fanfare for their presence. It was as if they were one of the regular, everyday citizens of the Harbor. Even with their patchwork skin, they blended in with the masses of people.

"Why is everyone's clothing like that?" I asked.

"People from various places find their way to the Harbor" Layli said as she hugged a few of the people standing around the hub. "Some come from well-off states like you, and others do not. Those from higher tracked states often come to us with clothes and shoes that fit, and they often come with multiple sets of clothing. Those from lower tracked states sometimes come to us with adequate clothing, but they are more likely to need clothing better suited for them. We try to engage in a communitarian effort within the Harbor, so rather than forcing those who have the least to suffer because of where they were forced to live and work, we throw all of our resources together and make clothing from all of our donations. It's a way for us to acknowledge each person's dignity, offer nurturing to every Endarkened who comes our way, promote amity between us, and foster positive group relationships. Plus, we all love a little vibrance, no?"

"Yes!" I realized all I've been doing for the past few hours was saying yes and asking questions, so I continued. "I see you all really work together here. I think that's great although GC would never allow such things."

"We work alongside each and every person here," Ebony placed her hand on my shoulder and looked right into my eyes. "Yes, we've been here the longest, so we have certain skillsets we pass along to those who want to learn, but we don't create rigid lines about who's in or out, who holds knowledge and who doesn't, or who's to be uplifted and who isn't. In fact, some of the most important knowledge comes from grassroots organizers like those kids over there. We're not restrictive like that."

Not … restrictive. I've never heard of such a thing, but I guess they make it work here. GC is all lines, boxes, and compartments. You choose a side, and you stick with that side. Your choice ensures you're positioned as an insider or outsider. Ideology is a rigid thing; it helps people maintain homogenization and exude control over people. Without it, wouldn't chaos ensue? What happens when people inevitably disagree because there is no ideology to hold them in place to what they should be agreeing or disagreeing with? What happens when people can't come to an agreement and begin fighting because each side believes themselves to be right? Without a prevailing ideology, how do we know who is right and who isn't?

"Don't hurt yourself, sister," Layli said soothingly after seeing the concerned expression on my face. "We talk to each other to both establish and negotiate our relationships, and because we choose to approach each person's thinking with care, our relationships can accommodate disagreement, conflict, and anger at the same time we accommodate agreement, affinity, and love. We harmonize our dissimilarities and respect how people express themselves, and we synchronize our differences by acknowledging the numerous ways people live rewarding and authentic lives. To make a comparison, GC requires rigidity. They present Endarkened people with an ultimatum—they must either succumb to GC's way of life or perish. Here, we acknowledge people's differences. We may not always agree on how things should be done, but we are always able to talk about why we think the way we do in hopes that we can see each other's point of view."

"I see," I responded noncommittally. I didn't understand how they maintained a community when everyone was allowed to follow their own spiritual and individual ways of thinking. I'll learn more, but the thinking behind this place is so different, and I'm not sure if I'd fit in like I hoped. I wonder if I have the capacity to think without limitations after having GC's ideology force-fed to me for so many years. I want to try, but it's scary to go against everything I know, especially when I've been taught that doing so means torture and possible death. Is freedom worth that?

As I continued thinking to myself, I mindlessly followed the Othermothers as they walked down a series of quiet hallways. The tunnels consisted of several long passageways, and I'm sure I'd get lost if left on my own. Eventually, they stopped in front of a door with the letters L J on it. It's weird because I didn't remember ever leaving the Othermothers, and I didn't remember them talking to anyone about me as we were walking through the hub. And yet, my chosen initials were carved into the door frame.

"Lauren, here is where you can sleep for the night. It's not much, but it's comfortable," Gholdy held open the door. "Tomorrow, we can fill you in on how everything works, but for now, I think it's important you rest. You've taken in a lot today, and you probably need some processing time. We do a lot of work here, but we also prioritize self-care. Right now, you look like you could use it. We'll be back for you in the morning." With that, Gholdy allowed the door to close, and the four women continued walking down the corridor.

Gholdy was right. I needed some time to think through everything I witnessed today, and I also needed some sleep, especially after the amazing meal we shared in the food hall. The Othermothers, the Hub, the unseen—it's a lot to process, and my brain is overloaded with new information. I am excited about this new knowledge, though. I wonder how they make this little society work and how many other societies exist across the country. I wonder why the Othermothers have patchwork skin, but the other Endarkened members of the Harbor seem to have one skin tone, like me. I wonder why GC is so scared of a place like this when it's just a space of Endarkened love.

September 20, 2085

I didn't want to get out of the warm comfortable bed, but I noticed there was a plate of food sitting on the table. Breakfast was a combination of fruit, vegetables, and toast. It was an odd breakfast, not something I would have put together for myself, but it would do. It was definitely better than the daily meal pills, or the oatmeal-like mush GC gave us for lunch. I guess it's hard to have processed food options when everything is underground, away from all of GC stores.

I finished my food and put on a pink, green, and brown Harbor dress I found in a wooden chest at the foot of the bed. It was much more comfortable than my light blue GC-authorized uniform. As soon as I was done getting dressed and putting my hair into a sleek ponytail on the top of my head, I heard a knock at the door. Venus stood there, with a huge smile on her face. She looked well rested and excited about the day ahead. It was weird because I don't think I've ever seen an Endarkened person smile so brightly, especially in the morning. It's hard to smile about a day you're not excited about.

"Good morning, sister! I do hope you slept well. The first night is always a little weird for new arrivals."

"I did. Thank you for asking."

"Wonderful. I'm glad you're rested because we have a lot to do today. Right now, I am going to escort you to our fellowship hall. It's the place where we welcome all newcomers and explain how we operate. It is also the day you can pick your classes if you choose to stay. Don't be alarmed, though. This is not like FirstHOME. We don't force you to stay with us, nor do we force you to take a specific set of classes. We encourage you to learn with other newcomers so you can find kinship because it helps the unlearning process go a bit more smoothly, but it's not required. If you're ready, please follow me." Venus finished her statement and began walking in the opposite direction without waiting for my reply.

I followed her down several hallways and wondered how she remembered which way was which. The living quarters of the Harbor were labyrinthian. As we walked, we passed several other doors with names on them. There must be thousands of people who live in this underground city, much more than were in the hub the night before. I also saw businesses. Clothing makers cut bits of fabric from worn clothing, dyed faded materials, and sewed them together to make new clothing options. There was a doctor's office with nurses bustling around inside. A daycare had kids of all ages running around joyfully as they played games with each other. Each business had an open door, where people could leave whenever they chose. No one was forced to work, but they were still working, and they seemed delighted to engage in their labor.

We finally got to a large, wooden double door with the words "fellowship hall" written in bold golden letters above the door frame. Inside, I saw Ebony, Layli, and Gholdy sitting at a round table at the front of the room. There were five other people sitting there: an Endarkened girl no older than eight, two Endarkened men who looked about 30, an Endarkened woman who seemed to be around Layli's age, and an Endarkened teenaged boy. There was such a variety of ages, and yet we all sat at the same round table, waiting to see who would speak first. The Othermothers looked thoughtful, while the rest of us looked anxious. If the others were given the same speech I was given, they had reason to be nervous.

After several minutes, Gholdy spoke. "Welcome everyone. We're so glad you were able to find the Harbor even with GC's constant surveillance. We know many of you had long journeys and went through much to get here. We acknowledge you and your hardship in this space. As you know, my name is Gholdy Jill Winn. My sisters are Layli Jane Walker, Venus Jill Collins, and Ebony Jane Womack. We're some of the Othermothers who take care of this place. There are more, but we take turns welcoming newcomers and teaching courses, so we all have time to rest. When we're well rested, we're better able to do our work. Anyway, we're going to tell you a bit of the history behind this place, and then we're going to talk to you about unlearning and the method we use to help you unlearn. We'll also talk about the classes we offer that can help you to not only unlearn, but to also learn to access the dreams hidden from you. Any questions?"

Silence.

"Good!" Gholdy exclaimed. "Ebony works in dream reclamation, so she's the best person to explain the maps. Ebony, you ready, sis?"

"Of course," Ebony said. "I'll start by asking each of you to say your names and terms, and then state the title of the book that led you here. I've found that to be the easiest way to start."

"I'm John–4758201. My term, I guess, would be sib. My partner, John–4792012 also uses sib. We found our way to this place using *Brown Girl in the Ring* after being told to find Hopkinson." I realize I didn't consider their terms when I first walked in, and I feel ashamed. I'm glad I know, and I'll make sure to wait for terms before assuming gender. It's all new to me, but I know I must do better.

By the looks of it, the Johns had a hard journey. John–4792012 looked so weak I wasn't sure they could speak if they wanted to. John–4758201 didn't look much better, but at least they seemed a bit stronger and were willing to speak for them both. I wondered if they decided to leave because GC doesn't tolerate variation in terms. GC and the other companies require a she/her or he/him designation. They/them and other terms are not accepted. I wonder if they left because GC didn't allow space for them to fully exist.

The 8-year-old had a strong voice I wasn't expecting from someone so small. "I'm Jane–8928394821. My observer told us to find double L to find our wonderland. I found L.L. and *A Blade So Black*, and then I came here. I use sister."

She stood up and looked around the room, focusing upon all of us as she spoke. After taking a few more moments to look everyone in the eyes, she sat down. There was an air of strength in her I don't have. I wonder how she got to that point. How is she so strong and still so young?

"John–190320938. Brother. *Tristan Strong Punches a Hole in the Sky.*"

The teenaged boy didn't seem too interested in the formalities, or maybe he didn't trust the Othermothers yet. I wonder if he'd already been forced into SecondHOME. If so, I could see why he didn't trust the Othermothers since they could be considered the observers of the Harbor. Some of the HOME observers consistently discipline Endarkened children for being themselves. If he had chosen to laugh too loud, talk with his hands, or use words unknown to his observers, SecondHOME would've been rough. I hope he never had to experience that.

It was my turn. I chose not to stand like little Jane because I was still trying to get a feel for this place and everyone in it. "Technically, I'm Jane–9675214, but I decided to change my name to Lauren Jane before I came here, so I guess that's my name now. I'm not sure if it will change again, but it works for now. I use sister, and I got here with help from *Parable of the Sower*." When I was done, I saw there was only one person left, the elder Endarkened person.

"I am Jill–54321. I prefer the term, sib, and I was blessed enough to receive help from *Beloved*. I am pleased to meet you all."

Many Endarkened elders command respect in their presence and tone, and Jill is no different. Their voice was a deep tenor, but the smile they held as they spoke lightened their words. Jill held everyone's gaze when they finished, as if to remind us of our manners. They were the only one to greet the group, and the look they gave each of us was a warning, prompting us to all say in unison, "Pleased to meet you, too."

"Thank you all," Ebony stifled a laugh as she watched our reactions to Jill. "I don't know if you noticed, but each of you was led by a different book. That is purposeful because we need a lot of maps to ensure the Dreamers don't catch on. Each of you also named a book that can fall within what some people call the speculative genres: science fiction, fantasy, magical realism, myth. I say some people because there are people who don't see anything speculative or imaginary about the books you read. Anyway, the writers of those books committed to engaging in an ongoing discussion with the past, present, and future by writing maps for future generations. Their goal was to assist us in finding, identifying, and creating places where Endarkened people are caring for each other and negotiating their existence on our own terms."

"More than likely, all of you were given hints at some point in your life," Ebony continued as she readjusted in her seat. "Our people can't tell you it's a map, but the goal is to provide enough hints to assist people in making the connection. The hope is that every Endarkened person who gets one of these maps will figure out where to go. Of course, some people figure it out early, while others take a little longer. So many factors impact people's journeys, from surveillance to intense feelings of fear. The good thing is that because so many different people come to us at different times, we're able to do some intergenerational learning, and we're able to learn more and more about how GC operates across time."

Layli chimed in. Her hands were folded in front of her on the table. "Another major factor is the dream extractions. We have not been able to figure out a way around those. The best way, it seems, is to read and view the works of others, but those are restricted. The surgery occurs at birth. The parents have no time to pass knowledge to the child. Both parents then undergo another dream extraction to ensure they lose the will to find the child. There's no way for us to get to them in time."

The room looked solemn. Even little Jane knew how Endarkened parents are treated. They give Endarkened children "the talk" when they're five because they believe us to already be knowledgeable of adult topics and sex by then. Endarkened men and women aren't allowed to have friendships, be in relationships, get married, live together, or even congregate in groups larger than three. We're consistently isolated. However, between the age of 25 and 30, Endarkened people are allowed to apply for a partner and have children if they choose, as long as it isn't a same-sex couple. GC uses their laws to criminalize them. Requesting partnerships isn't required, but if Endarkened people refuse, we lose our ability to have children later. GC doesn't want children or pregnancy interrupting our ability to work, and they believe our prime working talent begins at 30. They call this process Harvesting.

Many Endarkened people refuse to have children. This is what GC wants. The dream extractions and family separations began because the Endarkened outnumbered the Dreamers, and they feared we would treat them the same way we'd been treated for centuries. However, if Endarkened people aren't having children, the United States' population of Endarkened individuals might dwindle, possibly allowing Dreamers to outnumber us once again. So, although some people fight back by refusing to have children, others fight back by having them, hoping a revolution will start with the next generation. Jane's early journey to the Harbor proves it can happen, but we can't just leave it to the younger people. Adults have to do our part, too.

"The extractions definitely deter our efforts," Ebony said. She walked over to little Jane and sat next to her. "But that's why one of my goals is to talk about and help others fix the imagination gap caused not only by the extractions, but also by the long stint in GC's HOME system. For those of you who completed First and SecondHOME, you probably noticed a few things about your reading options. The books you read to find your way here aren't on the shelves at the HOMEs. They also remove all speculative media content featuring Endarkened people from television, film, streaming services, and the internet. Even realistic stories of joy, hope, resilience, and rebellion have been destroyed. They've restricted your access to these stories, only allowing you to become acquainted with the painful aspects of our history, rather than allowing you to access lands of imagination, joy, and hope. They never talk about the rebellions, the movements for freedom and equal rights, the resistance to GC."

"If they granted more access to these texts," Ebony looked toward the ceiling, "you'd have access to the dreams and imaginations of our ancestors. The goal is to break the ties connecting us to our history. That way, when you face the realities of GC's oppressive world, you have no idea how to find your way out of it. You have no idea how your ancestors found ways to fight back. You can only see yourself within GC borders."

I took in this information slowly. I remember being in FirstHOME and wondering why we didn't get to read stories showing Endarkened people dreaming. I never asked why because I just assumed they weren't out there, that Endarkened people never dreamed. But I learned later that it was orchestrated. GC knew we'd try to change things for the better if we had access to stories that taught us to dream for more than we had. They knew we'd rebel if they told us Endarkened people have a history of fighting oppression. So, GC restricted our access to these books because they knew reading them could help us challenge GC's oppressive institutions and find our way to a life of liberation. GC didn't want us to dream because it meant they could lose their ability to control the global majority, and they definitely didn't want that.

The other new members mulled over what Ebony just explained. Jill looked pensive, while the Johns looked sad and defeated. I'm sure I heard John–4792012 stifle a sob. Young John and Jill didn't finish their HOME training, but they stood stoic with their eyes downcast. I couldn't even hear them breathing. We all grew up in a system that suffocated our dreams. Some of us had less time in the system than others, but we all knew what Ebony said was true. The issue was how to fix it.

We'd all had dream extraction surgery. Some of us had a harder time fighting against it. Our eyes betrayed us. The older John had electric blue eyes like mine, so he had the surgery recently. Those of us in our late 20s to early 40s always seem to have the bluest eyes. The younger children often vary between deep and pale blues, mainly because they hadn't had the surgery since birth. Their eye color also depended on the observers and whether or not the observer chose to rebel against GC and attempt to teach them how to dream. That's why little Jane had powder blue eyes, and young John had a baby blue tint. The older Endarkened members are often confined to a separate nursery section of FirstHOME, and GC doesn't bother them too much unless they make trouble like Harriet–2 did. Jill's eyes were periwinkle. Maybe Jill's been off GC's radar for so long she was able to fight the extraction on her own.

"Basically, speculative stories are maps," Ebony said with a soft smile. "They led you to this Harbor, but there are many more spaces like this throughout the United States. We're located in California, Washington, Washington D.C., Oregon, North Carolina, New Jersey, Texas, Wisconsin, Tennessee, Nebraska, Missouri, Nevada, and Massachusetts. We even have one in Toronto. We can't house everyone in one place because we don't want GC to catch on, but we all work together to ensure everyone across the network has what they need. Also, each Harbor is cultivated to cater to a specific Endarkened group. The violence caused by GC necessitates spaces of individual and collective healing, so the goal of the Harbor network is to heal ourselves and then to work together toward collective freedom. During this process of healing, there are people like me who help Endarkened people learn to access their dreams."

That got everyone's attention. I've heard about failed attempts to dream, but I've never met anyone who succeeded. There are rumors, but as soon as a rumor began, the person attached to the rumor was removed from the rest of us, and we were told to shun the person for lying and bringing dishonesty into our lives. Sometimes, I think the companies started the rumors, but there's no way to prove it.

"That leads us to the next part of this conversation: unlearning," Venus said. She re-pinned her hair to move it away from her face, and I noticed her interlocking hair strands were a bit larger than Ebony's. "We offer a plethora of ways to help you unlearn, but they all take the form of classes to make things easier. I know it sounds weird to unlearn through classes, but the process works well. You can unlearn in various ways based on your individual interests: dance, drama, poetry, prose, musical performance, musical production, architecture. The list goes on and on."

"Your co-learners will guide you toward unlearning, toward dreaming, in ways that best suit your needs. If you don't know what style of learning best fits you, or you have no idea what your interests are, you may try different classes until you find what works best. If you select something and decide it no longer suits your needs, you may leave and select another. You can even go back to the first if you want to try it again. Essentially," Venus ended, "our way of teaching revolves around your needs and interests."

"We teach using a concept called Afrofuturist thought," Ebony added. She'd moved from little Jane's side and was back with the Othermothers. "It's an old form of knowledge based on how Endarkened authors created speculative texts centering Endarkened characters. These creators made books, songs, buildings, sculptures, and poems to reclaim and recover the past, counter negative and elevate positive realities in the present, and create new possibilities for the future. In each of the classes, our goal is to use the medium you choose to assist you in reclaiming and recovering aspects of the past GC has stolen from you; countering the negative ideals GC has instituted and elevating the positive aspects of Endarkened existence we're often told to ignore; and creating new possibilities for your own personal future as well as the futures of the Endarkened people. Once this occurs, you'll be able to access your dreams again. So, does anyone have any idea which class they will select?"

I raised my hand. "Um … you didn't tell us what classes we could choose from. You say books, and music, and architecture, but you don't say how those are courses. Can you tell us the names of things so we can select something? Also, what do you mean access our dreams again?"

"Oh! I should've explained a little better," Ebony laughed. "First, your dreams are still there. They weren't removed; you just don't have access to them because GC's procedure blocks them. It stops you from reaching the dreams you already have."

Secondly," Venus stood and smoothed the wrinkles on her dress, "you create your courses, and we find someone to teach you. The courses are based on what you want to learn. We have loads of expertise in the Harbor. Sometimes, your interests will be narrow, and you'll work with one person. Sometimes, you will have a broad interest, and you'll work with multiple people. It all depends."

My head spun. At HOME, we were told what to study. We never selected topics that interested us.

John–4758201 spoke up. "We would like to learn about Endarkened sibs who wrote poetry, and we'd also like to learn more about how the tunnels were made."

Those interests seemed so specific to me, but Layli looked over to them and said, "That can be arranged." She whispered to Venus who nodded. "Is there anyone else who would like to learn alongside John and John?" She waited for a moment, and Jane–8928394821 stood up.

"Wonderful!" Venus exclaimed. "Jane–8928394821, John–4758201, and John–4792012, please follow me, and I'll introduce you to your first co-learner, Samuel Jack Hunt."

When they left the room, I said, "I would like to know more about how the Harbor operates."

Layli looked over to Ebony and said, "Is there anyone else who would like to learn with sister Lauren?" No one stood and no one spoke. "I understand. We all have varied interests. Well, Lauren, if that is what you are interested in, then Ebony will be your first co-learner. She can help you learn more about how we have used Afrofuturism to build this space. If you will follow her, you can find a space to learn together."

I was expecting to be handed off to some other member of the Harbor since the Othermothers have so much to do, but I was excited to learn with Ebony. As I followed her out the door, I wondered what I'd learn and what I could offer her as a co-learner. I'd been doing a lot of wondering lately. Maybe this was what Butler meant when she wrote about change. I'd learn from Ebony and in the process, I'd change, but then, she may also change from learning with me. I have a feeling I'll be grappling with that phrase for a long time.

As Ebony and I walked, I tried to take in my surroundings, hoping I'd be able to figure out this underground maze without getting lost. There were letters above the doors similar to those carved above my room. Some doors had names, like The Fabians, The Fadleys, The Feagans, The Feists. After a few minutes, I realized that they had to be chosen names, especially since GC doesn't allow us to have family names. Our last names aren't important until we start working. At that time, we take on the name of the company we work for. It lets everyone know who we belong to. Based on the variety of names over the doors, the people choose their own last names. They choose their family members, choose who they belong to. It shows their individualism because I don't see similar last names carved above the doors, but it's also a way to form community because every person with that last name is now a part of a family.

In the Harbor, it seems like individualism and community are equally prized. They understand that having individual characteristics makes the community stronger. This differs greatly from GC because, for them, difference is a sign of chaos. They'd rather create one, unified whole devoid of Others to maintain a semblance of balance. This balance only refers to the Endarkened. The problem for GC was that we have too much difference amongst us which forced Dreamers to learn new terms, to honor our individual cultures, and to recognize other people and cultures exist. It's silly to believe everyone needs to be like the Dreamers in order to access humanity, but that's what the leaders of GC believe, so that's how they run the country they paid for.

We stopped at a door with the word "library" carved above it and walked in. "Tomorrow, we start our co-learning sessions," Ebony said. "We'll meet in here because it'll be nice to connect the authors to their works. These authors wrote books hoping we would read them, so I want to make sure you have access to the books if reading them is what you want to do. Tonight, though, think of specific questions you have. I want to make sure you get your specific questions answered." With that, she walked to the door and left me in the library.

The room was much bigger than the room I slept in last night. In fact, it was bigger than the hub we walked through when we first entered the Harbor. Bookshelves lined the perimeter of the room from floor to ceiling. There had to have been at least one thousand books on each shelf, maybe more. I had no idea Endarkened people produced so much literature overtime. What makes the space even better is there is no restricted section. I can pick up any book I see, and I can read it. It may not seem like a big deal, but it is. This library is freedom.

3

EXPANDING THE LITERATURE

Speculative maps, activated dreams

September 21, 2085

When I walked into the library, Ebony was entranced by a book. I didn't know what she was reading, but she was so enamored she didn't realize I was in the room until I was right next to her. "Um ... sorry to bother you, Ebony, but is this a good time to do the lessons? I can come back if it isn't." I know she agreed to work with me, but I also saw she was trying to learn more, too.

I had so many questions. Like, what, exactly, is Afrofuturism? Where did it come from? Why is it used to create maps? Knowing this information would help me better understand how I got here, but it could also help me understand why Ms. Jackson used those names and why Harriet–2 told me to find the Butler. There must be a history of stories like these which is why they are used to assist Endarkened people in finding the Harbor.

"Of course! I was just catching up on some reading." Ebony said without looking up at me. "New books are brought in daily, and I like to read as much as I can, so I have the latest information. You never know what people are going to ask, so I like to know a little of everything just in case. Plus, even though I use my knowledge to help other residents, I like learning new things and reading the words of Endarkened people who were writing in the midst of GC's rule. Their words give me hope. Anyway, you have questions for me?"

"I have, actually." I didn't want to waste her time, so I got right to it. "So, since you know so much about maps and Afrofuturism, I wanted to know more about that. I guess, a place to start would be to ask what Afrofuturism is. That would help me to better understand a little bit more about how people have found the Harbor overtime." It was better to start at the beginning rather than asking all my questions at once.

DOI: 10.4324/9781003159285-3

"Well, the first thing I should say is *this* Harbor was founded using Afrofuturism, but it's not the only way of thinking. Remember when we said we don't create rigid lines about who's in or out? Well, it works with Afrofuturism, too. People can choose to learn about dreaming through Afrofuturism, but they don't have to. Some people and Harbors use other speculative genres, and some follow more realistic ones. We have those, too, if you're interested. Like I said, this library has a lot of information."

"Based on your question, though," Ebony continued, finally closing the book and putting it on the table next to her. "I think there's someone who can give a better answer than I can. She's only been here for a few years, but I think she'll have the answers you're looking for. She's been really focused on this stuff since she arrived, and although I talk about it sometimes, I've been more focused on other things. Wait here a minute." Ebony left the room, closing the library door behind her. When she returned five minutes later, she had a beautiful, brown-skinned woman with a large afro walking beside her.

"Lauren Jane, meet Erin. I'm pretty sure she's the best person to learn with you today. She helped us figure out different ways to use Afrofuturism in the Harbor, and she's known for her interest in the speculative arts."

"Hi Lauren Jane!" Erin grinned as she extended her arm for a handshake. "It's great to meet you." Her grip was firm, and I thought she'd pull my arm off with her vigorous shake.

"Um … hi," I said, a little taken aback. "Did Ebony tell you my question?"

"She sure did," Erin nodded vigorously, causing her hair to flop over her face. "I thought about how to answer it while we were walking down here. I wasn't sure of the best way, and I'm not sure there is a best way since there's so much information, but I guess I'll start with my story."

"That sounds good to me," I said. As we all sat down, I wondered why Erin didn't restrain her hair with a ponytail holder or headband. Every time she moved, her giant hair flopped down and covered her eyes, and each time it flopped, she just flipped it back up and kept it moving. It was fun to watch.

"Ok. So, when I got here, I was fascinated by the innerworkings of this place. I wanted to know all about Afrofuturism … kind of like you. I talked to the head librarian, Edi, and she led me to short stories like 'The Goophered Grapevine' and 'The Comet' and novels like *Imperium in Imperio* and *Black No More*. These stories came out a long time ago, like almost two centuries ago, and seeing the dates helped me see just how long we've been writing this stuff. But, after reading a lot of the books … like almost all of them … I started to notice that even though Black authors in the 1900s were writing and publishing speculative fiction, their work wasn't considered as necessary as Black realistic fiction. Of course, this was before GC said everything we published was off limits."

I sat with this information, wondering when speculative fiction became important. If it wasn't important in the early 1900s, when did it gain more support? Or, maybe it had support and a large following of Endarkened supporters but Dreamers in publishing shrugged it off or something.

"Ok, so in the late 20th century, there were more Black speculative fiction authors, but not many of them were considered famous or anything. The small number of Black speculative authors caused a Dreamer, Mark Dery, to think about why we don't write speculative stories. But, of course, his question didn't allow for some of the nuance of publishing. There were probably lots of Black speculative fiction writers, but if publishers weren't publishing their works or only publishing one at a time, then of course people thought Black people weren't writing science fiction. But … I digress." Although Erin said she was going back to her point, I could tell she didn't want to. She was standing up at this point, as if she were preparing for a lecture. Her hair was covering her face, and she didn't even bother to move it. After a minute or so, she sat back down to finish her thought.

"Anyway, Dery's question encouraged him to interview some Endarkened scholars and authors—Samuel Delaney, Tricia Rose, and Greg Tate. This was before all the name changes. Their thoughts make up the majority of the paper, but from those ideas, Dery coined the term, Afrofuturism. He said it was focused on speculative fiction centering Black themes and addressing Black concerns in the 20th century. He even listed examples of Afrofuturism: the paintings of Jean-Michel Basquiat, the comics of Milestone Media, and the music of artists like Sun Ra, Jimi Hendrix, George Clinton, and Herbie Hancock. Basically, Dery coined the term, provided examples and such, and cast this word into the world."

"Wow!" I interjected. My mouth was hanging open at this point. Before coming to the Harbor, I didn't know this word existed, but there's a whole history behind it, one I would've never found if it weren't for the Harbor. "That's a whole lot of names. For something to not exist, there surely were lots of examples. And, if Dery interviewed Endarkened scholars to get to this definition, Afrofuturism must have existed before this word was created."

"Exactly." Erin agreed, holding the right side of her hair back with her hand. "Black people were doing Afrofuturism before a word existed to contain it. The word helps, but we didn't need a word to do it. I think Dery realized that, at least to some extent, because even though he provided a definition and exemplars, he said his work was only meant to map a small section of Afrofuturism," she looked as if she were far away, recounting the details of this word, remembering the stories before this word existed. "There is so much more work to be done to understand this idea."

"So … have people done some of that work? Have they mapped other sections of Afrofuturism?" I didn't want to bring her back from her thoughts, but all of this information fascinated me. Knowing Endarkened people have a legacy of dreaming and imagining was helping me see how I might be able to access that ability somehow. And, if Dery only mapped a small section of Afrofuturism, what else could be out there? What might I discover?

"Of course," Erin said, snapping back to reality and looking back at me. "Both Endarkened people and Dreamers came together to study it at one point and broadened it to be so much more than Dery initially imagined. From their work, Afrofuturism was able to take on many meanings because more Black people were creating speculative stories and more readers were attempting to categorize and theorize Afrofuturism."

"When the Othermothers brought the idea to the Harbor, they decided to do some research on their own. First, they looked at how everyday readers of Afrofuturism were defining the term because we center the everyday in the Harbor. They found that Afrofuturism was categorized as something focused on Black people's historical and present existence and highlighted how the past and present impacted our thoughts of the future. They also found that many people talked about Afrofuturism's ability to counter specific oppressions, and others talked about the need to not only place Black people in futures, but also ensure those futures were more positive. Once they saw this, they started to look into books and journals to see how academic people were defining it."

"It's so interesting they started with … what you call everyday readers. I thought they would, you know, start with the smart people, the academic people," I said in surprise. In GC, the people don't matter, those in power do. In GC, academics have both power and knowledge, and the idea is that we just sit around and wait for them to tell us what's important. How strange it is for an idea to start with the people.

"I mean, academics don't own that word," Erin replied with a smirk on her face, "the people do. That's an important part of how we operate here, especially since so many of us aren't allowed to be academics. Why only center the knowledge of a few when so many of us have knowledge?"

"That makes a lot of sense. I wish more people considered the everyday knowledge so many of us have." I realized I was looking down at my hands instead of looking into her eyes. I looked up again and gave Erin my full attention. "So, I know what the public scholars said about Afrofuturism, what about the academics?"

"Well, if you really have to know," Erin rolled her eyes. I guessed that she was giving me a chance to back out of the question since I already knew how people defined it.

When I didn't say anything, she continued, "Similar to public scholars, traditional academics said Afrofuturism was a means to combat oppression, a form of literature that countered negative realities. Other academics said it focused on recovering lost histories, analyzing history's impact on the present, and exploring how lost histories and cultures might influence the future. Still others said Afrofuturism wasn't going big enough, so they said it should address more topics, like the environment, gender, sexuality, and religion."

She paused to blow her hair out of her face. "Based on all of this information, the Othermothers decided to find a description that met the criteria of both camps. The definition we use in the Harbor is this: Afrofuturism is a cultural aesthetic in which Black authors create speculative texts that center Black characters in an effort to reclaim and recover the past, counter negative and elevate positive realities that exist in the present, and create new possibilities for the future. It's long, but it was a way for us to get everything in there."

That was probably the longest definition I'd ever heard, so I took a moment to process what the individual parts meant when she said, "I know I just said a bunch, but it's always best to start with the history and then go from there. I also have a habit of trying to share everything I know just in case people want more details. So, how are you doing with all of this?"

"I'm processing? Like, I follow everything you're saying, but it's just so much information that I think I need a minute. Can we stop for today?" I needed an information break. We've been talking for less than an hour, but within that time, I learned Black people had a history of using Afrofuturism, before and after the word was created. I learned this Harbor was built from speculative ideas that make space for Endarkened people to reclaim and recover our pasts, counter negative and elevate positive realities in the present, and create new possibilities for the future. I learned that I have a speculative history.

"Of course! I'm so sorry ... I kind of shoved all that on you. I can get that way sometimes because there's so much knowledge about Endarkened history they don't discuss in the HOMEs."

"I told you she knows her stuff!" Ebony laughed. "How about we allow you some processing time. What day do you want to meet again?"

"Maybe Monday would be good?" I was unsure of how much time I really needed to process Erin's information. I thanked her profusely and ran back to my room.

Once there, I decided to write down everything I'd learned in the last few hours. So far, I know Endarkened people have been writing Afrofuturism for almost two centuries, but the word was coined less than a century ago. I know it's found in books, artwork, and music, suggesting Harbor access points might be found in many more places, not just in books. I also know anyone can mold and shape the term, as it has continuously grown, and the power to alter the term doesn't belong to one group of people. This means GC can't control it. This also means that if GC took away one access point, there would be several others we could access to find Harbors around the country. I can definitely see why they use Afrofuturism as an approach to thinking. Afrofuturism can't be restricted by GC.

September 24, 2085

I decided to wander around the Harbor for a bit before meeting Ebony in the library. It's such an interesting place, filled with people from around the country. I met people from California, Nebraska, Michigan, Maine, and Alabama. I saw people of all genders and abilities who were thriving in this underground safe haven. They laughed, danced, played, chilled, and talked to each other, and they didn't have to worry about GC regulating how they looked, how they walked, or how they spoke. No one looked over their shoulders as they danced. No one cared about how loud they were when they joked. No one bowed their heads as they talked to the Othermothers. I could feel the sheer joy emanating throughout the place. It wrapped around me as I walked, blanketing me in happiness I never felt in GC. I wonder what stories the people have—how did they come to the Harbor? What speculative stories led them here? How do they see their future changing because they're residents of this place?

I wandered around the Harbor for hours, but I still got to the library early. I figured I'd use the extra time to learn more about how this place runs. So far, I've learned it's guided by a few things: a focus on everyday people, a nonrigid way of thinking, and a state of collective well-being. I wanted to know more, however, and although I could wait to ask Erin, Ebony, or one of the other Othermothers, I felt like it was important to read and learn some things for myself. I didn't want to rely too much on their intellectual and emotional labor.

I saw a woman sitting at a large desk in the middle of the room and decided to ask her for help. Her name tag said, Edi, and I knew I heard that name before, but I couldn't remember where. "Excuse me," I said a little too quietly. She didn't look up from what she was doing. I spoke a little louder and said, "Excuse me. Are you the librarian?"

"Yes!" She said, a little startled by the boom of my voice. "I'm Edi, the Harbor's head librarian, which means a lot to me since GC has all but destroyed libraries and the role of the librarian. I work with the spy network to bring in books by Endarkened authors and get them into the hands of the people of the Harbor. I kind of feel like I'm getting a chance to go against them, like I'm fighting them in my own way. Anyway, I say all this to say I am most definitely the librarian." Her eyes gleamed as she spoke.

"Great!" I replied. "Can you help me find something?"

"Sure! I can help you find whatever you need. What are you looking for?"

"I'm not exactly sure," I said lowering my eyes, "but I do want to know more about the origins of this place. Since I've been here, I've heard the Othermothers talk about how the Harbor honors everyday people, focuses on collective well-being, and allows an unrestricted way of thinking. I'd like to know more about that, but I don't where to start."

"I got you. There are two books I think you should read first, and then I have some other readings for you. The first book is on a theory called womanism and the second is on Black feminism. They ground a lot of the work done here although our foundation is mostly within womanism. I would tell you about how they differ, but I think it's important for you to figure that out on your own. What I can say is that even though there are similarities, they are different concepts. It works here because we don't require one theory or another. We just treat both as they were meant to be treated, as two modes of related thought … kind of like sisters."

"The articles I'll give you will help you think through it," Edi began rummaging through a filing cabinet behind her. "I always start with these because they focus on Black girls' literacy practices. The Othermothers first created this place to be a safe haven for Black girls, so we always start with this history. As you know, GC's United States is a violent space for us, and the Othermothers wanted to make sure we have a place where we can be well. They wanted to create a space where people listened to Black girls' words, their hopes, their fears … their dreams. Of course, Black women also experience violence, but our status as adults allows us to have more prominence in society. For example, before you came to the library for your unlearning session, Ebony told me that you used to work for GC. That means you had the ability to write and create even if you were constructing narratives for a violent organization. Black girls usually aren't given that much."

As Edi spoke, she increased the speed of her words. I don't know if it was because she was focused on finding whatever she was looking for, or if this was just how she relayed information to people because she was the only librarian and needed time to answer everyone's questions. Either way, she eventually began speaking at about 300 words per minute, and I gave her my undivided attention to make sure I didn't miss anything.

"Even before GC came in to alter—however slightly—the inner workings of the United States, there were award-winning Black female authors like Octavia Butler, Toni Morrison, and Alice Walker. These women used their knowledge to reimagine Black life and create new stories where we could safely exist. They used their political, social, and economic experiences to write themselves and other Endarkened people as the subjects of stories, rather than objects, centering us even when GC was determined to erase us. By writing about their lives, their experiences, their hopes, and their dreams, they were able to critique oppression and challenge any discussion that tried to silence or misrepresent them. They were able to use their writing skills to magnify their beliefs about inclusion and equity. Black girls, however, aren't usually afforded that privilege."

Edi moved around the room, piling book after book on my outstretched arms as she continued talking. My strength was going to give out soon. Thankfully, after the 12th book, she stopped piling and turned to look at me. "So, the Harbor was created with the goal of ensuring that Black girl's voices are uplifted. Got it? Good."

She finished gathering papers from the filing cabinet and started walking through the bookshelves before I had a chance to say anything. "Eventually, though, it was extended to include other women and girls of color and other Endarkened groups. Now, we help all people, those in need and those who wish to be co-conspirators in our cause. We started with Black girls and then we branched out, so that's kind of what I'm going to do with these readings."

Most Endarkened youth don't have access to the stories or even the names Edi mentioned, but I learned about them as an adult, so I know what Edi says is true. In Altered Truth, we learned that the authors Edi discussed were trying to challenge GC and make life for the Endarkened more difficult. That's why their works are restricted. To hear they were censored because they were reimagining what Endarkened life could be counters everything they taught us, which is probably why they didn't allow us to hear things like that in the HOMEs. As I thought to myself, Edi walked over to a shelf and grabbed two final books, one was extremely thick and the other was slimmer. She handed both books to me along with a stack of articles. I did ask for help, but I didn't know I was inadvertently giving myself this much work to do.

"Thank you for helping me with this, Edi."

"Of course. It's my job, but I also love helping my Endarkened sisters find whatever information they need. Let me know if you need anything else!" I hurriedly left before she could give me anything else to read.

On the way back to my room, I bumped into Ebony who was nodding and clasping her hands as she spoke with a young girl.

"Hey!" she said, pausing her conversation and looking up at me. "I'm headed to the library early if you want to meet before our scheduled time."

"About that," I said.

"What's wrong?" Ebony asked while the girl just stared.

"I just met Edi, and she gave me a lot of ... homework. I kind of want to dig into that over the next few days or so."

"I know Edi well, and she's always giving new community members loads of information. Knowing her, she gave you a wealth of great materials, so I understand the need to get reading, especially since GC has many of those books on the restricted list. Since you enjoyed *Parable of the Sower* so much, I'm sure you'll love the books you got in your arms. We can meet some other time."

I thanked Ebony and ran to my room.

October 12, 2085

It took almost three weeks to get my thoughts together about what I'd read, and I'm still not sure I understand as much as I wanted to. I guess the Othermothers knew it would take me a while because they haven't asked me to reschedule my sessions. Instead, I've just spent my time roaming the Harbor and reading the texts Edi gave me. It's been interesting to read the books and explore the Harbor because I get to see the ideals of the texts in action.

Throughout the Harbor, I see Black girls engaging in heated debates about the state of GC, discussing new hairstyles, creating new clothing concepts for GC residents, participating in Harbor governance, and discussing their dreams with the Harbor elders. I see Endarkened people who truly love the women around them; who appreciate women's culture, emotional flexibility, and strength; who are committed to the survival of all who inhabit the space and all who do not; and who are dedicated to nurturing connectivity between humanity and spirituality. I see Black women using their lived experiences as sources of knowledge, engaging in communal dialogue to create new knowledge, and utilizing emotion and care as essential to their existence.

These were the ideals I learned about in the books and articles I read over the last few weeks, and Edi was right. Although both seem to guide how people interact in this space, I do see differences in how womanism and Black feminism are taken up within the daily lives of the residents. The Endarkened people of the Harbor act as a community of Othermothers for the children, so even when the children aren't biologically related, they are still loved as members of a family. All residents, no matter their gender, age, sexuality, or ability, engage in acts of mothering. They are all caretakers, managers, nurturers, educators, spiritual, and communal mediators. They are all family.

I've also been able to see the communitarian aspect of the Harbor not only from observation but also from experience. As I walk through the halls, everyone greets me and asks how I'm adjusting. They don't care that I came here from one of GC's top divisions. They don't care that I don't understand everything about how things work. They welcome me with open arms. I've never been in a space where people are concerned for you even if they don't know you. I've never experienced a sense of community where ensuring the wellness of all members was essential. I feel like I belong here, even if I've only been here a short time.

In educating each other, some focus on challenging the narratives constructed by GC. They teach each other about how Endarkened people have historically challenged stereotypes, but instead of just listing the images GC created to confine us, they discuss how we often take in the negative images by adopting a politics of respectability or denying our inclusion as Endarkened people. They help each other think about how writing can be used to explore their identities and connect those identities to the world of GC and to the world of the Harbor. They work to define themselves even with GC and Altered Truth attempting to force a definition of self upon them. They talk about using their writing as a method of protest, a tool for social justice. From their conversations, I saw how the people of the Harbor use writing, community, and discussion to challenge GC and their lies. Although I read about it in the Black Girl Literacies articles Edi gave me, I see how all residents of the Harbor engage in these practices. I never knew writing could be so powerful. I never considered how my writing for GC was so powerful.

What stands out to me most is that even though the people of the Harbor center these educational experiences, they do so as a way to end oppression for all people. They are trying to restore balance between people, the environment, and the spiritual. It's kind of like the Harbor is trying to center the experiences of Black women and girls, but they are also focused on a wider commitment that extends beyond them to ensure the betterment of humanity and the world we inhabit. When the people speak, they don't just talk about personal freedom. Instead, they think about how all of us can be free. It's an idealistic goal, especially with GC's hold on everyone and everything, but I agree with it. It's an attempt to make the world—as a whole—a better place.

Maybe idealism is why Edi couldn't find more articles about womanism. I mean, the womanist reader was pretty hefty and covered a lot, but there were only three articles that mentioned this concept of womanism and Black girlhood. The Black feminist book was shorter than the reader, but Edi was able to give me over 25 articles to look through. I'm guessing not much has been said about Black girls in general; otherwise, I'm sure she would've given me more to look through. I wonder why more people aren't writing about Black girls and how they use reading and writing to critique, create, and conceive. I mean, I guess I know why—GC doesn't consider Endarkened youth to be important, so it makes sense to limit writings about them. Still, I wish there were more because what I've learned over the last few weeks is that the words of Black girls are assets. They … we have important things to say.

Right now, I think the issue is that GC controls the methods of communication, which allows them to regulate and often create the structures confining our beliefs, values, and norms. GC and the Dreamers who uplift them always have their voices heard, while Endarkened people and their accomplices are muted. GC silences our voices, overlooks our realities, and positions us as unimportant bodies who take up space in their dreamer–centric universe. Because the Endarkened are assigned to a lower societal status, there is an unbalanced power relationship between Dreamer and Endarkened, so even when we have something to say, we have little power to say it without getting into trouble. That's why we have the Change Room and the enforcers. In fact, our ideas are considered unintelligible unless we present them in a form acceptable to the Dreamers. Our words are disrespected even when we do speak the way they want us to because they think our knowledge is inadequate. I mean, just look at how my idea was accepted so readily when spoken from Charles' mouth. If I would've told them my idea during the meeting, they would've scoffed.

Regardless of GC's attempts, Endarkened people fought to use our communication methods, engage in our literacy methods, and talk about and critique our everyday experiences. We communicate through story, silence, speech manipulation, signifying, singing, dancing, acting, stepping, styling, crafting, and creating. We refuse to be limited to the methods of communication deemed acceptable by GC. We use our literacies to make ourselves relevant and build connections to people with shared life experiences. We pushed back against GC's silencing for decades, and I'm sure we also pushed back against negative experiences during King Trence's reign and even before he came to power. It's not only about how GC silences us, but also how we continue to use our voices anyway. GC doesn't authorize our speech or our existence. We are the authorizers of our stories; we are responsible for the excavation of our histories; we are the creators of our presents and futures.

As I've learned more and more about this place, I've been thinking about silencing, coming to voice, and accessing our dreams. Maybe, the dreams of Endarkened people disrupt some of the stories GC tries to tell about us. Maybe, the dreams of Black girls intimidate GC because they know our dreams enable us not only to critique but also reimagine this world. If we can reimagine, we can change it. I'm sure they don't want that. Right now, Black girls tend to have little power to say what's on their minds due to their race, age, gender, and/or various other identities. When we do speak out, we are punished or silenced, as the director made sure to remind me. Our speech is disrespected by those in power, and our knowledge is often ignored because we are deemed less credible than our Dreamer counterparts. But what if we listened to the dreams of Black girls? What if we read their writing and listened to what they said with the same fervor and resolve we use to listen to the lies GC tells us?

I now know what question to ask the Othermothers the next time I meet with them.

October 13, 2085

After learning about the concepts guiding the Harbor and walking the halls to discover how these practices are embodied in the people who live here, I finally decided to ask the Othermothers the question I've been holding onto. Reading and listening to people caused me to realize how much I want to help others do what Butler did for me. I want to help other Endarkened people write speculative fiction stories that challenge GC, reimagine Endarkened people's existences, and guide readers to find new Harbors, new hopescapes. Hopefully, I can also learn to access my dreams while working with them. In a way, this could be a co-learning environment that would be mutually beneficial to every person who participates in this project. Of course, I'd have to find people who'd be willing to work with me on this, but who knows what we could create if we unlearn together?

It had been a while, so I knew the Othermothers were probably busy, but I hoped someone was available to speak with me. I didn't know where they would be, so I walked to the library first. Edi was there, perusing a new stack of books. There were several other Harbor dwellers in the library, many more than I saw the last time I visited. Their colorful garb of vibrant orange, green, yellow, pink, and blue bounced off the black and brown bookshelves, bringing new light. On one wall, a group of Harbor folks, young and old, painted a mural of some sort. The colors they used in the mural were as lively as their clothing, the vivid hues melding to create a forest clearing filled with Endarkened people. It was a scene of confluence between nature and Endarkened life that would never be approved for the walls of any GC building.

The library's vibe was jubilant and energizing, but it was still a contrast to the hub because the volume was much lower. This library isn't like the GC libraries I'm used to where every person reads silently fearing an enforcer will harass them, where many librarians secretly help patrons access restricted books because, without them, we would be completely separated from the words of our ancestors. In the Harbor library, people talk to one another about what they're reading. Reading isn't an individual thing; it's a communal one, where people share their ideas about what they read while they're reading. It wasn't loud, but there was a cacophony of whispers throughout the room, and I could tell this wasn't an anomaly. People were too comfortable in their murmurs for this to be an irregularity.

"Edi," I said, interrupting her as she continued to shelve books. "Can you tell me what's going on here?"

"What do you mean? It's a library. People are reading." She gave a hearty laugh, and she followed it by saying, "Instead of asking me, why don't you ask them?"

"But wouldn't that be rude?"

"Nope. This group is here every Saturday and Sunday. They're used to new people asking what's going on."

I turned around and looked for someone I felt comfortable talking to. It's weird to barge into an established group and ask questions when they're in the middle of something, but the Harbor honors questions because everyone seems to want me to ask them. Sometimes they'll just give me the information I need, but most of the time, they want me to ask and learn. I guess they want me to be invested in my learning, so they wait for me to ask the questions, rather than just bombarding me with answers.

When I looked around the room, I found a group of four in the back corner at an oval table. There was an Endarkened adult and three young people writing something. It was the smallest gathering of people, so I walked over.

"Excuse me. Um … I'm Lauren Jane. I'm new here. Can you tell me what you all are doing?"

"Hi Lauren Jane, and welcome! My name is Kenny, and I use brother. We're writing right now. Would you like to join us?"

"What are you writing about?"

"Us."

"Us?"

"Yep. I host creative writing workshops for teens, and they focus on poetry, spoken word, and speculative fiction. To help us write, we often go out into the community—to the hub, to some of the local stores, and to our family units—and we learn from them throughout the week. Then, we come back here every Saturday and Sunday to write down the stories of Us. I hope all our young writers will discover the Harbor's stories, find their own stories within the Harbor and in larger society, and use their writing to talk about some of the important issues affecting Endarkened people. We work with any young person who sits with us, and at the end of the year, we host a celebration in the hub, where they share what they've written. It's kind of like we create written and oral histories of our pasts, presents, and possible futures."

"Is that what everyone does in here?"

"Not at all," Kenny replied. He looked around the room at the other groups. "On the weekends, the library is used for all sorts of reading and writing groups. For example, I work with youth who would be in SecondHOME, so like 14 to 17 Trinity," he pointed to another oval table in the far–left corner, "works with kids who would be at the end of their FirstHOME period, so they're between

12 and 14, usually. Her work is kind of like a precursor to mine because she focuses more on helping the youth celebrate themselves and their communities and express themselves through writing. She asks them to use their personal lives, their families, their neighborhoods, and current events as inspiration for their stories. Other groups just read together or discuss important business."

I turned to look at the other group of kids sitting at a table with Trinity. They intently scribbled on the papers in front of them, and I wondered what stories they were writing. I wondered if their lived experiences created the foundation for the stories they told. As I watched, one girl looked up and said something to the group. I can't read lips, so I had no idea what she was saying. All I knew was that as soon as she began speaking, the rest of the group looked up at her, listening, giving her their undivided attention. After she spoke, several others spoke to her, and she wrote as they talked. When the last person finished speaking, they all went back to writing. I had never seen a writing exercise quite like this.

"Thank you so much for telling me about this, Kenny. I have to go for now, but I'd love to learn more from you sometime if that's ok."

"It's fine with me, but I think you'd learn much more working with the youth instead of me. We all learn together, and they push me to think about things in vastly different ways. I'm pretty sure you would learn more from them than I could ever teach you."

I took in his suggestion. I wanted to learn from Black girls. I wanted to listen to their stories. I felt like I was being guided on a specific path that would lead me back to this place. "Thank you. By the way, have you seen Ebony or any of the Othermothers around?"

"They found a few new Harbor members yesterday or the day before. I think they're meeting with them today."

"Got it. Thanks!"

When I left the library, I walked toward the fellowship hall. That's where they took me on my second day in the Harbor. I haven't been back to the fellowship hall since I arrived. Outside of bringing in new recruits, the fellowship hall doesn't seem to be used for anything. I often wonder what it's for. It's a pretty big hall, and a lot of people could fit in there, but no one ever does anything in it. It's a big, spacious, empty room that remains vacant until one or more people are brought to the Harbor. They could probably do the introductions in someone's room instead since I've never seen more than ten new arrivals.

When I reached the hall, I saw almost 20 people sitting in a circle listening to the Othermothers give their welcome lecture. There were Black people of all shades, mimicking the various skin tones present on the Othermothers' skin. I even saw a Dreamer, but he stood outside of the circle. I don't think I've seen a Dreamer in the Harbor before. I heard the new members introduce themselves by using their names, both given and chosen, and giving their terms. Jill–562917608, Zora, sib, Jordan, brother, John–808742389, Tracey, sister. The next part was my favorite because the new members told the group which books helped them find this place. I repeated the names after they said them in hopes

I'd remember to add them to my running list of speculative books: *Legendborn*; *Kingdom of Souls*; *Dragons in a Bag*; and *Raybearer*. No two people read the same text, but they were all able to find this Harbor. Something about these texts helped them think beyond GC's barriers. Speculative maps are fascinating.

When the Othermothers finished with class assignments, only Gholdy was left in the room. The others had taken the new members with them, probably in the same way Ebony took me to my first learning site. I waved at her, and she walked toward me, her long black curly hair bouncing as she moved.

"Hey, Sis!" Gholdy said cheerfully, extending her arms for a hug.

"Hi, Gholdy. It's been a while!"

"It has. I heard you were talking to Edi, so I figured it would be a while before we saw you again. Every person that goes to her ends up with weeks of good reading material and a lot of information to sift through," she gave a high-pitched laugh that lasted for about a minute. "I'm guessing you've learned quite a bit about this place since I last saw you."

"Oh yeah … more than I thought I'd learn in such a short time. Actually, that's why I came to find you all. I had another question, and I think it's something you can help me with since you work with Endarkened children and help them think about literacy and writing."

"That's my specialty, Sis. What exactly did you want to know?" Gholdy asked, as she gathered her things from the corner of the room.

"Well, I was mainly wondering how it's been done. Like, how have Black girls used writing to combat GC to engage in justice work? And how can I help?"

"I think I can help … well, with the first part at least. I think you know how you want to help, but you have to think about it a little more. I'm sure I can give an answer to your first question pretty quickly if you're willing to walk and talk. Otherwise, I'll have to meet up with you next week. We have to get the new members settled in."

"Walking and talking is perfect. I can explore more of the Harbor as we go."

"Awesome!" Gholdy continued. She began walking down the hallway, and I walked alongside her.

"I think it's best to start with the history," she said. "If you haven't noticed, most of us do that. I think it's important since our history influences the present, and our present will influence the future. In fact, our beliefs and dreams about the future have impacted how we acted in the past and how we act in the present, so everything is connected!"

My head was spinning thinking about the cyclical nature of time, but I nodded my head and hoped she would continue talking as we walked further down the hall.

"Ok, so although GC tried to erase this truth," Gholdy resumed, "Endarkened women have always engaged in numerous tactics to create a socially equitable world. We organized Endarkened people and Dreamers to combat and challenge oppression, engaged in political movements by taking office, and used our words to promote justice. Some of our Othermother ancestors like Cherie,

LaDuke, Gloria, Fujiwara, Eve, Yamada, and Castillo wrote combinations of nonfiction essays, fictional prose, poetry, and academic papers to challenge GC and their predecessors. They wrote against their erasure, against settler colonialism, against removal. But even though many of our foremothers wrote to create a more socially just world, I tend to focus on Black women and girls because we have historically used our writing to advance society and progress justice movements. The issue is, as I'm sure you know, our words have often been silenced and our identities are often erased or minimized."

"What do you mean our identities were erased? Were we being sent to the Change Room?" I asked as we turned a corner.

"Oh no," Gholdy replied. "We were around well before Trence started the Change Room. Like, did you learn about Assata Shakur, Audre Lorde, Moya Bailey, or Trudy yet?"

"Nope. It wasn't until recently that I met so many people who didn't go by the name Jane or Jill. I didn't make the decision to change my name until a few weeks ago."

"Well, Assata Shakur wrote an autobiography to discuss how she was consistently surveilled, wrongly convicted, and forced to flee the United States and live in Cuba. We have a Harbor there. Audre Lorde wrote essays where she highlighted how she was constantly asked to focalize one aspect of her identity—Black, lesbian, woman—and marginalize the rest, rather than integrating all parts of herself. In the Harbors, we work against a forced separation of self, making sure every person is seen as a whole. Moya Bailey and Trudy invented the term, "misogynoir," a half century ago to describe racialized and gendered violence against Black women and girls, but their intellectual labor has often gone unnoticed, as most people fail to cite them when they use the word. In fact, GC co-opted the term and tried to say it was a positive trait a few years ago."

"So, these women used words to write themselves into existence all while challenging GC, and the Harbors infuse their ideas into the system?"

"Pretty much," Gholdy replied. "Even though they were doing all this thought work, their efforts were often minimized or silenced. Basically, Black women have consistently used writing as a tool for justice, and it helped others create knowledge, ask stimulating questions, propose alternate perspectives, and get other people involved in doing the work. We don't hear much about them anymore, and although part of that is because GC restricts access to the information, it's also because people often refuse to listen to Black women."

"But Black women still had more chances to write. That's what Edi told me the other day. What about Black girls? The director of Altered Truth told me about a few, but she also told me the division was responsible for changing their stories."

"Well, even though there is a rich history of Black women's writing in the face of domination and silencing," Gholdy opened a hallway door to let me walk through, "there is little information as to how and if Black girls mimic or differ from these writing practices. That's why I've focused on Black girls since becoming an Othermother. I actually focused on Black girls long before earning this title. I think it's important to see, read, and hear what's on the minds of Black girls because every time they put their pens and pencils on paper or speak their words, they are committing brave acts of self-empowerment, and we are empowered every time we listen. My goal has been to make sure people listen."

We stopped walking in front of the dining hall, and I asked, "Are you the only one who focuses on Black girls?"

"Of course not! There are several of us working towards justice, working to make sure that Black girls' voices are heard. Marcelle, Sherelle, Yolanda, Detra, Tamara, Delicia, and many others use writing to help Black girls analyze how they're socialized to believe certain things about themselves. Some, like Annette and me, use writing to help Black girls write about societal and institutional oppression. We use the historical legacy of Black women's writing to outline past and current resistance movements where Black women have used writing to promote change. Others, like Ruth and Maisha, build on discussions of individual identities and societal, cultural, and institutional oppression by using writing to help Black girls develop skills they can use to enact change. Some of us do it all. The Harbor has a collective that privileges work with Black girls."

"I think I understand," I said. "And I think I'd like to do that, too. I've been thinking about this ever since Ebony explained how the maps work. I think it started when I found Butler's book, but it was heightened after talking with Kenny this morning in the library. I want to know what speculative fiction stories Black girls would write if they were given more opportunities to do so. I want to know how they'd use their words to show us about the alternate or futuristic worlds they envision as well as the obstacles arising from the creation of such worlds. I want to know how they'd use their stories to promote justice and show how all Black girls can and do speculate and dream. My only issue is I can't dream. I can't amplify the dreams of Black girls if I don't know how to dream."

"Remember when we told you about seeing the unseen?" Gholdy asked, shifting her things from one arm to the other. "Well, you've been able to dream, Sis. You just didn't know that's what you were doing. Every time you dreamed of a world without violence, without capitalism, without oppression, you were dreaming of a better world for Endarkened people."

"So, thinking about possibilities is also a form of dreaming?"

"Of course, it is!" Gholdy replied with her eyebrows lifted. "From birth, GC participated in the asphyxiation of your social and civic imagination. The dream extraction procedure doesn't completely remove your dreams. There's no way they could do that. They don't have the power. What they do is block dreams, strangling them before they have the ability to reach the surface. For those of you who've read, seen, or heard the dreams of other Endarkened people, the block is gradually removed, and no amount of extraction can remove what you've learned if you engage with enough of it. That's why they restrict it.

They prohibit our books, vilify our songs and films, and limit how often we speak to each other. They do this because they know that once we engage with the dreams of our peers and our ancestors, we're better prepared to find community and challenge GC."

"So, I've been dreaming this whole time?" I gave myself an internal side eye.

"Yeah, Sis. But don't beat yourself up about it. Dreaming is more than just the thing that people do during sleep. It's more than just drifting off into space when your eyes are open. It's how we think about making things better for us and all people in this world. How were you supposed to know that, especially when GC consistently alters our histories?"

"You're right. I have a lot to think about."

"You probably do. Just remember we're here if you need us."

"Got it. I do have one more small question before you go."

"What's up?"

I was going to let this go, but I had to know. "In the Fellowship Hall, while everyone was introducing each other and talking about the Harbor, I noticed a Dreamer. Why was he there? Won't he compromise the safety of the Harbor?"

"Oh! That was Cody. He helped about ten people get to us."

"He ... helped them?"

"Yep. You don't think everyone finds this place on their own, do you?" She looked at me intensely. "Some people will need more help getting here, so some Dreamers work with us and other Harbors to get Endarkened people to safe havens. Some help by bringing people here, others by infiltrating the HOMEs and passing along names, and others by infiltrating the state owners, including GC, and providing us intel or engaging in company sabotage efforts. Social justice requires everyone to work together, but to truly make change in a world where Dreamers are uplifted and Endarkened people are not, we need Dreamers willing to put themselves on the line for a greater cause. You won't see many Dreamers around the Harbor because they understand the need for us to have spaces for ourselves. They understand we need spaces to heal without them, especially after the violence we experience up there on a daily basis."

"I see ... definitely a lot to think about." I shifted from foot to foot.

"I get it. It's a lot to handle when we come in here and disrupt everything GC tries to tell you about yourself and the world around you."

"I agree. But, more than that, I have a lot to think about in terms of what I want to do to help. This work requires everyone to labor together—including me."

"I know you'll figure out what you're supposed to do. Trust your spirit. It will guide you."

With that, she walked into the dining hall. Gholdy said to follow my spirit, and I knew my spirit was leading me to the library. It was leading me to work with Kenny and do something with reading, writing, and dreaming. It was leading me to dream with Black girls.

October 20, 2085

I spent most of my morning in the library, sitting with Kenny and Trinity, and I noticed something I missed the other day: all the youth were dreaming. They might not have those vivid sleeping dreams the Dreamers took from them, but they were writing about what they saw happening in the world and how they could see themselves changing it, just like Gholdy described a week ago. I wondered if Kenny and Trinity would mind me learning with their groups or at least with some of the youth who work with them. If I could do that, I could learn in community with Black girls who already inhabit the space, those who are already a part of the community. When I first arrived, Ebony said Black communal spaces are essential for our healing, self-affirmation, and growth. Based on what I read in the books Edi gave me and what I see in the Harbor, community is also important to help Endarkened people develop strategies of resistance, helping us to find more ways to fight against GC.

So far, my goal has been to learn from a group of people who are prized in the Harbor, to see the unseen. If I can learn with girls who made it to the Harbor at such a young age, I might be able to do just that. They were able to make it here and learn and dream in a place of safety before GC had the chance to give them another dream extraction surgery. I'm pretty sure that by reading and listening to their stories, I'll be able to see the unseen. Maybe, these stories can help other Endarkened people access the dreams they've been denied. Maybe, I can share these stories with coconspirators who live above. Maybe, the dreams of Black girls will help us create a better world, just like the dreams of the Othermothers helped to establish this place.

"Hey Kenny," I asked after compiling my thoughts into a cohesive plan.

"What's up?" Kenny responded.

"I have an idea …

4

INTRODUCING THE RESEARCH PARTNERS

Black girls and their world

October 27, 2085

My idea was to learn with some of the Endarkened girls in Trinity's group, and I'm so happy she agreed. But right now, I can't focus on that. I'm supposed to send Charles an update once every 2 months, and it's almost the 2-month mark, so I know he's getting antsy. His career is riding on this being a successful mission, which is probably why he granted me so much freedom. I expected him to find a way to reach out by now because GC doesn't give us free reign over our actions, but if he blew my cover in the process, the mission would fail, and his director chances would diminish. He knew this. He may not be as intelligent as he thinks he is, but he does understand power and how to get it.

The letter is difficult to construct, though. How do I give him enough information, but not enough that he'll find out about the Harbor and attempt to ruin the beauty of this place? I could give him an answer so vague it takes him months to decipher it, but that might cause him to rage and act irrationally. He and the other Dreamers at Altered Truth are known for raging when they don't get their way.

I decided on a short note that would give him something, but not enough for him to actually do anything. Hopefully, this will sate him for the next 2 months.

Charles:

> I have infiltrated the Endarkened enclave. To infiltrate the safe haven, you must see the unseen. To see the unseen, the spirit must guide you.
>
> *Jane—9675214*

It seems like I'm giving a lot of information away, but I know Charles doesn't have access to the Spirit, the commonweal guiding the place. Even if he did, seeing the unseen requires him to exist in community with the world. He

DOI: 10.4324/9781003159285-4

would need to honor his place as a community member who exists alongside Endarkened people as an equal. He would need to understand his place in community with the environment. But, Charles is incapable of balance because he sees Endarkened people as things, subjects, and property. He doesn't have the mental fortitude to work alongside anyone unless they're Dreamers—Dreamers who think and live as he does. He exists outside the commonweal, outside the balance, and in all honesty, he likes it that way. It's a disadvantage for him, but he'll never know it.

November 3, 2085

In a corner, at the oval table at the back of the library, I saw the girls Trinity told me about. They call themselves the Alfreda's: Amber, Talyn, Avenae'J, Terrah, Victoria, and Bailey. They found each other at the Saturday library meetings, and now, they consistently meet and tell stories about their experiences at FirstHome and in the world of GC. Trinity felt like they would be a great group for me to begin with because of their interest in Afrofuturism and all things nerdy. The girls are some of the newest youth members of the writing group, and they've been here for about a year. From what I hear, people are often fascinated by them because they came from FirstHOMEs all around Georgia and the Annex, hardly ever use the term Endarkened, and completely cast off their Jane and Jill names. They were also able to find the Harbor without any help, which doesn't happen often. As I walked up to the table, I noticed they were all engaging in an intense discussion. I sat down and immediately began to take notes on their conversation.

"We literally had to wear all black and all white to our graduation," Avenae'J said, moving her light brown arm from head to toe to denote clothing.

"The head observer focused more on how the school looks, but he didn't care about what students did," Talyn added. "At some point, he made a rule to where you had to only have solid color socks. You could not wear multiple colors!"

"That's what the handbook said. You're not supposed to wear those kinds of socks," Terrah explained.

"And then he was like, you can't wear certain types of shoes. Wasn't that a thing?" Talyn looked to Terrah.

"Oh yeah!" Avenae'J brightened, recalling the rule book. "One of the guys in our class who was wearing bright red and blue shoes got in trouble. The school cared more about how we looked than our actual scores."

"The handbook said you're not supposed to," Terrah said again. "Which I don't get because nobody ever enforces it at the Dreamer schools. If you're staring at people's feet, then you got an issue."

"We couldn't wear hoodies," Amber chimed in as she placed both hands on the table in front of her. "We couldn't wear red. We couldn't wear yellow. We couldn't wear all these colors."

"That's like the dress codes that are so against women showing their collar bone because they're sassy, but it's a collar bone!" Terrah said as she waved her hands wildly. Amber pointed her finger in Terrah's direction and smiled in agreement before standing up to stretch.

"That's what they did with our knees at our school," Avenae'J confirmed as she bit her nail.

"Yea, I hated that!" Victoria yelled. "I hated that! The schoolbook said you couldn't wear a sleeveless shirt or one that didn't at least have a 3/4 sleeve." As she said this, Victoria pointed to her tank top and wiggled her dark brown shoulders, showing how the clothes she wore in the Harbor would not be welcomed in FirstHOME.

Terrah also shrugged her shoulders and moved her arms around in a circle, as if to free them from the weight of dress codes. Then, she added, "You had to cover your shoulders and your collar bone."

Victoria sat with her hands clasped on the table, "I'm like, okay. So, when it's dress-down day, and you say we can wear what we want, we understand we can't wear short shorts."

"Yeah. Like no booty shorts or super high crop tops," Terrah interjected. She used her hands to show the proper length of shorts and shirts as she looked at the other girls.

"We know that much. But it can't not have sleeves?" Victoria questioned, her voice elevated to a high squeal.

"We weren't even allowed to wear ripped jeans," Avenae'J rolled her eyes. "Ripped. Jeans!" She clapped her hands to stress each word.

"We weren't even allowed to show our knees. Our knees!" Talyn stood and slammed her hands on the table.

"They were literally saying our collar bones were too flirtatious," Victoria winked at the other girls and laughed, and Bailey finally looked up from her notebook.

"What did they even mean? What if I didn't want to flirt?" Amber said, looking down into her notebook.

"We weren't even allowed to show half of our thigh because they said boys didn't know to act," Victoria said incensed.

"But … maybe teach them. Teach the boys how to act. Why were we losing stuff because they didn't know how to act?" Terrah clapped her hands and looked at the small group forming around the table.

"The observers were like 'girls learn how to dress.' How about you talk to guys about how not to touch girls?" Avenae'J said bluntly.

I remember how the observers were often more concerned with girls' outfit choices than they were about our learning. They were more concerned with the possibility of male arousal than they were about our rights to our own bodies. They were more concerned with our social decorum, rather than our academic triumphs. Apparently, the girls experienced the same things I did. The HOMEs haven't gotten much better. I guess that's what happens when they plan our entire lives.

FirstHOME doesn't need to care about our learning because we're already tracked to learn all we're "capable" of learning. Forcing clothing styles and colors just ensures the Endarkened who inhabit the schools look "respectable" to passersby. That's what they really want from Endarkened children: respectability based on what the Dreamers determine is respectable.

"You know what else I hated?" Avenae'J stood up and put her pointer finger in the air. "The one for all thing, like one person or a group of people does something, then the entire class got punishment for it."

"I hated observers like that!" Victoria adjusted her glasses as she yelled in agreement.

"That's how they did it at my school," Terrah sighed. "Like, there would be three people talking, and the observers would be like, 'okay, the entire class has silent lunch for the next week.' And I'm like, 'What?! You can't do that. I wasn't doing anything!' The majority of the class wasn't doing anything!" She clasped her hands together and shifted her body backwards, as if restraining herself from engaging with an invisible observer.

"Okay," Victoria said, standing in a storytelling stance—feet spread apart, arms ready for necessary hand motions, head leaning forward. "When I was in my seventh year, me and my best friends were the quietest ones in our class. I remember one day, the observer ... actually, he wasn't even a real observer, he was like a substitute observer that stays for the rest of the year. Anyway, so he was like, 'everybody has detention,' and me and my best friends went off on him. He was like, 'woah' 'cause we never did that before. We went off on him, like, 'How could you do that? We didn't do anything?' He was like, 'okay, um, I guess exempt you three?' He didn't know what to say. And I was like, 'thank you' and walked away."

As Victoria told her story, I thought of how cowardly I would've been in that situation. I would never have thought to stand up to the substitute observers at FirstHOME. More than likely, I would have sullenly taken the punishment because it's what I was taught to do. We were taught to be quiet and maintain respectability even if we knew the observer was wrong. Observers were allowed to demote an Endarkened's track at any time, and that demotion could result in a future I didn't want. Victoria was somehow able to undermine GC's silencing tactics, relying on her community of friends to address the fact that the observer's punishment was unjust. He couldn't punish all of them. Still, I feel for the children who are silent, the children who are too scared to speak up for fear of further punishment.

Victoria continued by saying, "I hate when a sub does that ... like you have a certain issue or something, and when it happens or when it comes to that time, they're like 'What are you doing? Where are you going?' Like, I understand they dealt with 100 kids that day, but still, one common courtesy, just listen to what I'm saying to you."

"Our math observer was like that," Talyn said. "One of our classmates had ADHD, so he had to take his medicine in the middle of class. For the first few months, she wouldn't let him go 'cause she didn't believe he had ADHD. And I was like …" She slapped her hands to her head, signaling her distaste.

"She wouldn't even let him go to the bathroom," Avenae'J added. "Every time he would walk to the back of the classroom to go to the bathroom, she'd be like 'sit down.' But then someone else would go, and she just looked at them and then looked away."

Talyn continued, "She did not like *certain* students in our class. She had grudges against them for no reason."

Because the girls' voices amplified throughout the course of the conversation, the small crowd had grown into a larger one. It's still jarring to see so many people interested and willing to listen to young people, but here they were. No one was listening to prove them wrong or respond. They were just … listening. Someone from the group, a tall dark-skinned person with a deep, gruff voice, decided to join in the conversation and said, "I wonder why they didn't pick up that type of behavior on the class cams. They could always catch the Endarkened kids doing something inappropriate, but they never catch the observers."

"They had cameras in the classroom?" Terrah probed, searching for the person attached to the comment.

"They did," said Avenae'J, adjusting her ponytail. "Ours was obvious. You could see it. They didn't care."

"They had those secret cameras in the classroom and on the bus and stuff, and they also put the cameras in the lights outside," Talyn shared as she pointed to the ceiling to show where the hidden cameras would've been placed if this were a FirstHOME classroom.

"Okay. Is it just me or did you ever look into FirstHOME cameras and feel weird, like, 'wait, they might think I'm doing something bad?'" Terrah searched the other girls' faces for confirmation.

"I did that on purpose," Talyn said, mimicking how she would stare straight into a school camera, daring them to accuse her of wrongdoing.

The girls' conversation reminded me of how GC is like a prison, how FirstHOME is like jail. Just like inmates are forced into monochromatic, institution-issued jumpsuits, the girls were forbidden to wear certain colors and certain clothing types. Just like inmate actions are consistently regulated, the girls knew classmates who weren't allowed to use the bathroom or take medication that would allow them to fully participate in the class. Just like surveillance cameras are secured around imprisonment facilities, the girls were surveilled to ensure compliance and respectability. The surveillance, the confinement, and the regulation never stop. GC knew my every movement. The enforcers monitored my every action. My time in the Harbor is the first time I feel free, like everything I do isn't under a microscope.

I know the days of heavy surveillance, but I'd gotten used to it. I'd learned to shrug off the consistent monitoring because it had become such a normal part of my daily existence. I remember how weird it felt for no one to be looking over my shoulder when I came to Savannah. I felt lighter, freer, and unburdened from the oppressive gaze of GC. The girls are talking about GC's surveillance state because they don't have to worry about being taken to the Change Room for voicing their opinions. In the Harbor, they are free to dissent, free to discuss, and free to dream. I have to unlearn, so I can feel free enough to do the same.

As I was thinking about their stories, Avenae'J said something surprising. In a quiet voice, she said, "I used to see student protests, and like, I would like to be in there, but I can't." Even though she spoke in a low tone, I could hear her pretty clearly. I must have missed when they began to quiet down. That's what I get for listening to take notes and make connections rather than listening to sit with what they were saying.

"People at my HOME in Illinois did," Terrah said. "Like, all the observers and the students, they all walked. They went to school for first period, and then they just left."

"Respect," Avenae'J put her fist in the air.

"At my school," Bailey interjected quietly, "they'd never let us do that." She turned her attention back to her notebook.

"We were all kind of afraid," Avenae'J added. "Like, we hated the head observer, but we were also kind of afraid of him because we couldn't have done anything without him. One time, the students decided we wanted to wear color. The observers went completely against what we wanted, and they had the authority to do that. That's why we couldn't protest. We wanted to do things, but someone always had more power than we did."

"You should have just shown up in color anyway," Terrah retorted. "Like, they couldn't just make you leave FirstHOME because you didn't wear what they wanted you to wear." She paused for a minute, thinking through what she just said. She looked far away. "They could actually," she said finally. "They could."

The conversation was interesting to me because of how quickly they moved from topic to topic. I'm pretty sure it's how people normally speak to each other in groups, but Endarkened people aren't allowed to gather in groups, so I'm not used to conversation jumps. Either way, I learned so much from them already. I know Altered Truth lies, but for some reason, I wanted to believe their story about FirstHOME getting better. But, it's getting worse. From surveillance to collective punishment, the girls endured much more than I could have imagined. Still, their discussion also included hope and rebellion. Victoria spoke back to a substitute observer who tried to put all of the students on punishment. Terrah joined a walkout even though I'm sure Altered Truth hid what they were actually doing. Talyn looked surveillance mechanisms head on and refused to feel monitored into silence. I see the horrors of GC, but I also see the hope of Black girls.

Something Avenae'J said really stuck with me, though. She wanted to protest, but she was afraid of the head observer and GC because she knew they ultimately controlled her every move. The comment makes me feel like no matter how much each of them undermined the system, they are still Endarkened people who exist within the system. They are still Black girls whose existences stand in contrast to the identities desired by GC. It makes me feel like what I'm trying to do won't make a difference. But the girls persisted. If they hadn't, they wouldn't have made it to the Harbor so early. That gives me hope that I might persevere, too.

They are helping me to see the unseen, to think past the lies Altered Truth fed me. I know my time with them will be life-changing. It shows in the way they've captured such a large audience with their words. It shows in the way I'm constantly reminded of my past when I hear them speak. Because I'm learning so much, I wondered if they'd written about their experiences. It might help more people to see the world through their eyes. So, I said, "I see there are still a lot of injustices in the FirstHOMEs."

"Yes!" They all answered at once.

"Have you written any of these stories down?" I asked.

"I didn't." Terrah said with eyes downcast. "I didn't realize it was so bad."

November 6, 2085

When I got to the library for our next meeting, I saw Terrah and Avenae'J sitting at the oval table. There was no audience today, and I was glad because I wanted to spend some time getting to know them better. As soon as I sat down, the other girls burst through the door.

"Yo, did you see the straight flag?" Victoria said as she and Talyn ran toward the table. "Did you see the straight flag? The 'hetero' flag? It's so ugly! It's white and black and striped. It is so ugly! Oh my God!"

"Hold up. I didn't see that yet," Amber said, running behind Victoria.

"It's black and white?" Terrah tried to stifle her snort, signaling her disproval of the color scheme.

"It has black and white stripes, and it has something between the stripes, and I'm like why did you need to do this? Just because you didn't feel included?" Talyn doubled over with laughter as she pointed at the picture in Victoria's hand.

"It is so ugly!" Victoria yelled, as she passed the photo to the girls who had yet to see the picture.

"Like, do you really need a straight flag? Like, they felt left out, so they made their own flag. They felt so un-included that they felt like they needed a flag." Talyn said, still holding her sides.

Avenae'J shook her head and said, "That lowkey looks like a Nazi flag."

"It looks like it belongs in a prison," Terrah joked.

"I'm guessing you didn't know about that one," I said laughing with them. In GC, another exclusionary flag shouldn't surprise them. GC is known for exclusion. It's the foundation upon which GC thrives. But maybe, the emotion isn't surprise. Maybe talking about it together helps them process feelings about the flag's existence, about why someone would need to create a flag for an identity they never had to hide.

"Ooooh … it says make America straight again … Oh no!" Amber covered her mouth in disgust.

Terrah pointed to another flag next to the picture Victoria was showing, "This is the ally straight flag, which is actually kind of cool."

Amber took a look, "I like that one better."

"Yeah … that one's cute," Victoria nodded her head in support.

The girls took their seats around the oval table. While everyone was getting situated, Avenae'J asked, "Why do you have to tell people you're straight?"

"I saw someone ask why we have a whole month for pride month when we only have one day for veterans," Amber recounted. "I was like, 'well probably because they may have fought for us, but gay people, you put them down, so at least we have a month because we've been through a lot, too.'"

Terrah looked at the picture and added, "There's a reason we have our pride parades, and that's because you guys made us feel as though we couldn't be prideful about ourselves."

"Exactly," Amber and Victoria said simultaneously.

"You guys have always been prideful about yourselves," Terrah looked down at the table.

Pride festivals still happen in GC, as do most of the pre-Trence holidays like Veterans Day, Valentine's Day, and Independence Day. Endarkened people are banned from attending the events, mainly because they don't want us gathering or finding community, but that doesn't stop Endarkened people from celebrating. Every June, I'd see small acts of defiance by Endarkened people I passed on the streets—a piece of flare behind the ear, a hint of glitter in the eyebrows, or a dab of nail polish on a finger. These were all small acts, but they made large impressions on me and probably on anyone who could discern the flare's hidden meanings. The funny thing is GC never figured it out because the acts could always be explained away as an accident. Dreamers could usurp the name and exclude Endarkened people who don't fit the Dreamer pride aesthetic, but they couldn't remove celebration from the hearts of the people. They block our dreams but they can't control our hearts.

"It seems like there are always people who want to counter anytime someone from a target group decides they want to bring community together to be prideful of who they are or to protest certain things." I said aloud after processing my thoughts a bit. "Somebody is always like, 'no, you cannot be prideful. You cannot have community. You cannot do that.'"

"It's not just that," Talyn said. "Sometimes, they just want the attention, and they want to be included. So, they make stupid things to feel included which is very bad."

"That is so sad," Victoria shook her head.

Surprisingly, the girls are concerned about more than just their experiences in the HOMEs. Like the other members of the Harbor, the girls want to critique all oppression in the world. Humor also seems to be a point of entry into much deeper discussions because they moved from laughing about the flag's ugliness to critiquing the negative aspects of the flag's existence. They discussed their need to feel pride for themselves and how this flag diminishes their ability to show pride in their own identities. Still, both Talyn and Victoria said the perceived need for a straight flag is a sad occurrence. They seemed to pity them more than they were angry with them. They showed compassion. It takes a strong person to continuously show care for others even when those others consistently try to dominate them.

"You know what I hate?" Avenae'J complained as she changed the subject. She seemed to be talking to Talyn, but she said it loud enough for it to catch everyone's attention. "I used to hate store clerks."

"I thought it was just me!" Victoria said.

"Oh my God!" Amber agreed, putting her face in her hands.

"I hated the ones who just followed you around the store," Avenae'J continued. "It's like, 'Do you need help? What are you trying to look for?' I swear that was always happening to me, and I was just like 'leave me alone!' I remember this one guy. I was just standing there looking around because I wasn't going to buy anything, and he just like kept scaring me because he kept saying, 'do you want anything?' Like, 'no! Please leave me alone!'"

"Same!" Terrah related. "Okay … did anyone else ever feel self-conscious about walking out of a store empty-handed?"

"I felt that way! It's like 'I'm so sorry for not buying anything,'" Avenae'J said, hands outstretched in a pleading manner.

"I felt like they thought I was stealing something!" Amber declared.

"I'm not the only person who thought that way?" Talyn asked the group.

"Why would you be scared to walk out, especially since you didn't want anything?" I asked, noticing the girls had all experienced this feeling. I had an idea, but I didn't want to assume. Because we live in company towns, we earn company dollars to buy essentials. Still, it's hard to walk into a store as an Endarkened person. We can't browse, or we're deemed suspicious. If we're looking for an item the store doesn't have, we have to think about the optics of perusing the shelves and leaving empty-handed. We don't even bother walking into stores with expensive items because we know we'll be followed from the moment our Endarkened feet step through the doorway.

"Like, okay," Talyn said looking at me. "The thing is usually when people walk out with nothing, it's like they stole something, or you assume they stole something, or you think the workers think you stole something. So, when you walk out the store with nothing, you feel bad and awkward because you don't know if someone thinks you stole something or not."

"Here's what happens to me," Terrah moved her chair closer to the table so everyone could hear. "I get really awkward 'cause I feel like people think I'm walking out of the store stealing something. So, I try to smile and make it look like I'm not stealing something, but then it just makes it look like I'm trying to steal something."

"For real," Victoria agreed. "Because it looks like you're trying to hide that you stole something, but you really didn't steal anything. You're just saying, 'I didn't steal anything.'"

"I'm innocent," Avenae'J put her hands up the same way Endarkened people do when an enforcer comes their way.

"Do you think everybody feels this way?" I wondered aloud.

Terrah turned toward me, "A lot of people feel this way."

"Yeah ... A few people feel this way," Victoria added.

As they were talking, I thought about surveillance. Whether they were at HOME or just existing in the world, there was no way to get rid of the scrutiny. They couldn't even go to a store without feeling obligated to purchase something. I know this feeling, the sense that everywhere I go, someone is watching me to make sure I know I don't belong. GC portrays Endarkened people as louts, so Dreamers believe we can't enter a place of business without stealing something. It's happened to me, but it's hard to hear about it from people so young. It's hard to hear they're categorized as criminals so early.

These girls are so much more than the negative experiences they've had, so much more than the damaging narratives GC uses to define them. They have rich lives that go beyond these narratives. Right now, I'm wondering how they might share aspects of their lives. I hear stories of rebellion and resistance when they talk against GC. I hear new narratives about Endarkened girlhood when they talk about themselves. I wondered if they saw it the way I did.

"Everything you all have been talking about in the last day or so seems to focus on justice. Edi gave me a book about it, but since I'm here to learn with you, I wanted to know what your definition of social justice is."

Terrah chimed in first, "Social justice? I'd say just everyone being treated like they're human. People always talk about freedom and equality, but I don't think a lot of people realize what equality means. If people could learn to understand equality is everyone being treated the same way, no matter their race, gender, sexuality, all that stuff, then we will reach social justice. But until then, it's just not going to work."

"I wouldn't have much of a definition if I'm being honest," Amber said after a pause. "But I can pull the two words apart. Social, I'd say everyone coming together, and at least being nice and helping each other instead of making people feel bad and putting each other down. Because that's what everyone's doing right now, especially in HOMEs."

"I guess when everyone lets other people be who they are without judging them as much or judging people out loud," Bailey added. "They can judge in their heads as long as they don't say anything to other people, I guess."

"Just making sure the person who did the crime did something wrong," Talyn commented. After waiting a few seconds, she added, "That's what they deserve whether that be a smack to the face or a kick to the balls. It does not matter as long as they get punished for the actions."

Victoria looked around the table to acknowledge everyone else's comments and said, "I think I would say people being allowed to be who they are. Like, you look at the news and you see people having to be scared because they're Black or people having to be scared because they're in the LGBTQ community or whatever. I am who I am. Why can't you accept me for who I am? People being scared of Black people because of some type of stereotype of 'Oh they wear their pants too low, so they must be gangsters,' or 'I have to hold my purse because I don't know if they'll rob me or something,' or 'I don't understand gay people, so I'm against them.'"

She paused for a moment and looked down at her hands. When she spoke again, her voice was lower. "It's kind of like, 'You are this, and I don't understand you, so I'm either going to be afraid of you, or I'm going to hate you.' And me, being who I am, a 14-year-old who is African American and bisexual at the same time, I see all this going on around me, and I'm not scared of being who I am. But at the same time, it's like you never know what could happen." Terrah placed her hand on Victoria's shoulder.

"I also think it's where people are able to be themselves," Avenae'J claimed. "Social justice is where people are able to be themselves and not worry about other people doing anything. A lot of people can't be themselves because they don't think anyone will approve of them. We just need people being able to be themselves out in the world. Like, if they're gay or if they're a lesbian, they can go out and hold hands with their girlfriend or boyfriend and go on dates and not have to worry about people staring at them, or being extremely rude to them."

The girls seemed concerned with making sure all the people in the world could embrace who they are without fear of exclusion or revenge. It's the idea of the commonweal again. The girls focused on race, gender, sexuality, and community. They wanted freedom and equality for all. There was also a requirement for niceness. Bailey talked about wanting people to be able to be themselves without judgment, but she also thought people could continue judging as long as they kept it to themselves. Amber said social justice meant people had to be nice. Based on what they said, I wondered if they saw themselves as people who engaged in justice work, especially considering what they said about GC. "You all have such varied definitions," I began, "but I also see so many connections. As I'm trying to figure out what all this means, I'm wondering if you consider yourselves to be activists, especially since you made it to the Harbor and have been really involved in the work here."

"I see myself as a person who can empathize with others who have been through it even if I haven't been through it myself," Talyn looked pensive and placed her light brown hand on her chin. "I think I can understand what it's like to feel like you've been in the wrong because you're a certain age or a certain type of person, you're this color, you're this gender, you identify as this person, and you like this certain thing. I can understand that, and I feel like I can get to some of the people who don't. I can help them understand because not everyone is always informed."

Terrah nodded toward Talyn and added, "If I were able to go out to marches and stuff I would because it's a good way to stand up for what you believe in without hurting anybody. There's just so much people in the world don't accept about other's identities, and the quicker they learn to accept some of these things, the easier it will be for them.'"

"I'd see myself trying to speak up," Amber said in a low voice which drastically differed from tone she used in earlier conversations, "but then at the same time, I don't know how I'm going to do that because I don't like talking in very public places. I'm still shy, no matter how much I talk, so me speaking up, I wouldn't say a lot. I'd get the jitters trying to talk, and then I wouldn't say everything. Then, when I walk away, I'd be like, 'I could have said more.'"

"Honestly, I don't think I've ever been in a protest," Victoria sat with her hand resting under the right side of her face. I could tell this conversation had been hard on her, and it was draining her energy. "I mean, there's always a movement focused on justice for this person and justice for that person. And I'm like, 'Yeah, they do deserve justice because their killer shot them or they're still out there kidnapped.' But at the same time, I don't think I've ever done anything about it."

"I wouldn't be in any parades or anything," Bailey said as she stared at the table. "I'd probably just agree with what they were saying and go on with what I was doing. I probably won't have to do anything like that since I'm going to be a doctor when I grow up, or a writer. I'm going to either be at the hospital, or at book signings, or whatever."

"Right now," Avenae'J took a deep breath, "I'm just showing people I can be smart, and I can be sweet, and I'm not going to rub it in their face, and I'm not going to make them feel bad. I'm showing that Black people can be smart; we can lead; we can be kind; we can be anything. We can be anything we want to be. Basically, everyone can be. We're not just restricted. GC and its followers have never taken the time to actually get to know us. I'm just trying to show we're smart and we're beautiful and we're just like you."

I wasn't ready for their answers. I never seem to be ready when people tell me things. They approached my questions in open and authentic ways, and each time, I saw something I hadn't seen before. I saw they were grappling with what it meant to be an activist. Is it protesting? Is it speaking out? Is it agreeing with others and going about your business? I think it can be a combination, but I'm not sure. Maybe there are levels to it. We've only met once, and my mind is already spinning in so many directions. I realize how working with this group of girls is going to be more intense than I initially thought it would be. Still, there was one thing bothering me, something I didn't notice when I saw them yesterday: why did each girl have one blue and one brown eye?

November 10, 2085

I wanted to focus today's learning session on social justice issues most salient for the girls. So far, they'd discussed racism, homophobia, and sexism in the HOMEs and in the world at large, but I wondered what they would say if I asked them directly. When I walked to our table, they were already deep in conversation. I swear, every time I have an idea of how I want the sessions to go, they upend my plans. Learning in community means it's not just my decision, and that's something I need to learn.

"Didn't they take a picture of a kid putting something in the amnesty box?" Talyn asked.

Terrah squinched her face. "You're not supposed to take pictures of people without consent. You're supposed to ask permission."

"They took a picture! They took a picture of a kid putting something in the amnesty box," Talyn rose out of her seat for emphasis.

"What's an amnesty box?" I queried. I'd never heard of such a thing. I mean, I can guess what it is based on context, but I'm not sure why FirstHOME students would need an official pardon for any reason.

"An amnesty box …" Victoria hesitated. It seemed like she was trying to figure out the best way to describe this object. "It's for … if you have something you're not supposed to have at FirstHOME. You put it in the amnesty box, and they'll forgive you for it, but it's supposed to be anonymous. Nobody is supposed to know you put it in there. Basically, you're not supposed to take pictures of someone."

"I don't think my HOME had one of those," Terrah said as she started rebraiding her long hair.

"It was in the hallway to our cafeteria, just sitting there," Talyn responded nonchalantly.

"I think ours was hidden in this little section of the hallway. In the front door, there was this hallway that went to the left, and it was hidden in that corner. I don't think anyone ever used it," Terrah thought out loud. It seemed as if she was creating a mental map of her FirstHOME as she described the possible location of the amnesty box.

"Ours was in plain sight," Talyn confirmed.

"No one used ours," Avenae'J added.

"Ours had a picture of enforcers," Amber exclaimed. She lifted up her notebook and pointed to the middle of it, suggesting the picture was centered on the amnesty box.

Victoria said, "If you walked to the front of our school and went to our connections wing, the amnesty box was just sitting there. Nobody knew what it was, though, because they didn't have a sign over it or nothing. It was just a black box that looked like a mailbox, and you just put stuff in it."

"It's supposed to be for weapons," Amber declared, her long braids moving back and forth as she looked for confirmation from the other girls.

"Like, if someone brings a lighter to school, they could put it in there," Talyn concurred. "If you brought drugs to school, you put it in there."

"Someone put some trash in there before," Victoria laughed, and the other girls laughed with her. "And I was like, 'that's not what that's for.' And they were like, 'it doesn't say that.' And I was like, 'that's the amnesty box,' and they were like, 'it doesn't say that.'"

"I've never heard of this thing," I said.

From what I'm hearing, GC believed Endarkened students would bring weapons or other illegal paraphernalia to the HOMEs, but even if they brought something, accidentally or otherwise, would they be willing to put the items in a box controlled and monitored by the observers? Also, the presence of an enforcer photo attached to the box implied it wasn't an amnesty box. Instead, it was another way to police and surveil the students under the guise of forgiveness. That's why the kids just put trash in it because the whole concept was, essentially, trash.

Selfishly, I redirected our conversation. I learn so much from them about the Harbor, and I wanted to know more about this Afrofuturism and womanism thing. "So, we know there's always been a lot going on in the HOMEs in terms of the one-for-all policies, these amnesty box things I've never heard of, and dress codes. So, I'm wondering if we can do an activity. Could we all just make a list of some social justice issues we've see in the world? The issue can be as small or large as we'd like, from a sib getting on your nerves to global warming. Then, we can pick one thing we think needs to be fixed right now and we can also think about what might happen if we don't fix the issue in 10 or 50 years. Does that sound ok?"

This was definitely a random redirect, but my hope was to see if this might recreate what the Othermothers did. They saw an issue in the world, and they thought about ways to fix it. That's how the Harbor network came to be. I wondered what it would look like to reconstruct that scenario, and for me to participate in it in some way. There are so many issues within and beyond GC, and I want to think about some ways I could help to fix the problem. I also want to think with the girls I'm so privileged to learn from. I think this will help me think through my role. Where do I fit in? What is my role in the commonweal?

Thankfully, the girls nodded, signaling their willingness to do this random writing activity. In fact, some were already writing things down. It was peculiar to me to see the girls using pen and paper so freely when everything was digitized above ground. However, I know using too much technology means the Harbor could be hacked, their secrets revealed to GC. There are a few computers in the library because they have to connect with other Harbors and coconspirators, but they're used sparingly.

We wrote for about 20 minutes, and then Amber decided to share. "I'll name some of them, the bigger ones. Discrimination against women sometimes, and a lot of the time, it's Black women who still aren't getting treated fairly. The crime rates are going up. I mostly see young or older Black men. That's what I see on the news. Everything I've written down is actually what I used to read or see on the news. Crime rates was actually one of the biggest things I chose."

Amber flipped the page of her notebook and continued, "In 10 years, the crime rates could go higher, death could occur more often, violence and gangs showing out more. In 50 years, I think peace could try and grow, but it's not going to be as strong as we really want it. In a bad way, I'd say war because most of the time it's off of conflict, and conflict can turn into war. Then, crime could go even higher than how it was. I have some other things, but those are some of the major things I wrote down."

"I have something. It doesn't completely correlate with crime rate, though," Terrah said. She moved her neck back and forth in preparation. "I remember you mentioning something about Black men being a huge part of this. Like you mainly see them in it, and I just remembered I saw this post about these three Black men. This white guy driving a truck hit three Black men who were walking across the street, and the Black men were the ones getting arrested because they weren't wearing safety stuff, and I'm like, 'that doesn't make any sense. Why are they getting arrested for that?' They didn't do anything except walk across the street, which anybody could do.'"

Terrah's story sparked a thought, so I offered an extension. "Since we're talking about what we see on the news, think about who makes the news and what stories they may put on there more often than others because, of course, they choose what stories they want to share."

I didn't want to say specifics, like how Altered Truth was probably responsible for the newscasts they'd seen. News reporting had changed from what it used to be. It used to focus on various happenings within a specific locale, but overtime, it began to rely on sensationalism. Analyzing the content presented to us onscreen wasn't a focus in the HOMEs because it caused us to ask too many questions. Instead, they just left it to the masses to figure it out. Some could see through the drivel, but not everyone had those skills.

Terrah continued the discussion, "Okay, so in big letters I wrote underrepresentation because a big thing to me is people not getting represented for what they need to be represented for. I have a bunch of subcategories. My other one was people being told to act or people saying people are acting like a color. Like you say, 'you're acting Black,' and it just doesn't make sense to me. But I went with underrepresentation, and I kind of put a subcategory to help me know who really doesn't get a lot of attention in the press and stuff, or who is discriminated against."

"Like good attention?" Victoria asked.

"So, like bad attention," Terrah answered in a matter-of-fact tone. "So, I said Blacks, women, disabled people, the LGBTQ+ community, and sexual assault victims. Those are like the main things I have. So, in 10 years, I said the people who are overrepresented are going to have too much power, and the underrepresented are going to start lashing out, probably causing a war. Then I said in 50 years, people have now separated themselves into factions, so the community they're in matches like who they are."

"It is true what you're talking about," Victoria said solemnly as she looked toward Terrah. "Like the disabled and LGBTQ+ and the sexual assault because sexual assault victims don't get that much press. If you think about it, like they'll talk about it for maybe a week, and it'll be done with, and then they'll be like, 'okay don't care anymore.'"

"Okay. It's my turn, right?" Victoria asked as she moved the conversation from Terrah's writing to her own, possibly attempting to lighten the mood after a heavy topic. "So, some of the problems or issues I wrote are poverty, racism, hate crimes, violence, homophobic people because they are a problem in themselves, murder, mental illness, suicide, more kids going into the system like foster care, more people in jail, and bullying. The one I starred was suicide, and this one was hard for me."

She moved her finger down the page to find her place. It seemed as though she had written her comments nonlinearly. "For 10 years later, I put there will be no real future because death rates would skyrocket, and the economy would sink. There would be no more of the human race, and no one to save the planet from full destruction. For 50 years later, I put the remaining people will live on space, and everyone will have to be alike, and if you're mentally ill, you will not be able to harm yourself, which means you would literally be guarded by someone every day you're on wherever you are."

"You could also talk about bullying as well," Avenae'J said.

"Yeah. It's a main cause of suicide," Talyn added.

"I think they coexist with each other," Victoria agreed. She scribbled something down in her notebook.

"I think you can feed that into there because a lot of people get depression because of that," Terrah said, her mouth downturned.

Thinking about what Terrah added, I said, "I would also look into ... like which groups are committing suicide more than others because there is a lot of information about who. That may even affect your 10 year and your 50 year because everyone is not committing suicide, but there are certain people who are."

"I did it wrong," Talyn lowered her gaze. "So, I didn't write about the 10-year thing and the 50-year thing. I just erased all of it. Like, not erased, but I crossed it out, so I have nothing to share."

"Okay," I said. "Hopefully, you will have something to share later?"

"I will," Talyn replied.

Avenae'J decided to share what she wrote next. She started and stopped several times, but eventually, she began. "Okay, so there are murders of certain races, genders, or ethnicities, not because they did anything but just because people feel a certain way towards that group. Observers are giving every student a bad grade, like a 50, just because of the one-for-all thing. There are also social issues or important issues, such as murders, that are not talked about because it relates to different races, genders, or ethnicities. People don't talk about it until other people start talking about it. Most people only talk about it because they don't want to look bad ... Then, I put bullying."

"I went with the social issues thing," she continued after flipping through several pages to find what she was looking for. "I don't know why, but that's really important to me. I went real into this. In 10 years, there will be more murders of certain ethnicities, races, or genders because people think they can because it's not being talked about. Racism would grow out of hate because they hate certain things or groups. Then, in 50 years there will be a civil war between groups. A solution to that would be people have to cover their entire bodies from head to toe, so no one can tell their color, race, gender, or ethnicity. People have to speak and be spoken to in a certain way, so no one can tell an accent or deepened voice. If they cannot speak in that way, they'll have a genetically modified voice or robot speak for them. No one can date or have feelings whatsoever, and no one can represent their religion."

"I can see a movie and also a book made out of that idea!" Talyn's eyes widened at the thought.

"Yeah. That's a really cool idea. Like, that's great," Terrah agreed.

"I think you could also bring up the point that if a white person were to murder somebody, it wouldn't be like talked about very often, but if like a Black person were to kill somebody, then automatically it's all over the news," Terrah murmured. "You see it everywhere. It's the only thing people are talking about for weeks on end."

"I'll do mine," Bailey whispered. "So, I chose poverty because my brain wasn't working, and I didn't think of a lot of other stuff. I said in 10 years, if we didn't fix it, then something might happen to where the government or whoever's in power might think there's an overpopulation problem, and then they would enslave the people who have no place to stay. And then in 50 years, they'll probably start killing people or maybe helping the people who are about to be homeless or whatever."

"So, I have something I want to say," Terrah interrupted. "You already kind of have a plot line for your story, but I kind of thought of something while you were sharing. I think a cool idea—because you said they would be enslaving the people who are in poverty—would be to take it from somebody ... it could be anybody who is one of those people who is rich but has a place to stay. They recognize all the poverty, and they're just trying to help all the people who are being enslaved out of it ..."

"Kind of like an abolitionist but for poverty!" Avenae'J interjected excitedly.

"Yeah. It's kind of like, you know, 'Here, I'll, I'll take you in. I'll give you a job at my house or whatever, and I'll pay you,'" Terrah pretended like she was giving money to someone.

"You could also do like a before the Civil War type scenario, like where the slaves are starting an uprising, that type of thing," Talyn suggested.

"Yeah, you could do that too," Terrah nodded her head in agreement.

"I could also make it something else where they're saving the people by taking them where they're not being enslaved," Avenae'J proposed.

This is such a collaborative environment. Even though we were talking about issues that were important to them individually, the girls provided assistance to their sisters, helping them to delve more deeply into the issues. They were using their everyday experiences—watching films, watching the news, reading books, and living in the world—as a way to teach, to unlearn. All of this made sense because, in this underground enclave, most of the learning comes from books, films, newspapers, and news reels the library has acquired over time. Still, it was amazing to see the unlearning happening in real time. I was able to see how the girls used their personal knowledge and the information gathered from outside sources to help each other see the unseen. What does it mean for me, though? I've always been so isolated. I don't know if I can be collaborative in the same way.

"I guess it's my turn," I said. I paused a moment then began. "The biggest one I put was representation. I decided to focus specifically on Black people, so I said in 10 years we still see Black people in civil rights and history movies, and they'll always have a white savior in it. I said people will think of anything with Black people in fantasies and futures as not possible. Then, I said in 50 years, Black people will forget how to dream or how to think of these futuristic or fantastic things, not just lose their access to them."

"Ugh," Terrah sucked her teeth.

"Everything is going to have a white savior," Amber repeated. "It is very true because every show I watched it was like 'Oh, there goes that white guy. Oh no, he's going to save us. Great. I could have done that. No, I couldn't have in the story they wrote, huh?'"

"You were talking about how the white guy will save African Americans, and it's like very predictable," Avenae'J said. "I really hate that because you thought it was going to be the one way, and then you saw a white guy come in, and then it was like, 'oh, we know how this is going to end.'"

"Like, everyone in the theater just simultaneously says that," Talyn added.

"It's like 'Oh my God! We finally have a Black movie!' Sees a white guy … collective sigh," Terrah described, mimicking the dejection that rests on Endarkened faces when they see another white savior in a Black movie.

"We're not trying to be rude, but it's so predictable. Can they change it up a bit, so we can be surprised for once?" Avenae'J questioned.

"What if it's like a white civilization and then a Black man comes and saves them all," Terrah asked.

"They're not gonna do that," Amber answered.

"That would be unpredictable," Avenae'J replied.

I welcomed the girls' commentary, especially because I didn't expect them to talk with me the same way they talked with each other. I felt like this was my unofficial welcome into the group. I mean, yes, I'm part of the group, but I still felt a barrier between us because I'm a newcomer and an older person. They didn't initially speak to me as if I was a part of the group, but after their commentary, I see things are changing. Maybe it's because I shared with them. I participated in the same writing activity and talked about what I wrote, just like they did. Maybe, they always welcomed me, but I couldn't see it because GC always made me feel like an outsider, and I don't know how to accept inclusion. Who knows?

Just like they did with each other, they used their everyday experiences to help me think through my ideas. They said how much they disliked savior narratives, critiquing how the Dreamers always save the Endarkened from ourselves. They talked about the predictability of stories focused on Dreamer saviors because those stories are told so often. Even when Terrah tried to present a possible counter to the norm, Amber let her know GC would never allow that. An Endarkened man would never be cast as the savior in a Dreamer story. Still, I wonder what it would look like for Endarkened women and girls to be the hero. I wonder if it will ever be a possibility.

5

RESEARCH PARTNER STORIES

Bailey

November 13, 2085

After a couple days of learning together, the girls decided it might be time to write speculative stories. I thought it would be too soon for me, but the girls said I could listen and learn from them in hopes that I'd gain some speculative writing confidence. We worked collaboratively, so we made the decision to continue working together through the story creation. From this point forward, we'd focus on two stories each week, one on Saturday and the other on Sunday. On Sundays, we'd help our sister flesh out ideas, if that's what she needed. If she didn't, we'd just listen to whatever she wanted to tell us about her story. Then, on the following Saturday, we'd listen to the speculative fiction story she created. In some ways, we'd have an author reading each week, and each story would be both personal and collaborative.

I really liked this plan because I'd get behind the scenes information about each story. It's a way for me to see things I might not have been able to see just by reading it. It'll also give me time to learn more about the girls individually. How did they get here? What are their lives like? What do they care and worry about? What do they fear? What brings them joy? To figure out the answers to these questions, I asked the girls if, during the week, I could meet with the person who was telling their story on Saturday. I'm hoping that connecting their personal story to their fiction story will help me figure out how to see the unseen.

Bailey wanted to go first because her story was based on other stories she'd created in the past. Because we made the decision to alter our learning sessions, we added a Wednesday meeting this week to provide feedback before she reads her story on Saturday. Bailey said we could meet up today because of the condensed schedule, and I'm excited to learn from her.

DOI: 10.4324/9781003159285-5

We planned to meet in the Harbor's gaming room. I didn't know the room existed, but I do know the Othermothers try to make welcoming spaces for all residents, no matter their interests, so I wasn't surprised. I am starting to realize how love is the foundation for the Harbor, though. Creating a space like this takes a lot of love and flexibility since so many people live here, and no two people are exactly alike. The Othermothers seem to understand that Endarkened people have varied interests, that we're not all the same, and it seems like a focus on the diversity of Endarkened interests impacted how they structured the Harbor. It was a labor of love, a commitment to loving Endarkened people.

I saw Bailey walking down the G hallway. She was wearing colorful sweat-pants and a vibrant baggy shirt, and her dark brown hair was in small braids tied into a ponytail. She was several feet away from me, but she turned when I shouted my greeting.

"Hi Bailey! Ready to tell me your life story?"

Bailey slowed her stride to match my pace. "Hey, there. I sure am!" she gig-gled, and several laugh lines formed on her caramel-colored face. I noticed her voice was a bit louder than it was in the learning sessions.

When we got inside the game room, we walked over to some chairs in the back corner, and Bailey grabbed a game and controller from a stand at the side of the room. For an underground enclave of Endarkened resistors, they sure did have a large gaming area. It was pretty dark in the room, possibly to create the optimum game experience. Even in the low light, I could see several old gaming consoles from the late 20th and early 21st century—Xbox, PlayStation, Nintendo, and Sega systems-were set up around the room. There was also a wall of board games that covered the right side of the room and another wall of puz-zles on the left. Chairs and sofas were stationed strategically around the room so people could play alone or with a group and others could watch the players if they wanted to.

Bailey easily found her game and grabbed an SD card from a case in a side cabinet. She found an open PlayStation console, sat down, and motioned for me to sit next to her on the sofa. I sat down and asked if she could talk and play simultaneously.

"Of course!" she said, as if I'd asked a ridiculous question.

"Got it." I brought out my notebook so I could write down the important things she said. I didn't want to forget anything. "So, can you tell me about you, like who you are and what you like?"

"Um … Let's see … I was born August 12th in a Delaware hospital some-where. I like baking cookies, and cakes, and brownies. I don't know how to make anything else. I haven't watched movies in a while, but I like *Tokyo Ghoul*, *Attack on Titan*, and *Noragami*. They're all action based, and the first two have a lot of gore and stuff. I also read a bunch of old Wattpad archives, and I play a whole bunch of video games." As the game loaded, she twisted around in her seat to get comfortable. "I like games, but one time, I was playing an online game, and something happened where all the people got out, and they blamed it on me, but I didn't do it. I don't have a headset, so they couldn't hear me, and they all blamed it on me. That's what happens most of the time. It's horrible, so I just leave the game."

Although I'm not a gamer in the same way Bailey is, I do know how difficult it is to be a Black girl gamer because the only "safe" way to be one is to hide your identity from the Dreamer players. "Why would they blame it on you?"

"Well, all the people on my team were guys, for one." She said as she leaned to the left, moving her body in unison with the character she controlled on screen. "And two, I didn't have my headset on, so they couldn't talk to me to communicate or anything. Girls play, but they're never on my team. I can pick my team, but I don't have any friends that play games like me."

"I see. So, what do you think you're good at, and what would you say are your weaknesses?"

"Well, my strengths are writing and reading and sometimes playing video games." She stopped her answer to yell at some monster on the screen, but one second later, she was back to the Bailey I was used to seeing. It was amazing to see the gamer side of her. "My best talent would be reading fan fiction because it's easy. Weaknesses would be talking to people because I don't like talking to people. I don't know. I'm kind of weird, especially to people I don't know. Another weakness can be just talking in general because even though I knew my observers, I really didn't like talking to them either. It just depends. If you're good friends with me or I know you for a little while, I'll be fine. If not, I won't talk to you."

Considering she brought up the observers, I asked, "Can you tell me what you remember about FirstHOME?" The girls talked about a few collective experiences, but I knew they had individual stories to tell. Plus, Bailey was so quiet in the sessions, which made sense since she doesn't like talking to people. I'm hoping this conversation will be easier for her shyness since we're not in the larger group.

"Well, there was a time when an observer thought I did something when I actually didn't," Bailey furrowed her brow, hiding her brown eyes in a squint. "We had a cart where they sold a bunch of snacks, and people kept stealing. The observer thought I stole something, but I didn't. Almost everyone around me knew I didn't, so they told on the person who did it. The person that did do it was 'way nicer than I am'—that's what the observer said—so she didn't think they did it. I got in trouble for it even though I didn't do anything at all. The person who did steal eventually got in more trouble since there were more witnesses who saw them doing it and not me. The observer still thought I did it, so she yelled at me, and then yelled at the other person more."

"Did the other person come forward, or how did the observer eventually find out?" I asked. Of course, I was livid, especially after hearing how the observer told her she was guilty because she just … looked like she was. This young, quiet, brown-skinned girl, who is always humble and always kind "looks" like she is guilty.

"They didn't come forward. Everyone was on their phone since it was the end of the year. They were recording it for some reason, so they had it on video and everything. The observer still yelled at me."

"Oh … wow."

It took a recording of the event for the observer to believe Bailey's words and the words of several of her classmates. If Black girls are too loud, they get in trouble. If Black girls are too quiet, like Bailey, they still get in trouble. They look like they're guilty just because they exist. We can't win in a system like that.

"Yeah … then, I think it was in the sixth year, I got in trouble for spraying perfume out of my gym bag when I did it on accident. My bag was on the ground, and I accidentally stepped on it, and then perfume went everywhere, so I got in trouble."

"You got in trouble for accidentally stepping on something?" I said incredulously.

"Mm-hmm. My HOME was supposed to be one of the better HOMEs, too."

I'm glad the Harbor is shielding her from those negative experiences, but I can see they're not easily forgotten. The Harbor is shielding me, but I still feel the weight of GC hovering above me at all times. I wonder if she feels that presence, too. I wonder if we will ever get away from that feeling.

I'm also wondering how we decide which HOMEs are good and which aren't, especially when they've all been harmful to Endarkened children. Maybe she can help me understand. "I see. Well, were there any redeeming qualities?"

"My homeroom observer was nice, and then my social studies observer was nice. My math observer … it depended. The math observer on the other team, she didn't like me. My reading observer was just mean."

"Why didn't she like you?"

"I don't know. I had her for a seventh-year class, and she never talked to me. I don't think she liked my class in general, but she liked all of her other classes. She just kept moving our seats and complaining that we talked too much, but there was a bunch of other classes that talked way more than we did."

"What made your reading observer mean?"

"She gave random people silent lunch for standing up, and she marked me on the board for standing up even though I wasn't." She put the controller down and looked at me. "I knew I wasn't! If I did stand up, it was probably to open the door for an observer because I sat by the door. So, I got marked for that, and I couldn't get a snow cone on 'snow-cone day.' I don't eat them, so I didn't care, but I couldn't have one."

"Hmm. So, you had a few nice observers, and a few who were not. Still, I see a lot injustice." Bailey was consistently punished for things she didn't do, and I didn't understand what about her made her a target for the observers, other than being an Endarkened girl. I did notice how she never spoke up to the observer. Her classmates told the observer who stole the snacks, and she silently took her punishment for standing even when she didn't do it. "Do you consider yourself to be an activist, like someone who speaks out when injustice happens?"

"I don't think so." She walked to a cabinet and picked a new game to play. "I mean, I'm not going to go talk to people about things because I'm not the type of person to talk to people about stuff I don't like. If I don't like something, I usually keep it inside because nothing happens. There's nothing I can do to change it."

"I understand. But like, who do you think is responsible for making sure there's justice in the world?"

"I think everyone is responsible because one person can't change everything in the world." She shrugged her shoulders. "Like, GC can't just change everything and make everyone do something because that wouldn't be right, and not everyone agrees with it. People working together makes social justice happen."

"You're right. We do need to work together to make change. I think those are all the questions I had, but is there anything else I should know? Maybe something about your story?" I asked. She had already given me so much, but I wanted to make sure my questions didn't limit what she shared.

"Um … I was writing fanfiction before working with Trinity." She said without looking back at me, her focus on this new game. It looked like one of those team games she talked about earlier. "Most of the time they were on anime, but there's this one exception where it was about creepy web stuff. I have one for *Fairy Tail*, and I just restarted the *My Hero Academia* one because I got tired of it for a little while. I think I started writing them in sixth year, but they were horrible because they had no description or anything. It was just telling what happened, and that was it. I still use the characters I made for it, though, because I feel bad if I don't use them."

"I didn't know it was fanfiction at the time." Bailey continued, still giving her attention to the screen. "I just thought I was writing my own story. I would just watch a show for a few episodes to see if it had enough room to make an original character, or OC. Then, I would make a few OCs for it. They all have totally different personalities most of the time. They look totally different, and if they have any powers or anything, I put that in there sometimes. Sometimes I don't. In my *Attack on Titan* one, I have two OCs. Two of them can shapeshift into Titans, and one of them is just different sized. I started writing it, and then after a while I slowed down on writing. I reread it a few times, and I edited it a bunch. Then, when I got to the end of the season, I was done."

"So, you were writing alongside the season as it was going?" I'm not sure when fanfiction is normally written, but I always thought the writing would happen after the season ended. There's so much I need to learn to honor Bailey's fanfiction author identity. "How is building your OCs different from building characters for the learning sessions?" I asked, repositioning myself on the sofa.

"The characters I did in the learning sessions are … I guess you could say … they're more well written than the other ones because I didn't have all the scenes to go by. Most of the time I base it on the series, and then I add stuff on as I get through it. But for the sessions, I had everything in the beginning."

So, Bailey had a writing identity for much longer than I have, and she completely embraces her love of anime and gaming. It shows up in her hobbies, and it shows up in her writing. Her gamer and fanfiction identities are a part of her, and I'm glad she is able to call upon those skills as she writes her story in the group.

"I'm super excited to see what you create this weekend. I'll leave you to your game for now. I hope you pass this level today!"

Bailey paused the game and looked back at me as I stood up to leave. "Before you leave, you also need to know that I really like plushies, and I hate water," she grinned.

"I'll make sure to write that down for my fanfiction story about you!" I laughed. I walked out of the room wondering what plushies have to do with her story.

November 14, 2085

We had Bailey's collaborative session today. I was the first to arrive in the library, so I sat at our oval table and waited. There weren't many people in the library this morning, just me and two other sibs who were sitting at a large table in the middle of the room. The light beams from the ceiling highlighted their brightly colored clothing, which glimmered in the fluorescent glow. I don't know if this was intentional, but the colorful Harbor clothing make this underground safe haven brighter. We may not have access to the sun, but we create the sunshine just by being together.

The girls walked in together, talking loudly, and waving their hands. When they sat down, they let me know our collaborative sessions would follow a strict format. First, the lead author would explain how their story came to be, and collaborators could ask questions or provide commentary. Next, the lead author would describe where they were with their current story, and once again, the collaborators could discuss. Last, the lead author would ask any questions they had for the rest of the group. If they kept it in this format, the author would have loads of feedback as they finished their story.

"My character's name is Kenzi. She is 16 years old, and I think she's mixed, but I don't know yet," Bailey began. "She has short curly hair that's light brown and a whole face full of freckles. She has hazel eyes and super long bangs that cover her eyes. She wears bland t-shirts that sometimes have words on them, and she wears black or white jeans. She wears a chain around her neck since she doesn't know what she is yet, like a vampire or a fairy or whatever. When they know what they are, when they turn 17, I think, they get like a crystal or whatever on their necklace, so everyone knows what they are."

"I have a question. Does the crystal just appear?" Talyn asked.

"No. They have to go get it."

"Interesting," Avenae'J said, nodding her head approvingly.

"I also wrote that she has a bunch of weird habits," Bailey looked up nervously and quickly turned her attention back to her notebook. "Like, she has to do something, or her brain has to be working on something, or she shuts down. She also loves books, her siblings, puppies, tea, social studies, and her hair, and she hates her eye color because she wanted it to be green since all of her brothers have green eyes. She hates what her siblings do because they're super obnoxious. She hates anything cold and pink. She dreams about equality, but she's too shy to do anything. And because humans are super rare, all of the leaders and stuff are hybrids. She really needs to find out what she is because she's getting nervous because all of her siblings know what they are. Well, most of them. Her oldest brother is a soldier, so he gets all the money."

"Okay. I just have a question for your story," Amber said. "How are children born into this world? Are they just, 'Oh look,' and pop out?'" She put her hands in front of her like she was catching a baby.

"I haven't exactly thought of that," Bailey answered, speaking a little more confidently.

"That's something important you could think about," Terrah said.

"Make it funny. Make it less depressing," Talyn suggested.

"You don't have to make it funny," Terrah disagreed.

"Make it however you want it to be," I added. I wanted to make sure Bailey didn't feel pressured to make her story ours. She could write whatever she wanted to write, and we'd still appreciate her words.

"Or it could be morbid where they just genetically modify children," Avenae'J pondered. "Or they could do it where they take two people and they make them reproduce, and then they give them a memory serum, so they don't remember anything. They don't remember what happened. You know, like they do to the adults."

"Yeah … they already do stuff like that," Terrah agrees.

"That's almost like *The Giver*, except they … well no," Amber thought aloud.

"Kenzi's usually quiet most of the time because her siblings do all the loudness for her." Bailey interjected. She didn't look annoyed, but she did look like she wanted to get this part over with. She had been doing a lot of talking. "Her siblings are class clowns and everything, and she is the nerdy type, I guess, but she doesn't let people bully her. That's probably how she got injured because she fought back when someone tried to bully her, and then her brother got suspended, too, because he did something to them. She's bullied for, I guess, just being her because she's one of the weirder ones. She stands out for not being a class clown like her siblings. But her siblings know if she gets bullied, they'd fight for her. The HOME kind of mirrors my old HOME because the HOME I went to is supposed to be a good one, but it's not because everyone gets bullied a lot."

"The setting is 3050," she was speaking faster now. "Kenzi messes with her sister's VR headset. She puts a random game in, and she ends up in a haunted place with a bunch of killer plushies, so she needs to find an exit. The plushie kind of like teleports and only moves when the lights are off. It's always really dark, so you don't know where it is until you see it. It's going to start from the end and go through like that. So, she almost finds an exit, and then she almost dies, and then she almost dies again, but her friend, no, her sister takes the gear off, so she doesn't die."

"I hope she finds an exit!" I said.

"She almost dies twice?" Amber exclaimed.

"Killer plushies?" Avenae'J yelped. "I have stuffed animals in my room, and you're going to make me scared of them."

"Well, I need names for plushies," Bailey said. "They're scary plushies."

"It's like Chucky, but worse," Talyn said.

"Anamina?" Amber suggested. "No, spell Chucky backwards. Let's see how that goes."

"Chucky backwards would be," Terrah thought aloud, "Yeah … Chucky backwards is not anything."

"Yucky?" Talyn offered.

"Could it be Yucky? Because there is no, Y," Amber asked.

"Oh wait. No, I'm spelling it wrong," Terrah rethought.

"You know what Chucky backwards is?" Amber asked Avenae'J.

"No, sorry," She replied.

For some reason, naming was really important to the girls. Bailey could have asked any question of the group, but the only question she had was to ask for a character's name. Yes, the character was a scary plushie who would torment the main character via virtual reality, but that ability to name her character and share the naming with her sisters was important.

I guess naming is important to all Endarkened people, though. I changed my name when I decided the name GC gave me was no longer acceptable. I wanted to name myself, to decide who I am. How good it felt to choose who I was, rather than having someone choose for me. I just wish Endarkened people outside of the Harbor had the opportunity to share in their own naming, too.

November 17, 2085

The reading of Bailey's story was the only thing on the agenda today, and I was excited to see how her identities, collaborations, and interests showed up in what she created. What will I learn from this scary plushie story? What elements will open my eyes so I can see the unseen? I'm so anxious to hear what she will show me about herself and about the world we're living in.

"Exit"

> I push myself down the dark hallway as fast as I possibly could. My heart raced a million miles per second, and I felt as if I could pass out at any second. I kept going, though, and I saw the exit I had to go through.
>
> "Yes! I'm almost out of here," I thought to myself, and I pushed harder, having a newfound burst of energy. I was going to get Amber back after this...

I watched out the window to see my siblings leaving for school. I couldn't go since I had an arm injury that was so bad the school told me not to come back until tomorrow. Mom was at work, probably helping with a pregnancy. Dad was out of the picture. I shifted around on my bed and looked next to me.

Amber left a game for me to play since she knew how bored I would be. It was a sit-down virtual reality (VR) game, where you'd move in the game even though you didn't move in real life. It was a really good illusion, too.

The game choice was either a racing simulator, a school simulator, or a plushie rush. I chose the plushie rush because it sounded better, let's just say. I put the game in the VR set, and I put the headset on. The new game screen immediately came up.

It was brightly colored with a cutesy yellow plushie bunny in a circle in the middle. The circle was a dark red which stood out from everything else. The only other dark thing was the words "fun with plushtrap" on a dark blue ribbon underneath. The plushie was yellow with blue eyes and an innocent smile. One of its long ears was bent, and its head was tilted slightly to the left.

I went on and clicked new game, and the title screen flashed a different color. The backdrop turned black and white with even darker splotches on it. The plushie was different, too. Its ears had pieces missing. Its eyes were wide and unblinking. Its smile literally spread across its whole face, showing its really pointy teeth.

I blinked twice and the rules danced across the screen. Everything was dark now. Nothing had color.

- Rule one: No use of weapons, or you die. I blinked, confused.
- Rule two: You must find an exit before Plushtrap gets you. I tried taking my VR off before noticing that I couldn't.
- Rule three didn't come until I was literally dropped into an empty security room: you can't escape.

I looked at the static monitors before I heard a laugh. Deciding that laughter in a haunted game was so not good, I ran out of the left door and down a hallway.

The room the hallway opened up to had a bunch of tables with birthday cone hats and a huge stage. The stage had the demon plushie on it. There was a door to somewhere, and I jumped in there before the demon plushie went to get up. I jogged down the hallway until I realized halfway that it was a dead end.

I turned around and Plushtrap was there. He was sitting and super small, of course. I was cornered. The hallway lights went off and on each time Plushtrap moved. I took this chance to find a vent or something. This just can't be a dead end. I can't die now.

My frantic banging on the walls led me to hit a vent. I traced it with my shoe real quick and saw that I could easily fit through. I yanked it away and threw it behind me. Then, I crawled sonic fast, hearing weird echoes. Suddenly, not paying attention, I fell out of the vent into squishy red stuff. I jumped up immediately, ignoring all of the horror clichés, and I ran.

I noticed I was in the office. I ran back down the first hallway, and this time, I went to the right and slammed open the door.

Bailey received a standing ovation. Her work both scared and thrilled us. I could definitely see how parts of her story mirrored some of what she told me in our conversation yesterday. There's gaming and virtual reality. There's also a slight critique on horror films, as the characters often accept their fate, standing still and waiting for danger to arrive instead of getting out of the situations quickly. We didn't talk much about horror, so I wanted to know more.

"How did you come up with the idea to do like the scary underground ... well, not underground, virtual reality plushie thing?" I asked as I followed Bailey out of the library.

"I got it from *Sword Art Online*, and the fact that it's a VR game you can't log out of, I guess. And then, I had it from FNAF ... um, *Five Nights at Freddy's* because of the creepy plushie thing. There's a plushie you have to get in a mini game. And then I took the characters and stuff from the story I wrote. It's not a fanfiction, though."

"Got it," I said. I know about the game and the anime from other conversations we've had in the sessions, so it was nice to hear how these interests connected. I wanted to know about the groundwork for other ideas, so I asked, "What happened to the main character's arm? Like, why was she in the house for the arm? Was there any backstory to that?"

"Oh yeah. She was being picked on, and one of them grabbed her arm." Bailey gestured to her right arm as she continued walking. "So, now it has a huge bruise on it. But, before the bully could do anything else, her siblings showed up, and they yelled at them, and the bullies disappeared."

"I see. So why was she being picked on?"

"Because she's not like her siblings. Her siblings are super popular. She's not."

"Okay. And then you also said the mom is at work helping out with pregnancy. I'm guessing the mom works in childcare, and the dad's out of the picture. Why did you make that choice?"

"The mom, I based off of my Harbor mom, and my Harbor dad wanted to be a villain in the story, so I was like 'okay.' So, there is no dad."

"How is your dad the villain in the story if he's not there?" I knew I was asking a lot of questions, but this was the first story reading, and I wanted to make sure my notes were clear, so I had all the information I needed to think through what I heard. I kind of felt like asking these questions was my ... responsibility. Like, I needed to know these details so I could share them with others someday.

"He's the villain in the actual book. I took the mom from an existing mom I created in another story, and I took the siblings from already existing siblings, so I didn't have to make a whole bunch of characters again."

"As for the characters, is the younger sister, Amber, based off of your younger sister?"

"One of the siblings is, but she isn't mentioned."

"Oh, okay. Who is Amber based off of?" I asked.

"Amber is kind of based off of me because she's a gamer with all of her games everywhere." She stopped walking and turned to face me. We were close to the game room, so I guess she wanted to give me her undivided attention. Once she went inside, I'd be more of an afterthought, with a game taking center stage. "Her face was based off of a video game I wanted to make, but I couldn't. It's like a dating game, but the dating game isn't really a dating game. It's a horror game."

"I see that horror writer keeps coming out," I laughed. "I know we didn't have 18 years to write the short story, but there was a cliffhanger. If you had more time to write, what would happen next?"

"She'd probably go a different way and end up getting out," Bailey said. She paused for a long moment, and I waited silently to see if she wanted to add more to her comment.

"Wait, no," Bailey continued, "she wouldn't get out. Her siblings would take the headset off of her, so she could live instead of her getting caught by the thing. She'd almost get caught, and she'd almost have the game over thing, but then her siblings would take the thing off of her. I didn't want to cramp the ending into like five minutes, and I didn't know what to put in the end, so I just left it on a cliffhanger because, I guess, it just sounded better than me cramping it all up into one space. I don't really like cliffhangers, so I plan on finishing this eventually."

I see how Bailey's life and interests surround the story, as she includes elements of horror, anime, and gaming, but she's also showing me what's needed to see the unseen. Throughout the story, death, in the form of a demonic looking plushie, looms all around the main character. It hunts her, and she is forced to run in order to save her life. Although it seems like the main character will find a way out by herself, Bailey said her siblings will save her. The inescapable plushie seems to resemble the oppressive state of GC. Like the plushie, GC promises physical, psychological, and/or emotional death for all Endarkened people, and it's hard for us to get away. However, there is hope in community. We may not be able to find the exit alone, but our siblings can help us to get free and truly live. To see the unseen, we can't just rely on what we know. To see the unseen and find our way out of GC's clutches, we must rely on each other.

We can't find the exit on our own. I can't find the exit on my own. But what is my role in this? Am I Kenzi, needing to be saved from evil forces? Or, am I a sibling, destined to help others escape? Maybe, I'm both.

"Thank you for walking and talking with me," I said, not wanting to keep her from her afternoon plans. "I'm so sorry for keeping you from the game room. I know that's your thing after we meet."

"It's fine. You're welcome to play with us if you'd like."

"Us?" I asked.

"Yeah. The Alfreda's play Minecraft together now. You can play, too, if you want."

"I'm horrible at that game, so I'll sit this one out. Y'all have fun!"

"We will. See you tomorrow!" Bailey said as she walked into the game room, and I heard the girls' laughter as the door closed.

6

RESEARCH PARTNER STORIES

Victoria

November 18, 2085

Victoria was scheduled to lead the learning session this time. She told us she already had the foundation for her story because she planned the plot and created the characters immediately after Bailey's session. She was happy to go second because she was able to participate in Bailey's session first before she chose to share. I guess it gave her more confidence because being the first to share is always hard to do. Because she had a better understanding of how the sessions would go, she was ready to show us what she had been working on over the past week or so.

"I've decided I'm doing a suspense story," Victoria proclaimed once everyone settled down at our table.

"Lovely ... I would like to read that," Avenae'J said as she settled into her usual seat next to Terrah.

"So, someone is going to be kidnapped and taken to a whole 'nother realm where she realizes she's the queen," Victoria said smugly. "I was just thinking about all the things I could write about. Then, for some reason, my mind went to *Princess Diaries* and *Twitches*. So, I was like, 'hmm.' Then, I'm watching a show called 'Grey's Anatomy,' and she's a doctor, so I fit that in."

"That's cool!" Terrah leaned forward in her seat to hear more.

"I know, right?" Victoria agreed. I could tell she was feeling herself because she paused for effect. "I can't think of a name for my person, though. Can I tell y'all what my story is about and the conflict, and y'all help me pick a name from that?" The girls nodded their heads in agreement. "Okay, so my story is about a young woman who lives a normal life until one day she's kidnapped. When she starts to be aware of her surroundings, she starts to get flashbacks to when she lived there a long time ago, and in the end, she reclaims her place as queen."

DOI: 10.4324/9781003159285-6

"Athena!" Talyn suggested, pointing her finger at Victoria.

"Oh yeah!" Avenae'J nodded her head in agreement.

"You would say my favorite goddess," Victoria smiled.

"Why do I feel like Athena's everyone's favorite goddess?" Terrah pulled her glasses down and looked at everyone quizzically.

"Because Athena is the goddess of wisdom and battle strategy, and she's such an awesome goddess that is over-powered," Talyn looked at Terrah as if to say, "duh!"

"So, what do you think the character's name is going to be?" I looked at Victoria.

"I'm thinking of picking Alexa because it says the meaning is defender of mankind," Victoria explained. "That makes sense for my story. Her name will be Alexa Fairchild."

"Well, there you go," Terrah slapped her palm on the table, a little louder than she anticipated.

"That's a very pleasant name," Talyn agreed.

"I don't know where I came up with the last name," Victoria said. "But, she's a general surgeon, and she dreams to one day be the best surgeon in her hospital and to have a family because she grew up in the foster system. Her mom and dad were living in the kingdom, and she was in the normal world by herself, so she dreams to one day have a family and be the greatest surgeon in the world. She's an outgoing person, but introverted at the same time. I kind of based her off of me."

That comment gave me pause. Victoria was creating a fantasy world, where the main character was a princess whose personality traits mirrored her own. Bailey did the same thing in her story when she gave one of the characters her personality traits. I had to wonder—what other story elements mimicked events in her life? What other elements of the main character's life reflect Victoria's life? Why are the girls including parts of themselves in these stories?

"We're both introverts, but extroverts," Victoria continued. "If my first plan for a career of becoming a restauranteur does not work, I want to become a general surgeon. And basically, her whole personality is like mine because she's goofy but then serious sometimes. Then at some points, she just wants to be alone, but then she doesn't want to be lonely. She has long black hair, and she has dark brown eyes, and she is fit and not fair skinned. She's like mixed ... a mix between a lot of different ethnicities. Like, she is basically like her kingdom. She's African American, which is her mom's side, and then her dad's side has a little Vietnamese, and somewhere, her family is Greek and stuff. Basically, she's just a whole mix of everything, and she loves different cultures."

She sat back in her chair and got comfortable before continuing. "The conflict is her kingdom was taken over by her evil uncle, and he's run the kingdom into the ground and now she has to reclaim her spot. Her uncle has a whole 'nother kingdom, but when the princess, which is Alex, went missing, he took over because the mom and dad were getting older. They're still alive. They just don't have any real power because the uncle is there, and he's ruling. But, um, he overheard one day that the princess is coming back, so he starts running the kingdom into the ground, so she won't have anything to rule. So, basically, she has to hurry up and come back and become queen before he makes the whole kingdom crash."

She really put a lot of thought into her story. Of course, I'm wondering about certain choices, like why the character is a mix of everything when Victoria is a dark-skinned Black girl, but this is her story, not mine, so I decided to ask a different question. "Why did you choose that conflict?" I asked. The girls all laughed as if I missed some important component of the story.

"Because, like I said, *Princess Diaries* and *Twitches*. If we want to get technical and compare him to something, the uncle would probably be like the uncle in *Twitches*. But, if you want to just have him in words, he has a nice-looking persona, but then when you really get to know him, he's more sinister. He doesn't really care about anything. He's just greedy and wants their money and power. That's the whole reason why he wants to take over. I added that part, and it was a little bit from my imagination."

I guess I could've taken more time to figure that out because she did tell me that her story was inspired by *Princess Diaries*, *Twitches*, and her own life. Still, I don't know much about those movies other than what she's told me, so it's an understandable slip.

"And," she continued, no longer looking at me, "like I said, the main character is based off me, and the mom is based off my Harbor mom, and the dad is based a little bit off my Harbor uncles because my uncles are my father figures. The mom in the story just wants the best for the daughter, and she wants her to have her own choices. At the same time, she needs her to be there for her kingdom. That's kind of like my mom because she lets me make my own choices, and she's like my best friend, but at the same time she's the mom when I need her to be. The dad is like my uncle because my uncle is a really cool, laid back person, and he is there when I need him to be. Like, if I need to talk to someone, and I can't talk to my mom, I'll talk to him."

It's interesting to see where the girls get their inspiration from. Their lives provide some of the groundwork, but they also seem to be influenced by family, movies, television, and even games. They've taken the information from the media, from their lives, and from each other when they're creating these stories. It's truly a collaborative process on so many levels.

"I also can't think of a name for a kingdom," Victoria said, as she ran over to a computer.

"Magic Kingdom?" Avenae'J suggested.

"It should be Chesapeake," Amber offered as she walked over to Victoria.

"Wait. I found a kingdom name!" Victoria's eyes widened as she turned toward Terrah. "The Kingdom of Afnia. I was going to call it the Kingdom of … well … No, because that means smart in Greek, but no, not all of them are smart."

"Is there anything else you want to ask or share with us?" I asked as she feverishly typed.

"I'll share my rising actions," Victoria said. She continued typing as she spoke. "Okay. My first rising action is she has a big surgery to do on a new trauma patient who just came into the hospital. Then, my second rising action is she gets kidnapped and taken to her old kingdom where she used to live but doesn't remember."

"Got it. So, what is the uncle doing that's causing the place to crumble?" I probed.

"Um, well first, he's the evil person, so he's doing it deliberately. He feels like he's the rightful owner, but he also realizes she's coming back. He says if he can't have it, no one can. So, he starts trying to make all of their allies become the enemies, so it could just be one big fight even though they're going to lose. So, he's just doing it to hurt the kingdom. I really need to focus, though." With that, Victoria dismissed the group and let us know her story would be ready on Saturday.

November 19, 2085

I met Victoria in the dining hall for our individual chat. She works there most days, cooking and getting management experience she'll probably use to one day start her own restaurant. The dining hall schedule is strict, with meals beginning and ending at specific times, although people can always stop by for a snack between meals if they want. Because of the strict schedule, Victoria knew the dining hall would be empty, so it would be the perfect place to meet and talk. We found a table at the front of the room because she wanted to be within earshot of the kitchen. She didn't think they'd need her, but she wanted to be prepared just in case. Talking with me was cool, but she had other priorities.

At first, we chatted about her story, and I watched her dark brown eyes light up as she shared the connections between the main character and herself, the queen and her mother, and the king and her uncle. She told me her Harbor mom was her best friend and support system, a strong and caring person who is also hardworking because she does her best to make sure they have what they need. I could tell she and her mom had a strong bond because she spoke about her mom with such joy in her heart, a happiness that emanated from her whole being.

After a few minutes of chatting about the story, I figured I should ask my questions. Who knows when food prep beings? "I have a few questions for you, if you don't mind. I want to make sure I ask them just in case there's a kitchen emergency you must attend to. Is that ok with you?"

"Mmhmm," she said, nodding her head simultaneously.

I pulled out my pen and journal so I could take notes. I swear this book is becoming a treasure trove of stories. "Okay, so although I'm there for our meetings and hear about your lives within the group, I don't know much about your lives outside of the library. I think it's really important to know you better if I'm supposed to learn from you. So, can you tell me more about you?"

"Hmm … well, I am an African American, 14 about to be 15-year-old girl. I wear glasses. I have dark brown skin and brown eyes. I have very coarse black hair. Let's see … I'm more into comfort than fashion, so I wear sneakers more than flats and stuff like that. I am also very weird. When I'm at HOME or in public, I am deathly afraid of being alone because I never know what could happen. When I'm at home, I like being with people, but then at the same time, I want to be by myself. I like being left alone at home but not in public. I'm very indecisive."

Victoria glanced at the kitchen to make sure no one needed her, and then she continued. "I think I'm more of a natural born leader because I have a lot of leadership skills, and I don't steer people wrong. I can also be a very patient person, and I like to help people a lot. That falls under leadership skills. When I help people, it's pushing them to do more or do better, and it helps me along the way because at the end, we all get to the finish line."

"I do consider myself to be a very insecure person, though," she said as she fidgeted in her seat. "I can be the most confident person, but on the inside, in my brain, I'm like, 'Do I look all right?' or 'Do I need to fix this? Do I need to fix that?' I'm always … I always care about people's opinion about me, and I consider that a weakness because I always want to make sure everybody else thinks something nice about me. I'm very self-conscious about a lot of stuff. I'm self-conscious about my weight because I don't like my weight. I try to fix it, I guess you could say. I really care what people think."

Her confidence in her leadership skills and intelligence was magnetizing, but she was still insecure about whether other people would see those amazing traits. I understand her, though. I used to wonder how my clothes and actions affected people's perceptions of me. I still wonder about it. How can I not when everything about me is villainized in GC's world—my clothes, my hair, my skin, my existence. Either way, I'm glad the learning group is a welcoming space for Victoria, a space where she doesn't have to ask if people will welcome her, a place where she knows there's nothing she needs to fix because she is perfect just the way she is.

"So, you know I've been learning about Afrofuturism, sci-fi, fantasy, and such since I've been in the Harbor. How did you get into it?" I asked.

"Well, ever since I was little, I loved to read," Victoria said. Her eyes brightened as she continued, so I figured reading must be an important part of her life. "By the time I got to first year, I was reading on a fifth-year level. Then, I just started reading different types of books, and I found out what intrigued me more. That's when I realized I was into fantasy. By the time I got to sixth year, I read at least two of the Harry Potter books, and then I started getting into old movies like *Star Wars*, and *The Hobbit*. I actually like watching the movies because it's like you see it from a different perspective than the book."

"I see." I appreciated how she was so open and willing to talk to me about her interests. "So, you've had a lifetime connection to this stuff. I'm so jealous!" I really was. I know the books and movies she mentioned were Dreamer-centric, but she was still able to find joy in reading and watching them. I liked them, too, when I was younger, but they didn't alter my world the way Butler's book did. I don't have a reason for that, but it is something I'm thinking about now that Victoria shared her past with me.

"I do have one more question that kind of goes with some of the things we talked about in the library. Basically, we talked a lot about the HOMEs, and I know you were a part of those conversations, but do you have any other HOME experiences that didn't come up?"

"I mean ... Okay so, in eighth year, we had this one boy in our class, and he said something very homophobic," Victoria answered sullenly. She was looking in my direction, but she wasn't looking directly at me. It seemed like she was journeying back to her eighth year. "A lot of the girls in my class, the ones I really talk to, we're mostly part of the LGBTQ community. I'm bi, one of my friends is pan, one of my friends is ... I don't really know what she is because she likes boys and girls alike, but she also likes a lot of other people, too, so, I don't know. There's a lot of different groups in the LGBTQ community. Some of my friends are just supporters of the LGBTQ community. Anyway, we all ended up getting on him, and he was just like, 'What are you upset for? Blah, blah, blah, I didn't say nothing wrong.' So, we basically just had to tell him why what he said was wrong and politely ask him to fix it."

"Did he fix it?"

"Yeah, he fixed what he said."

"I see. It's great that you all were able to stand up to him and help him see why it was wrong." I said this aloud because I saw how proud she was of herself for standing up for her friend, but it still saddened me to hear how the youth were responsible for teaching each other about their differences. Hearing how she stood up to her classmate made me wonder how she saw herself in justice work, especially since I'm trying to figure out where I fit in all this. Rather than sit quietly in wonder, I asked, "based on what happened and how you all stood up for each other, I'm wondering ... do you consider yourself to be an activist?"

"It's not that I don't fight for stuff because I do," Victoria said, pushing her glasses back into position. "I just don't feel like ... I just don't feel like I ... I don't want to say fight hard enough, but I don't necessarily tell people, 'you should do this,' or 'this is not the way you should do it,' or stuff like that. There are always movements about justice for this person and justice for that person, and I'm like, 'Yeah, they do deserve justice because a killer shot them, or they're still out there kidnapped or something like that,' but at the same time, I don't think I've ever done anything about it. If I did, I think I'd want to stay back and help out, either helping them get information or something like that."

"So, you don't consider yourself to be an activist?" I inquired further.

"I'm going to say no."

Her answer surprised me, especially after hearing her story just moments ago. If she's not an activist, who is? "Okay, so who do you think is responsible for making sure that there's justice in the world?"

"I think everybody is," Victoria said. "Because at the end of the day everybody needs to be punished for doing the bad thing."

"Who gets to decide what's bad or not?"

"I don't know," she looked puzzled. "Like, how the enforcers get away with shooting people. They either get suspended, or they don't get the right punishment. The enforcers don't go to jail for shooting people. There's a lot of examples, and it's mostly African Americans. But, even if you do something minor, like just cheat on a test, or litter, or something, you shouldn't do it because this is everybody's world, not just yours."

"I definitely understand." I still can't wrap my head around her not considering herself to be an activist even though she's engaged in justice-oriented actions. She strongly discusses her beliefs and points out the enforcer's wrongdoing. She and her friends stood up to a fellow classmate who made homophobic statements. Those are the actions of an activist. Of course, you don't have to identify as an activist to be considered one, but maybe we should rethink how we define the word. Maybe there's another word I should be using. Maybe our definition of what an activist does needs to be broadened. Maybe we need to reconsider how we teach young people about the goals and processes of activism.

"It'll be dinnertime soon, so you probably need to get in there, huh?" I said, wanting to be respectful of her time, but also needing some time to process what I learned from her.

"Yes! All the culture and all the feelings you get from cooking just come out in your food and then you make people happy, and it's just a really awesome feeling. Cooking good food takes time."

"Well, I'll be back in a couple hours." Victoria ran toward the kitchen, so I yelled, "I know whatever you cook will be amazing!"

November 24, 2085

Victoria planned to read her story today. After hearing more about her narratives, the written one and her personal ones, I couldn't wait to see how it all came together. How would her personality shine through the main character? How would her interests be aligned with the interest of her protagonist? How will her story be similar or different from Bailey's? What will I learn about the seen and unseen? As I thought about all I could possibly learn, the girls trickled into the library and took their seats. They knew Victoria's story would be read today, so they all sat silently and waited until Victoria was ready to begin.

"Another Boring Day"

"Another boring day," Alexa thinks as she puts on her scrubs to start another day at the hospital. She gets in her car to go to the hospital to start another day of trauma and blood. She starts to do her normal surgeries and handles her ER. She goes into the on-call room to get some rest after the big surgery she just had.

When she wakes up from her nap, she sees two men in suits hovering over her body. She perks up in the bed she was just laying on. The two men grab her and take her to a black SUV. She fights them the whole way there. When they get to the SUV, she tries to run, but one of the men catch her and throw her into the car.

"Sorry princess," he says as he gets into the passenger seat.

"Princess?!" She yells at him as she tries to open the back doors, but she realizes it's on child lock. She tries to go to the back windshield and scream for help, but as soon as she tries, the man sticks a syringe in her which causes her to fall asleep quickly.

She gets up groggily and hears voices before she sees people.

"She has to learn how to be the proper queen for the kingdom," she hears. She gets up to see one of the men who kidnapped her and a lady wearing a maid uniform. When she sits up, she realizes she is laying in a big unfamiliar bed in an unfamiliar bedroom. The people notice that she is awake and stop talking.

"Who are you? Where am I? What do you want?" she asks in confusion.

"I am Gideon. You are in Francara, and we want you to take your rightful place as queen," Gideon says.

"Queen? What are you talking about, and why am I here? Take me home."

"I'm sorry, princess. I can't do that," Gideon says.

"Why not? And, stop calling me princess," Alexa says.

"Because I can't, and you are the princess. What do you want to be called?" Gideon says.

"Fine. But I am not the princess," Alexa says.

"Perhaps you need some sleep, dear. It was a long ride," says the lady in the maid uniform who has been standing there this whole time. Alexa drifts back off to sleep.

Flashback:

"Mama, Papa, look at the pretty butterfly!" little Alexa said.

"I see, Baby Girl. Let's go inside now," said the father.

All of a sudden, a loud boom goes off inside the castle. The queen takes the little girl in her arms as the king advises two guards to take them somewhere safe. The king runs into the building with 15 other guards. They run to the sound, and they never come out. A month later, the queen goes to the kingdom to find out that her brother took over the kingdom. When she goes to take back the kingdom, he kills her. The guards take little Alexa far away to a new place and leave her there.

Flashback over:

"No!" she yells as she wakes up, and the maid comes to her side. "We have to stop my uncle. I remember everything now."

Flash forward to one year later:
"All hail Queen Alexa!" says the kingdom. The uncle is rotting forever
... or is he?

The girls and I sat still, waiting for Victoria to continue her story, but she just
grinned at us, holding her storied secrets within. I was pretty sure the rest of the
girls had questions similar to the ones swimming in my brain: how did Alexa
become queen? What happened to the uncle? Is the uncle really gone? Did the
uncle kill her parents?

I thought she was just going to leave us with a cliffhanger, but then she started
talking. "Since it is a short story, I really like where it stops. But, if I had more
time, I would add a training part about how they change her to be a queen. Then,
I would add her fighting the uncle herself, and then at the very end I would put
her winning and taking over her kingdom. The training montage would basically be them teaching her how to have etiquette and how to ride horses and
fight and stuff. The actual fighting part would be her using her wits and creativity to defeat her uncle, basically just to make him feel that he's not good enough
to be the king, so she wouldn't have to physically fight him. At the end, when she
actually rules, it would just probably go to a flash forward of probably five years,
and it just shows her kingdom prospering. Like, she has a whole bunch of allies
and everybody wants to be part of her kingdom."

I figured since she was giving us more background, I might as well ask some
of my questions. "So, there's a whole story we don't have yet! Since you're giving
us the inside scoop, can you tell me why she wanted to use her creativity and wit
instead of using strength? Like, why'd you make that choice?"

"Because she doesn't like violence. She feels like violence isn't always the way
to go. Words, most of the time, are more powerful than strength. If people talked
more, then we wouldn't have to worry about how much violence we get now."

I was glad Victoria chose to share a little more information with us, answer-
ing questions before we had a chance to ask them. Still, I'm wondering what
would happen if we had more time, if I wasn't bound by GC's time constraints.
I wonder what they could've created if this form of storytelling were an everyday part of their HOME experiences. I know that's a farfetched idea because
that would mean observers would have to be willing to teach this skill, and
most Dreamers would be against it, but I'm still hopeful. I mean, Ms. Jackson
tried to help us, and the Othermothers said there are many coconspirators in
the world above. Maybe ... just maybe, there are enough who will take up the
call to engage Endarkened children in this ... Endarkened storytelling. Maybe,
I need to be willing to go back to the world above and be a part of that work.
If I do, that will mean leaving the Harbor and going back to GC. If I do, that
will mean risking my life to make sure other Endarkened people can find freedom. It's too scary to focus on right now, but now the idea is in my head, and
it might be hard to shake.

For now, I'm focused on Victoria and her stories. I'm thinking about how even though she doesn't see herself as someone who brings about social or political change, her story, whose main character is based on her, brings about political and social change in the kingdom. This character advocates for nonviolence as a way to bring down oppressors. She becomes a queen in a land historically ruled by kings. Just like the character, Victoria doesn't see herself as an activist even though she stands up for her friends. She also advocates for nonviolence, promoting discussion over viciousness. Victoria may not see herself as an activist, but to me, she most certainly is.

But ... am I?

7

RESEARCH PARTNER STORIES

Amber

November 25, 2085

Even though my hand is cramping from all the notes I've taken on their conversations and stories, I have learned a lot. The girls are all so different, and yet, I still see similarities. I feel like the Harbor allows for that. GC wants all Endarkened people to be alike, to be a part of the melting pot. That's why we aren't allowed to have our own names, why we are only allowed to know certain parts of our histories, and why only certain stories are told about us. In the Harbor, I've learned what it means to embrace my Endarkened identity, but I also know I won't be punished for honoring my whole self. I can acknowledge and uplift the numerous identities that make me who I am. I can acknowledge the myriad emotions I feel—joy, pain, anger, love, happiness, fear, sadness, disgust, pride, and so much more. I'm learning that I can only see the unseen if I embrace all of me. I must hold tight to my name and my history and uncover the stories that have been locked away. I can't see the unseen if I don't know who my people were in the past or who I am in the present.

When I arrived at the library, the girls were waiting for me. They positioned themselves in their normal places around the oval table, Victoria to my right, followed by Terrah, Avenae'J, Talyn, Bailey, and Amber filling out the circle by sitting on my left. Amber told us she was ready to start our session.

"It's the year 2120, about 35 years from—well not really today—but 35 years from now." Her voice was low, as if she was setting the scene for a movie trailer. "Crime has progressed more than 20, no 40%, making it really dangerous to go outside. The main character's family is just her, her mom, and her dad. Her dad is from Western Europe in Germany, and her mom is African American, but they live in America. She's Black, but she's not really dark, but then she's not really light. The main character has blue eyes, light freckles. Her hair is just a mess. It's

DOI: 10.4324/9781003159285-7

not an Afro. It's not a puff. It's a mess. It's a brownish color. She's always wearing these solid colors, and most of the time, she'll wear red and black."

She seemed to be checking off a list in her notebook. I think she wrote each of these items as bullet points and was walking us through each one. "She goes to school since she's a highly privileged Black person. She uses her really high-tech skateboard, which she loves, and it helps her get out of a lot of trouble. What she really dreams and hopes for the future is that crime and hate are not words in their vocabulary, but she will fight back if she has to."

"So, not a lot of people want to go near her because she looks so different. It's rare for even white people to have blue eyes in this time. She has blue eyes, and she's emo. For them, emo is a good and bad thing ... yes, emo will still be a thing. But, it's not like they're wearing dark colors and just listening to emo rap and stuff like that all the time."

As I wondered what emo meant, Talyn joked, "She's listening to rap ... the devil!"

"Let her finish," Terrah wagged her finger at Talyn.

Talyn cut her eyes at Terrah, but she was quiet, allowing space for Amber to finish. As Talyn brooded, Avenae'J and Victoria looked at each other and smirked. Bailey, with her jacket pulled up to cover the bottom of her mouth, raised her eyebrows to no one in particular. Somewhat flustered, Amber continued to tell us about her story.

"Um, what she ... what she needs is someone to see her for her because everyone sees her as this really dangerous person with a really bad background because a lot of bad stuff happened where she used to live. She needs someone to love her for her. Oh ... yea ... she doesn't figure out she has a dangerous life until somewhere later in the story." She paused for a moment after double-checking her list. "I do have a question related to what I'm writing, though. Does Marco sound like someone who's feared? Like does he seem like he could be feared in some type ..."

"DeMarcus sounds better," Talyn interrupted again.

"I feel like if somebody said Marco, then I would go Polo," I said trying to shift the focus back to Amber's question. "That's not really a scary thing. I feel like people with scary names have hard sounds, like Declan or something."

"Demetrius!" Terrah offered.

"Declan is not scary because I know someone whose name is Declan," Amber replied. "He's not scary, but he tries to be scary."

"See, he tries to be scary because Declan just sounds very hard and hardened," I shrugged my shoulders and laughed. Then, I added, "It doesn't matter what the name is. It could be Charles. That's the name of my boss ... former boss? You could make it Jessie, and then even though that's not a scary name, you could just make it scary."

"Markus with a K!" Terrah exclaimed.

"I can't do DeMarcus because someone in my family who just passed away is named DeMarco. So maybe something that starts with V. I get really sensitive,"

Amber said looking down at the table. I wondered who DeMarco was, but I didn't ask. It didn't seem like she wanted to talk about it.

"Lucifer!" Terrah jumped up and her glasses fell off her face.

"Ooooh! Okay. Another question: anarchy or monarchy. Which one? Anarchy or monarchy?" Amber rubbed her chin and looked up to the ceiling.

"It depends on the situation," Terrah said.

"After World War 3," Amber moved her dark brown hand from one side of her body to the other to signify the movement of time.

Amber didn't say it, but I was wondering what caused World War 3 in her story. We learn about the world wars in school. Like, how the former United States was quick to declare war on Germany during World War 1 because we have always stood on the side of justice and justice could never be neutral. We also learned about how peace talks between Japan and the United States broke down after years of trying to repair the relationship, thereby causing World War 2. They tell us that even after Pearl Harbor was bombed, they tried to maintain peace and refused to engage in violence. Eventually, they had to declare war on Japan to ensure the safety of all Americans. Even after declaring war, however, they tried their best to make sure there were minimal casualties on both sides. You know, no bombs, no assault weapons, only necessary fighting. I think Altered Truth had a hand in this history, but I'm not sure.

"Okay. So far this is what I have written down," Amber said. She looked down and read from her notebook. "Violence has become the number one effect from World War 3. Ever since, the US turned to anarchy with rising leaders, including Maya's father. That is as far as I've gotten."

"What's anarchy again?" Victoria asked.

"Anarchy is complete chaos. No rules or anything … like Egypt," Amber said.

"Yea," Talyn looked at Victoria. "Total chaos is anarchy and monarchy is like a king and queen … you know … British."

When Amber said Egypt, I had to take some time to process the words. Talyn's description of monarchy referenced Britain as the example, while anarchy and chaos were tied to Egypt. I know Britain is a common one, and I know FirstHOME and GC create these narratives, but I wish the girls knew about kings and queens who existed in Africa, South America, and Asia. I'm not saying monarchy is a good thing, but I am saying we should know Europe wasn't the only continent to have kingdoms and empires. We should know that Africa is not filled with chaos. What does it say about the current system of education that Dreamers are tied to order and a hierarchy of rule, but countries full of Endarkened people are connected to chaos and ruin? What does it say when our imaginative stories continue to tie Endarkened history to chaos?

"I actually am glad I chose anarchy," Amber said. "If I had a monarchy, then I would have to think of other names, which I don't feel like doing. I still have to think of her father's name. Oh! I forgot to say something about this. I actually have the protagonist's name. I looked up Western European names. Maya

Adrianna, that's her first name. It's like two names because her father is Western European. The last name is Hundre. I don't know how to say that, but we're going to be okay with that."

"So, violence is actually one of the number one effects from World War 3," Amber continued. "Maya is really against all the violence, and she wants it to just leave. Ever since World War 3, the USA has turned into an anarchy. Her father wants to fight against that, but he also wants to take control of the US. So far, he took control of half the country, but he didn't take over the whole country … just half of it. He's pretty mad about that."

Amber flipped to a different page in her notebook. "Anyway, Maya wants to fight for the greater good of humanity on her killer hoverboard/skateboard."

"Oh My Gosh. I cannot get enough of that!" Bailey exclaimed. She looked up at Amber with wide eyes, showing her enthusiasm.

"Which side did he take over? East or west?" Victoria asked.

"North or south?" said Talyn.

"Heaven or hell?" Avenae'J laughed.

"I still haven't thought about that," Amber replied. She wrote something down in her notebook, probably making note of the questions coming up in our discussion. "Right now, I feel like they should take over where California is. The climax will be when Maya finds out her mother was killed during a protest for fighting for peace, so we'll get more information about why she doesn't like violence or why she doesn't want to do what her father is doing. In the falling action, she learns she wants to become the president to stop violence in the US. She wants to turn it back into a democracy, which was before all this anarchy stuff. Um, and the resolution is that Maya uses her father's control to climb towards a democracy and becomes the youngest female president."

"How old is she?" Talyn asked.

"Okay," Amber looked up from her notebook. "So, she is actually … at the end of the story, she is actually 17 because there's like a bit of a time jump. It's not like the Trojan horse thing that happened overnight."

"So, it's going to do a time jump from when her father takes it over to … " I start.

"Well, in the story she starts out as 15, so it really isn't a huge time jump, but it's a time jump because we are going years into the future. I'm just thinking the beginning of the anarchy would start in 2020."

"I mean, we still had elections in 2020," Talyn pointed out.

"Yes, we did," I said.

We haven't had a president since Trence handed over the government 40 years ago, but he ruled over America from the time he was handed the presidency to the time he died. He was elected by a majority of Dreamers who believed Endarkened people were trying to replace them. They had parades, caravans, and rallies of support, and many of them showed up to voting places with weapons to intimidate Endarkened people. They probably didn't need to do that because the states moved all polling places outside of Endarkened living areas and made it illegal for people to assist with transport. They also kept changing the voter ID and signature laws, which made it impossible to vote. We needed a notarized copy of our driver's license, a familial witness to accompany us to the polling place, tax stubs from the last 10 years, and county fingerprint records just to get a ballot. In order for our ballot to count, all 12 ballot signatures had to match with 99.78% accuracy.

When Trence lost his reelection, he decided not to abdicate his throne. He ruled until he died, and then he willed the presidency to his son. No one thought he was bold enough to do that, but he did. The family just kept doing that until the last Trence decided to share the wealth with his buddies. I know we had presidents before the Trences came into power, but they only teach us about certain ones. At one point, I heard an Endarkened man had become president, but it was just a rumor.

"My mom said, 'If you don't have nothing nice to say, don't say anything at all,' So, I'll just say he was the president," Victoria said in a hushed tone. "I just didn't like the way he shamed certain people. Like, at my old HOME, I had a lot of friends that were not from America. When we learned about him at HOME, I didn't really like the way he talked about immigrants to people. It's not like they wanted to move to America to take people's jobs and stuff; they just moved to America to get a better life for themselves."

"And then another thing is," she increased her voice a bit, "I don't like what he said about how transgender people couldn't fight for their country. I'm not saying I want to go fight for my country because that's scary. But if anybody wanted to fight for their country they should've been allowed to. If they wanted to do it, then we should've let them do it. They were legit fighting for him, if you think about it."

"I don't really agree with everything he said," Amber said looking at Victoria. "I'm not really fond of him. I didn't agree with everything he was saying about building the wall. Honestly, first off, this is the United States of America. We were not supposed to be building walls. The word, united, means together, not apart. I find that really hard to understand why he wanted to build a wall. If people were coming to America, it was probably so they could get away from something bad. Like, he was sending families back to somewhere they were possibly trying to get out of. This is the United States of America, and united means together, not apart, and building a wall is basically the definition of pulling something apart."

"I really didn't like him," Bailey said. "But I figured he would start building a wall, and then it wouldn't be finished until the next president. The next president wouldn't want it or something, so then they would tear it down, and all the money would go to waste." She shrugged her shoulders as if to suggest the ridiculousness of the whole process.

"I feel like he knew what he was doing was wrong," Avenae'J started, angrily. "I think he was just being petty. He was going along with countries who were doing bad things, sitting down with a candidate who killed and tortured his opposition. He was 70 something! He should have known what to say and what not to say. The things he said were just really hurtful and harmful. What he said about immigrants and what he said about building a wall. Did he realize those are our people, too? People from Puerto Rico were coming to Florida because he wouldn't help them. They had water pollution, air pollution. They hadn't gotten better after the damage and the hurricanes, and he was not helping them. He expected them to not come here? Puerto Rico is a U.S. territory. We're supposed to help them!"

"I just believe we should always trust the office even if we don't trust the person who's running it," Terrah said bluntly. "But, in this situation, I didn't trust the person who's running it. I think some of his ideas weren't well thought out. I didn't think he was very good at representing what this country was supposed to stand for. And I didn't think he was a very good person in general."

"Well," I said. "Even with all the other mess that happened with GC, I'm glad Amber's World War 3 didn't happen in 2020."

"It could have happened when 45 didn't get his act together," Avenae'J argued.

"In everything I read and watched from that time, somehow, it seemed like World War 3 would be the result of everything happening in the world. I don't know why. It just seemed like it was a ..." Amber started.

"Like World War 3 was out to get us?" Victoria asked.

"Like a consistent presence?" I added. The girls nodded their heads in unison.

November 28, 2085

Amber wanted me to meet her at her house in the J hallway. When I got to the door, I knocked. I tried not to knock too loudly, but it was pretty quiet in the hallway, so it sounded louder than I wanted it to. The door opened, and a short, brown-skinned woman smiled up at me. She must have been Amber's mother. She had the same long hair, the same dark brown eyes, and the same grin. For this woman to be her Harbor mother, the resemblance was uncanny.

"Welcome to our home!" she said. There were five kids playing behind her, and I wondered how they managed to take in so many Harbor children. I don't really know the process, but I did know most of the kids have Harbor parents, and many adults connected with chosen families, destroying the nuclear family trope of two parents, two kids, and a dog. I spotted Amber waving to me by a table in the living room.

"Come in, Sis!" Amber's mother said. "Don't just stand there. I know there's a lot going on in here, but our house is always full of life."

Amber came to the door, grabbed my arm, and pulled me to the table. "You've got a lot going on today!" I said to her.

"Always," Amber laughed. "So, what did you want to know?"

I'd been asking the same questions over and over again, so instead of giving my speech about why I was doing this, I started with the first question I always asked. I know the girls talk to each other outside of the group, so I figured that this was a way to save some time. "Can you tell me more about yourself?"

Amber paused for about 3 minutes before she began. I remember her check-lists during the group session, so she seems like the type of person who wants to have her thoughts in order before she speaks. "I'd probably describe myself as shy, but then when people get to know me, I am nowhere near shy. I am very talkative ... *very* talkative. I dress a little odd. I don't like to dress really girly, so I don't wear a lot of dresses. I'm like 5'5 and a half. I'm dorky but then at the same time I don't like to be a dork sometimes. I'm kind of athletic because I play a lot of sports, but that's only if it's team sports. I don't really like to play solo sports. Compared to everyone in my house, I'm like a goldish brown color, but then it's still kind of dark. I'd say I'm Black although I don't know a lot about my heritage. I'm still Black and strong. I'm not independent, though, because I still live with my parents."

Amber was interrupted when her younger sister came to sit on her lap. She looked to be about one year old, and as she put up her hands to be picked up, Amber smiled and obliged. She bounced the young child on her knee for a few minutes and then continued talking.

"I think my strengths would be my friends and family because without them, I wouldn't really be where I am today," Amber continued. "My strength is the people who are around me supporting me. Another strength is that I've been writing stories since around third year because I really like telling stories, and sometimes I'd write them down and tell them to my friends. Now, I show my family. After I'm done writing, I'll show it to them, and they'll say, 'oh, that's good' or 'you could add something more to it,' or 'you could take something out.' So, it would be a mix of them helping me and me just telling them my story."

I took in this information. Like Bailey and Victoria, Amber thought she was weird, and I'm still trying to figure out exactly what that means. What does it mean to be weird? What does it mean to be normal? Who decides who's weird and who isn't? Either way, I notice how she found strength in her family and in her friendships, so weird or not, she felt supported. Because she said she shared her stories with family and friends, I wondered if she had always been one to share her writing with others. So, I asked.

"I used to not talk, because if I didn't, people didn't have much to say bad about me," Amber replied. "Now that I'm older, I talk a little bit more. I've changed a whole lot. My worst memory would be at HOME because I didn't like talking. People would make fun of the color of my hair or the length of my hair. Then, they'd laugh at the way I'd talk, because I had some kind of weird accent. I only had about two friends. I was bullied for a really long time. I only got braces because people laughed at the gap I had between my teeth."

"I remember in third year, they'd pull my hair and say, 'Is that a weave?' I would be like, 'No.' I didn't even know what weave was at the time." As she spoke, she tugged on her long braid, mimicking the moves of the children from her past. "I didn't know until I was in sixth year what weave was because

I never grew up with that kind of stuff. I'd say one of my worst moments was people teasing and pulling my hair when I was younger. I wanted to cut my hair. I wouldn't necessarily say I believed them saying I was ugly, but I didn't like hanging out with people because they said I was stupid or ugly. I didn't really like going to school, but I did because my observers, they'd at least stand up and tell them to not do things like that."

"There was one point where people were saying so much about my teeth that one of my friends went to the counselor and told her," Amber said proudly. "They all got called to the counselor's office, and then they didn't like me because they thought I talked to them. I was like, 'My friend did that, that's what we're supposed to do.' I was really hurt, though. I couldn't even tell my favorite observer. Sometimes, she could just tell. She'd pull them aside and ask, 'What are you doing?' She'd tell me she talked to them, so they shouldn't be doing it anymore, but kids will be kids or teens will be teens, too. As I got older, I realized I don't need their opinions, because the more I let them say I'm stupid or ugly, the more I feel like I am, but I know I'm not because they're the stupid ones for calling me that."

I looked into the eyes of the beautiful Black girl in front of me and tried to figure out why she was forced to deal with bullying behaviors that caused her to hate her lovely features. Of course, "kids will be kids" is something so many of us learn at FirstHOME, but what aspects of the world socialize us to assume that Black girls plus long hair equals weave? What aspects of the world cause children to hate the unique gaps that form between their teeth? What world have we created when a young Black girl has to internally fight feelings of ugliness because the kids and society consistently tell her that she is not beautiful?

"I guess I'm a little sensitive when it comes to a lot of things," Amber said, disrupting my question spiral before it fully formed. "I try to be a little strong about it, but later on by myself, I get really upset."

I understood her point. It's hard when you're forced to be the strong one, especially when you know there aren't many people who are willing and able to be strong for you. She shouldn't need to apologize for embracing softness in a hardened world. "I'm so glad your friend stood up for you when those kids were bullying you. Do you speak up when you see injustices happening?"

"I see myself trying to speak up, but then at the same time, I don't know how I'm going to do that because I don't like talking in very, very public places. I'm still shy no matter how much I talk," Amber whispered. This seemed to be a question she's considered before. "I'm still shy, so me speaking up, I wouldn't say a lot. I'd get the jitters trying to talk, and then I wouldn't say everything. Then when I'd walk away, I'm like, 'I could have said more.'"

"That's understandable. I mean, I think we also have this idea that in order to be a part of justice movements, we have to go out and speak, or protest, or hold signs. There's so many different ways to speak up."

As I said this, I thought about what it really meant to me. How else can people be a part of justice movements? In a world where Endarkened people are consistently maimed and murdered and in a society that relegates us to the lowest rung on the ladder of humanity, how do we speak up? How do I speak up? I've lived a life of compliance, and I'm not sure how to engage. The only thing I think I'm good at is writing. Maybe … maybe writing can be how I engage. Maybe writing can be how I do justice work. But, does that count?

"Yeah, you really don't have to. It can start with your family, or your friends." Amber said. Her sister was begging to get down to play, and she put her back on the floor. "It doesn't have to be out there, out there. I am active on things like helping out society and things like that. Right now, I am helping out at the Harbor's senior centers. I'm also planning on doing a radio show soon. It's basically going to bring up things for teens in our community, asking them to help with society. I honestly just want everyone to not have a bad life. I want them to have a good one where it's still the United States of America because the way we're going right now, there isn't much peace going around. There are still people treated unfairly. Like, we are Black, but we should all have equal rights and it's unfair how we're still being treated unfairly. I know it's kind of cliché to say world peace, but that's what I want most in life … for everyone to be equal."

Her sentiments ring true throughout the group, but I can see how her comments might impact the story she's writing. From the collaborative session and from this individual chat, I know she's discussing the violence happening in GC. The main character wants peace, wants to avoid the violence and the chaos. She wants democracy in action, not in name only. She wants a world where Black girls can avoid ridicule, a place where they can be well. Just like Amber, the main character wants equality for all.

December 1, 2085

On Amber's storytelling day, the group was buzzing with excitement. The girls were talking amongst each other, making predictions about what Amber's story would entail. What would we learn about Maya and her hoverboard skateboard? How would her story be written? What would she show us about the seen and unseen? These questions were at the forefront of my mind when Amber began her story.

"World War 3's Effect on Society"

> It's 2120, 35 years since World War 3 ended, 20 years since the USA turned to anarchy, 15 years since Maya-Adriana Hundre was born to someday return the States of America back to the United States of America.
>
> Maya was never one for the violence and chaos she grew up with. Her father, Marco, only wants to control the chaos. There have been many outbreaks of protest over gaining peace. No successful attempts.
>
> As Maya skates to school on her hoverboard, with her long, dark brownish hair flowing freely, she passes by the other kids' teasing and criticizing words. Maya tries her best to not take their words to heart.

"It's dangerous to be walking around without your mom," they would say, as well as, "Oh wait, you don't have a mom."

Every time they would make those remarks, she thought of retaliation, closer and closer to fighting back. But as she thought about retaliating, she remembered what her mother used to tell her.

Letter # 23
Dear Dylan,

The students have individual desks with holograms to do class work at their own pace. Talking is very limited. Interaction is also limited. These precautions are to make sure that no violence or chaos is brought into the school environment. Since you left, so much has changed. The air tastes of defeat and no feelings. Sour.

—Maya-Adriana Hundre

After school let out for the day, Maya was getting ready to hover away to her dark mansion of a house. The house of a feared man, her father. Before she could leave, she felt a shove to the back from a hand strong enough to knock her down by surprise.

One second later, all Maya could feel was the cold and hard concrete. The next thing she heard was false sorry's and laughs as they said, "Oh no! Do you want your Mommy? Wait, you can't. She's dead. Sorry." The next thing Maya knew was that she was swinging. She hit the boy so hard he's on the ground groaning in pain with hints of blood. Maya set course home on her hoverboard.

Flashback

Every day, Denise would tell stories of how peace should be free. She never liked the thought of violence. Maya loved that about her mother. Denise always said that violence should never be fought with violence. Maya, as a little girl with light freckles starting to fade, took her mother's words to heart.

1 Year Later

Ever since Maya's father gained control of over half of the country, everyone has been looking down on her when they once just looked at her like she was a girl on the street.

Letter #120
I don't know when I will come back, but remember: don't let them look at you as just the scariest man alive's daughter. Tell your father I said gut gemacht (good job).

—Dylan 'Dilly'

2137
Denise Hundre, a brave woman. Had she not been murdered during a peace protest, Maya would not have found her lost thoughts. Today is the 13-year anniversary of Maya's mother's death. Upon Maya finding out, she thought of ways she could change this anarchy.

Before we could clap for her, she told us there was more to the story. Terrah and Avenae'J sighed in relief because they had questions.

"My writing is always, somehow, about me, but not a lot because I don't like talking about myself," Amber said as she shut her notebook and took her seat. "I'll talk about myself if someone asks what I like or what I do, but I don't really write a lot about myself because it's not something I like to talk about. The part about having her mother die was in my head because I always think about how it would be if I didn't have my mom. I depend on my mom a lot, so if people were to start bullying me about something, they'd probably say something about my mom. I talk about her more than I talk about myself."

"Maya's mom didn't like all the violence, so she was protesting," Amber continued. "But one day she was protesting, and they were actually on the news, so everyone could see. The government came out and basically shut it down by shooting all of them. Everyone saw that. Even Maya saw that. That's why people tease her about it because she doesn't like to talk even though she'll talk every once in a while. I'm not sure if I put that in her bio."

We all shook our heads to nonverbally let Amber know she hadn't given us that detail. Amber acknowledged us and continued discussing other aspects of her story. "Dylan is an old friend who moved out of the United States of America, not United, because we are now in anarchy. He is a friend from the States of America. He's moved recently, and they write each other every day. So, I think the first entries I put on there is like 20-something because it's been 20-something days since he's left and he's moved to Europe, which … I don't know why. I just wanted to go to Europe, so I was like, 'let's just put this in here.'"

"The father isn't really a major point until close to the middle or the end of the story. I think I forgot to say that," Amber added sheepishly. "In the middle, I'd probably give more details on how he took over because people were scared. He basically had his men take over all these states, and he can't really take the rest of it because there's another side, another man trying to take over States of America, too."

She concluded her list of extra information, and the girls began clapping. She got a few high fives from the other sci-fi writers in the group. I assumed their burning questions were answered because no one asked anything, and they all started making their way toward the door. As they walked, the girls discussed details for Talyn's collaborative session scheduled for the next day, and I thanked them for working with me again.

While the girls hugged each other and prepared to leave, I thought about Amber's story. It may not have been all about her, but parts of the personal story she told me popped into my mind as she read. Bullying was a major part of her life. She was bullied for her teeth and for her hair. Although her main character was bullied because her mom died, there was still the element of kids being kids and teens being teens. But rather than wanting to cut her hair, Maya's hair flows freely. Rather than having a friend stick up for her, Maya fights the bully herself.

It may not be Amber's story, exactly, but I see how it could be. In fact, so far, all the girls' stories reflected aspects of their lives. It may be speculative in nature, but the themes are definitely realistic.

In so many ways, blending the speculative and the realistic together is like seeing the unseen. I can't see the future or the fantastic because these do not exist, at least not yet, but the girls are guiding me to these other worlds through their words. They are blending the seen, the realistic, with the unseen, the futuristic and fantastic. I'm thinking about the book that led me here, the speculative books leading all of us to the Harbor, and I'm realizing how the codes work. Somehow, by reading these books, we unlock the codes to the maps. How? I'm not sure. All I know is it happens. It's like we have codebreaking technology locked into our brains.

How wonderful it is to realize we can tether the present to futures and other-worlds. How free it is to realize we can write about our lives by relying on our imaginations. How sad it is to realize this might be one of the reasons why GC takes our dreams away from us.

8

RESEARCH PARTNER STORIES

Talyn

December 2, 2085

Talyn was waiting for us when we walked into the library. She had quite a few documents in front of her. I was pretty sure they weren't pages from her story, but who knows? Talyn told me she likes to build worlds for her characters, and sometimes, worlds need extra pages. Before she began telling us about her story, she prefaced her content.

"Mine is really weird because my character lives in an alternate universe. It's in the same universe, but it's like the Earth got hit by a meteor, everyone died, and then they like reformed and got bigger."

"The Big Bang Theory!" Avenae'J exclaimed.

Talyn disregarded Avenae'J's comment, "I was inspired by a book. I think it's called *All's Quiet* ... something like that. It's a book where the main character goes into war, and there's this British kid who knows nothing about what war actually is, and when he gets there, his life changes completely. Then when he gets home, he's like, 'I have nothing to do. I don't have anything.' Like, his whole view on life kind of just changes who he is because he felt like wars were a prideful thing. But then he saw his friends die, so that kind of changed everything."

I hadn't read that book, and based on the other girls' silence, I don't think they read the book either. Nothing about it sounded intriguing, but I found it interesting it was part of Talyn's story. We remained quiet, listening, waiting for Talyn to begin again.

"Okay," Talyn continued. "The world is also kind of based off of Greek mythology. This girl looks like the water girl from *Avatar: The Last Airbender*, but she's taller with heavier coats. Her hair is all the way out, and it's dark brown. She lives in a forest on a country of islands because she doesn't like

DOI: 10.4324/9781003159285-8

people. It's always cold; it's basically Antarctica, but with trees that have leaves. She lives by herself—no pets, no family, no nothing. She hunts for food. She doesn't technically go to FirstHOME. She's 15–18 years old. I'm still trying to figure out what range, what age I should put her in. Um, she wants to go into war so she can be respected and find out what she is because she thinks war can make you realize who you are as a person."

I don't want to interrupt Talyn as she talks, but I am wondering why her character feels like she isn't respected. What happened in her past that made her believe war was one of the only ways to figure out who she is? I made a note about how violence shows up across the stories I've heard so far.

"In the world, there are different races," Talyn continued. "And it's evenly distributed between the army she's in, but there are two people who are extremely racist and they're white. I'm making them blonde, white people who know nothing about the actual outside world, and they refuse to learn anything else. These people came for glory, and they're always blaming whatever bad happens on all the Black people in the army. Then, the other white people are like 'get them out of here!' They get reported for that, and then they are no longer part of the military. There is a war going on between two different countries, and you have time to bully Black people because they're Black? We do not have the time or energy for that."

"Is there a reason why you made the characters white and blonde?" I asked.

"I guess it's because it's a stereotype," Talyn replied.

"Well, you definitely went in depth on your characters," I complimented.

"I've been working on this person since like the end of last year," Talyn replied. "I've had an idea of this person for a very long time. Oh, I also forgot to mention my character is Black, but it's like the lighter shade of brown. It's like, um, your skin color," she said, pointing to Terrah. "And she also has really long light brown hair down to the bottom of her shoulder blades. Her name is Kokolane. I still don't know where the name inspiration came from."

"The year is … I haven't come up with the first two digits, so I just put Xs."

Talyn laughed as she showed everyone the two X's she wrote instead actual numbers. "The story is about becoming a soldier and getting respected by the people around her. The major conflict is between two countries. They're fighting over Kokolane's island because of the minerals and resources it has on it. So, they're fighting over the island, and whichever side wins, they get it."

Avenae'J jumped in to ask a question, "So, she lived with her family, but then she wants to live alone?"

"I mean … Yeah," Talyn responded without looking at Avenae'J. "I'm going to start at the end which is in the middle of a battle with Kokolane and the bad guy of the story. Then, she is actually going to become a soldier, and she will discover what she is. Then the resolution is just her liking who she is because I cannot think of anything else more fitting for that character. I like to make my characters overly powerful. When you have that, you can make battles kind of interesting. My characters don't know they have powers yet. So, if I have them fighting someone, I can make it to where they unleash this giant explosion of things or make the story about them finding out what their power is."

"Respect," Avenae'J said. "I like that. It's actually really nice, like the ending."

With more stories being told, I'm starting to connect threads. It's like the girls' individual stories are a part of a larger quilt, and my job is to read the patches, follow the threads, and figure out how all are woven together. I made another note about both Talyn and Bailey's characters needing to discover their powers and kept listening.

"So again, yes, I started off in the middle of the battle, and then like I did 'year jumps,'" Talyn continued. "It jumps back to when she got into the army, and then two months after that, and then a few days later, and then two days before the battle happens. I'm working on the buildup for the climax to show she is a god, more or less. I'm trying to see how that works. So far, I think it's good. I got her in a fit of rage because emotions can heavily influence magic, and that is something consistent in so many places."

After hearing Talyn's synopsis, I wasn't sure how we could help her. She had been working on this character for much longer than we'd been meeting as a writing group, and she seemed to have a grasp on the characters' world as well as the main character. Maybe she just wanted us there for moral support, to listen to the premise of a story she had already written.

"So, what's a type of mean girl plastic name?" Talyn asked. I think she was using plastic to describe someone who is popular, materialistic, and mean.

"Karen. Gretchen. Brittany," Terrah offered.

"I put Cassie," Talyn said.

"Rebecca?" Avenae'J suggested.

"Okay, now I need one for a mean dude. Just like … " Talyn started.

"A guy?" Bailey asked.

"Chad," Avenae'J said.

"All the names are going to have Cs, Cassie and Chad," Talyn proclaimed. "They're the bad people."

Those were the only questions Talyn had for the group. Still, I couldn't help but notice how the naming of characters came up again. Even though Talyn had the name of her main character, she wanted us to help her think of names for the racist Dreamers who antagonize characters in the story. I think naming is essential for Endarkened people. I've said this before, but each time I meet with them, it becomes even more prominent. That's got to be the reason why naming keeps coming up in our sessions. Naming ourselves and naming those who attempt to oppress and antagonize us is vital. Naming helps us figure out who we are and, possibly, who we should avoid.

December 4, 2085

Talyn wanted to meet in one of the Harbor classrooms. I had never been to the classroom section before, but I was excited to see it. FirstHOME classrooms look

like jail cells, with desks lined up in rows and silence listed as an essential requirement. When I walked into this classroom, I noticed there were no desks, no
sterile color palettes, and lots of noise. They call these spaces classrooms because
so many of the Harbor kids and adults go there to learn. According to Talyn,
it's an open space that doesn't require people to silence their voices or adhere to
arbitrary rules, a space where they teach and learn from each other. There are
some specific classes given here—Endarkened History, Music, Dance—but most
of the time, there are just groups of like-minded people coming together to share
knowledge.

"So, why did you want to meet here?" I asked Talyn as she came in the room.

"FirstHOME didn't allow me to have the imagination thing. It was a science,
technology, engineering, and math school, so it didn't have arts. It didn't have
any of that. It was just straight up factory learning. It was not fun."

"Oh. That makes sense why you'd want to be in a place like this, then," I said.
Of course an organization bent on "Helping the Omnipotent Manufacture
Efficiency" would revert to factory learning since the HOMEs job is to
ensure Endarkened youth aren't dreaming and Endarkened people are ready to
enter GC's workforce. It also makes sense why she'd want to meet in a more
welcoming space.

"You've probably spoken with the other girls already," I said. "So, you know
I'm just trying to learn more about your personal story before listening to your
speculative story. Whatever you want to tell me is cool."

"Well … my earliest writing memory is when I was seven, and I was copying
words out of a Dr. Seuss book. I think it was *Green Eggs and Ham.* That was the
first time I remember writing something down. I think I was just bored and had
nothing else to do, so I did that. I haven't actually written my own stories in a
while, but I do have stories. I just tell them to my friends. When I write, I'll
make a character and figure out what I want them to be like, and then I'll center
the story around that, and then it just flows. I don't really have a system to where
I stop, think of something, and go again. It just comes out, you know? That's
how I write it up. I'll make corrections later."

"For the story you'll hear on Saturday, I got inspiration from *Fairy Tail,*"
Talyn continued, her brown eyes lit up with excitement. "Which is an anime/
manga and one of the first actual cartoons I watched. It's a show where basically
every single technology is somehow integrated with magic and is powered by
that. I take some of the different types of magic from it—celestial, requip, and
dragon slayer magic. I take that and the concept of guilds from that show."

"Your writing process reminds me of Bailey's," I said. "She also gets some
inspiration from anime and manga. Is there anything else I should know about
you? Like, not about the story you're writing, but about your personal story?"

"Uh … I mean … I used to hide in my closet a lot," Talyn answered with
an unconvincing smile. "The time I was most scared was around the time my
Harbor brother started to have more anger issues along with depression. He was
really angry, and he wanted to get a device from me. I knew it wouldn't work,

so I didn't give it to him, and he kept trying to bang down the door. So, I put my bike, this computer hardware thing, and a few other things against the door. Then, I hid in my closet. He was yelling, and I was crying tears. It was not a good experience. Then, he also had friends over, and they harassed me."

Outside of our collaborative sessions, Talyn often talked about her brother, and it was usually a conversation about something mean or ignorant he said in conversation with Talyn and their mom. Many people in the Harbor become Othermothers to kids who make their way to the underground safe haven. Some take in numerous children, like Amber's mom, and others take only one or two. Talyn's brother is only a year older than she is, and they came to the Harbor at about the same time. It seems as though her brother was having a harder time adjusting, though, because Talyn often interrupted the other girls to tell stories about a problematic thing her brother did that day.

"It seems, based not only on this story, but also the other days where he's been mentioned in random conversations, that you have lots of stories about your brother. How is that relationship?"

"How is that relationship?" she tilted her head back and let out a sad laugh. "I don't like him very much. I care about him, but I don't like him."

"Why don't you like him?"

"The first few years, he acted like he was better just because he was the first one. But, one time, my brother's friends came over, and I recorded them saying stuff, and I sent it to my mom, and he got in trouble. That's something I was proud of. They all said very inappropriate things, except for one guy. The rest of them were very inappropriate and not respectful in any way. I don't know if that was because I was a girl or because I was his sister or whatever, but I did not like it. It was not okay."

"If you don't mind me asking, what inappropriate things were they saying?"

"Like sexualized things," she said somberly with a tinge of anger. "I don't remember the exact words, but it was like 'you wanna hop on this dick' … stuff like that. There were a few girls, and they told them to stop. My brother was not in the room, but I don't know if he would've stopped them or anything. I don't know what he was doing, but he was not doing anything. Then, I threatened them, and they didn't stop, but I was recording, and then they got in trouble. I felt happy."

I was appalled. "They should never have been saying that," I said.

"And they were like the same age as me!" she exclaimed. "How?! That's not okay!"

I'll be wrestling with this knowledge for a while because even though her home in the Harbor should be a safe place, there is someone in the household who no longer represents safety for her. At first, her brother was her friend, an ally of sorts within the Harbor. Now, especially in lieu of these two events, he's a traitor. I know the Harbor has people from all over who are still grappling with their time in GC. I know people come to this space with GC views that must be unlearned, but until the most vulnerable of us are protected, none of us are safe. Talyn's story about her brother showed me we have a lot of work to do on ourselves even as we fight against GC. It showed me just how much GC can corrupt Endarkened youth.

"It's not okay, but I'm glad you were able to record them. You took a stand. You stood up for yourself even though your brother wasn't around to speak up for you. To me, that's activism. Do you see yourself as an activist?" I didn't want to change the subject, but I also wanted to make sure the conversation didn't just center that relationship and the negativity it brought.

"I see myself as a person who can empathize with others who have been through it even if I haven't been through it myself," Talyn answered. "I think I can understand what it's like to feel like you've been in the wrong because you're a certain age or a certain type of person, you're this color, you're this gender, you identify as this person, and you like this certain thing. I understand, and I feel like I can get to some of the people who don't. I can help them understand because not everyone is always informed."

"So ... you see yourself as someone who's responsible for justice?" I asked.

"I mean ... the people who realize there needs to be change are responsible," Talyn said. "The women who started the #BlackLivesMatter movement, Martin Luther King, the people who got out and said LGBTQ people are very much needing of things because we are human beings. Those people who realize human beings are just human beings, and they're not going to be anything other than that, no matter what you are, who you are, and what you prefer."

I think I know what she meant, but I thought it wouldn't hurt to get some clarification.

"I get you. So, the people in more targeted groups are responsible for making sure the people in the more dominant groups are socially just?"

"No. I feel like it's the people in the target groups who help themselves and help each other. The agentic groups, when they start helping out, makes things get more attention, so it's kind of both of them working together."

Talyn basically summarized what happens at the Harbor. Endarkened people work together to make sure they're all taken care of. They help each other learn. They uplift each other. There are other Endarkened enclaves working to uplift their members. Although the Harbors can exist on their own, they also need the help of Dreamers who understand we all need to work together to have justice. That's the purpose of the commonweal.

All of this reminded me of what the Othermothers said the day we met. Layli said to protect the Harbor's residents from harm, Savannah—the city—alters what people see. The Othermothers exist in community with the world and see it as it wants to be seen. I couldn't see the unseen because I lived separately, isolated from the world and from my people. What I'm learning, though, is I need to work in community with others to truly see. My spirit needs to align with the spirits of the people in the Harbor and with the spirit of the city. Until we are all aligned, I will never see the world as it what it can be, what it wants to be. I will only see it for what it is. The balance provides sight.

December 8, 2085

"Before I start," Talyn began, "I have to say a couple things. With more time, I would've gotten more into detail. I would've put more logs because the style I'm writing in is basically her putting logs in her book and then in her diary or journal. Sometimes something happens on a day when she can't write in that journal, so it's not a day-by-day journalism thing. If it was, it'd be like 2000 pages long because it's a long time."

With that introduction, Talyn began her story.

"Kokolane Signing Out"

> Clash! The sounds of swords beating against each other. Glares are thrown between the battling. Sparks of metal hit the ground before fizzling out.
> "You've gotten better, Kokolane."
> "And you talk too much," she swings her sword at his head.
> **Three and a half years ago**
> June 15, XX03
> It's been a while ... I haven't written in this thing in a while. I finally got to be a soldier. One step closer to being a part of my village. So far so good. No one has said anything to me. I guess that's how I like it.

—Kokolane signing out

> **Two months later**
> August 15, XX03
> Recently, the Eoduunal army has advanced. I was put in my first battle, but what I noticed is that whenever I shot an arrow, it looked like the energy that it gave off was drowning the enemy. Sometimes, when I dodged, it seemed like I was floating.

—Kokolane signing out

> **A few days later**
> August 20, XX03
> Someone has been caught trying to steal a few data files today. I'm just glad no one is blaming me. Well, almost no one. Cassie and Chad ... they are the most racist pieces of s*** I've ever met. They are blaming me and everyone else my color. I don't know why the general doesn't kick them out. Besides, Cassie is the worst liar. She once tried to blame Tony (a good friend of mine) of stealing her undies, when it was likely some animal that got in.

—Kokolane signing out

> **Three years later, before the battle**
> "Alright troops, you're the only ones I have," says the general. "Mindala, since you're our last healer, you're in the back. Kokolane, you're the best

with a sword, so you're in front, and Thomas, you're our last gun man, so you're the middleman."

"What about you sir?" Kokolane asks with a slight panic in her voice.

"I'll be with Tom, Koko. Don't you worry. Now, let's move!" he says with confidence. Thomas, the general, and Kokolane get their weapons. Mindala grabs her healing staff and a weapon of her own. Kokolane gives a small offering to the goddess, Aquarius, and they set off to the battlefield.

The mud soon turned dry. Kokolane is deep in battle when she hears the general's screams. "This feeling," she thinks. "It's like a running river." Her moves flow more and more as water splashed up from the ground. Another yell for help. "Mindala." Rage. Rage! RAGE!

A yell and a blast from the sky. The sky turns gray as if a storm is coming. The wind stirs, and it starts to rain. As Kokolane attacks, the storm winds get faster, and the snow on the ground flies up in the air. Kokolane yells in pure rage, as she plows through the enemy army. She watches as her friends … no, the last drop of her family, is killed. The snow then turns into a type of tornado. It combines with the water coming down and wipes out the rest of the enemy army when …

"Kokolane!" she hears the general yell. She looks to see the general struggling to keep up a fight. She quickly goes over to kill the orc he's fighting. She hears an arrow. It came from behind her. It killed the general. She grabs a dead man's bow and arrow, then kills the last soldier.

"Kokolane … do you realize what you are?" a deep voice says. It sounds like the voice of a shadow.

"You … you're the mole Arkasan?" She turns to him. He looks more like an Eoduunal soldier without all the makeup. It was more disturbing than before. And to think, she used to think of him as an ally. As a friend.

"Let's finish this. And, let's see how long you last." He unsheathes his sword. It looks like a katana with a black handle and a silver blade. Kokolane picks up her sword.

Mud mixes with blood and bone beneath their feet. Her sword felt lighter. Her eyes glow blue, and his turn purple. The sky screams out as the fight breaks out.

Sparks fly. Blood is drawn. Lines are crossed.

Dodges and hits. Missing and getting. So close to a win.

Then, Kokolane is pushed back by a blast of energy. Arkasan smiles as Kokolane has trouble getting up. She stands and glares at him. She stands fully and charges.

She jumps up and …

Clash!

The two swords are sliding against each other. Kokolane throws him back and she lands on her feet.

"You've gotten better, Kokolane," he says panting.

"And you talk too much," she snaps back. She swings her sword over his head. The force of a god can kill anything. Who says it can't kill another god? His head falls to the floor. The storm clears.

Kokolane, injured and tired, falls to her knees. In all her life, never had she thought she'd be able to do that. She smiles, but the smile turns to tears, and the tears turn into small patches of snow. She wipes her tears. This battle is over.

Back at the base, the other generals let her go home. She needed rest. She's seen what anger can do, what people can do, what she can do. It was time she went home and relaxed.

After a few hours, she opens the door to her house. It was warm. She sits on her couch and relaxes, and she pulls out her journal.

June 15, XX06

I've fought in a way I've never fought before. It was the first time I understood what I can do. I feel better about myself. Anyway, I should sleep.

—Kokolane signing out

The girls clapped for Talyn as she bowed to her audience. While she gave her victory speech, I thought about the connection between her story and the personal story she told me the other day. Yes, I know her story was based on war and Greek mythology, but I couldn't help but notice how the main character was forced to defeat a traitor to find her true power. When Talyn spoke about her brother, she said he'd changed. He put her down because she was a year younger; he made her cry when he violently tried to take her device; he didn't stand up for her when his friends were harassing her. In various ways, her brother, a person she once considered an ally, ended up being a traitor in the same way that Arkasan was a traitor against Kokolane. She didn't tell me about that connection, and I'm not sure if she's made that correlation herself, but it's definitely something I'm thinking about.

I think what's making this story so hard to consider is, up to this point, I saw the Harbor as a place of safety for everyone. I think it's more complicated than that, though. Even though the Harbor is a safe place for many, we come here with different life experiences, with different pasts, with different baggage. That doesn't go away just because we've found some semblance of safety. How do we heal in a world that consistently uplifts our pain? How do we protect Black girls to make sure they don't have to continue fighting in supposedly "safe" spaces? What is my role in this? How can I … no … how will I help?

9

RESEARCH PARTNER STORIES

Terrah

December 9, 2085

Terrah wasn't sure how much help she needed, but she still wanted us to listen and give input. In some ways, that's how all the girls used the time. Most had their stories mapped out before we even began to talk about writing stories, but they still wanted to meet and talk about what they planned on writing. I think it's just an excuse to get together, but that's more than fine with me.

"So, Zorella is generally a really shy, kind of awkward person or girl, but she's really, really smart," Terrah began. "She focuses a lot on schooling and that's why going to this college was a big deal because after America split, all the colleges on her side of the country kind of crashed, but the colleges on the other side … they crashed, too, but eventually, they got better. The colleges over there are better than any of the colleges on her side, so it's really important she goes, so she can find her place in the world."

The girls nodded their heads to let Terrah know they were listening. "She lives with her mom, dad, and younger brother. She's pansexual. She doesn't talk to very many people, usually only her family and best friend. She dreams of having her own successful musical one day and raising a family, of escaping her everyday routine and meeting someone from the other side of the world. She dreams of everything going back to the way it was, or how it was before, I guess. She feels like she needs to stop dreaming, but what she really needs is an outlet, a way to let go. She needs someone to listen. She needs motivation. She needs someone to love. She's tired of being lonely."

"She's short with very long hair that she often straightens or puts in two Dutch braids." Terrah pointed to her braids to make sure everyone knew what hairstyle she was talking about. "She's Black, and she has rounded doe eyes and small lips," she continued. "Well, she is a mixed girl. Both her parents are mixed, Black and white, and so that makes her half Black, half white."

DOI: 10.4324/9781003159285-9

Terrah paused for a moment. She seemed as though she was considering the character description she just shared aloud. "I feel like, in a way, she kind of relates to me. I feel the same way about wanting to find my place and where I belong in the world. Her going to college far away from her family also represents me because I want to go to a college very far away. If I go to Harvard, Stanford … and I forget the name of the third one, I'm going to be far away from my family which is the only thing I'm hesitant about. They're all far away from where my family will end up. I know that for a fact because they don't want to live in the Northeast or all the way on the West Coast."

Terrah's character was like the real Terrah, and the character's situation resembled events in Terrah's life. Like all the other girls, there are elements of truth embedded within the speculative story. I don't think anyone taught them this technique. It seems like the storytelling ability, the capacity for placing the real into the realm of the fantastic was innate. I wish the HOMEs recognized this genius, rather than forcing compliance. Of course, I know that will never actually happen.

"Okay. I'm deciding between the names, Thea and Lydia. Which one?" Terrah said. The girls all shouted which name they preferred, creating a cacophony of sound. Through the roar, the final verdict was Thea with three votes. Lydia trailed close behind with two.

"Okay," Terrah said, writing down something in her notebook. "So, I have a name for one of the sections, which is actually good. The section she lives in, the one that started with underrepresented people, is Japanese for invisible, but I changed the spelling a little, it's pronounced Mee-eh-nye, so that's what it's called."

"Don't you love when you get those breakthroughs," I said. "Like 'I have a name for something. I know why this is this thing?' I'm guessing it's going to work some way into the characteristics of that place."

"Yeah. That's how they came up with the name," Terrah replied. "They were in the government, and they were like, 'Okay, we're a different country now. We gotta figure out what we're going to call our country.' And, you know, they used some language other than English because that's kind of the point is that it's supposed to be underrepresented. It's Japanese, and it's invisible."

"What's your conflict?" Avenae'J asked.

"My conflict?"

"Like, in your story," Avenae'J clarified.

"Oh! So, the plot I've come up with is this girl lives in the underrepresented part, and she's Mienai—now that I have a name for it. She's just a really average girl, and there's really nothing special to her. She's really basic, I guess. She lives every day pretty much the same, but she's like, 'I don't want to live like this anymore. It's boring.' Then, for some reason, the other part, they're like, 'Hey, we want to pick some of you to come to college and take some of you to come to school in our area.' She qualifies for it, but because she's so close to her family and her friends, she doesn't know whether or not she wants to go because she doesn't want to leave them behind."

"This may sound very childish, but like that kind of reminds me of like the first *Descendants*," Victoria interrupted. "Like, the descendants, like all four of them, were chosen because they're overrepresented for their parents being the worst villains. So, this kind of reminds me of that old movie, where she's chosen to go, but she doesn't want to go for the reason her mother wants her to go."

"Yeah!" Terrah brightened as she looked at Victoria. "Okay. So, when she's at the college with all the other people, she has a choice of whether or not she's going to have a roommate the rest of her college years. She decides she would because she can easily get lonely. So, she signs up for a roommate, and then they give her a room with another person from her section. I haven't made a character, exactly, but I know it's gonna be a boy. They put them together because he's gay. Then, there is somebody from the section they're in now who asks them to come to a welcome party. Her roommate goes, so she decides she'll go as well. At the party, she gets a call from her friend back home. She tells her friend it's actually really nice here. It'll take some getting used to, but it's going to be fun. And that's kind of where it's resolved because her friend is like, 'You're gonna do great.' And she's like, 'I feel good about this choice I made.'"

"Basically," Terrah took a deep breath after talking for several minutes. "I wanted to think about what the country would be like if all these people who felt like they were being oppressed against just were done and kind of fought against it and started their own country where everyone was equal, which, for the most part, ended up well, but there's always going to be people who hate other people for no reason. I wanted to see what would happen if after this long time of being separated, they decide to bring people back together."

Her story reminded me of what the Othermothers said about the common-weal, that state of collective well-being for humans, animals, and the environment. The Harbor is a commonweal because the Othermothers designed it to be this way, but America is not. The world is not. America was built on the destruction of the commonweal, so it cannot exist here. At least not right now. It may not be as separated as the country in Terrah's story, but it's not whole. Many of the Dreamers continue to uplift their own interests to the detriment of everyone and everything else. Some Endarkened people do it, too, often to gain favor with GC or their Dreamer employers. But the world Terrah envisions is trying to come together, to forego separation based on arbitrary things. I can't help but think that this story shows how Terrah wants the world of GC to come together, to break down the wall that never should have existed in the first place.

December 11, 2085

I met Terrah in the Harbor doctor's office. It's nothing like any office I've ever seen, and it's where all the Endarkened health and wellness people meet. There are no sterilized wall colors, and there are no long lines waiting for insurance payments to be handled before someone is able to receive aid. Instead, a person can walk in, tell the receptionist what they need, and then be taken directly to a specialist. There are many health and wellness scholars in the Harbor who focus on preventative measures, and although they may not be working in the office every day, they are always available when someone needs help. It's a weird system, but it works.

Terrah wants to be a doctor, so she is apprenticing in the office. She mostly works with the nurses right now to learn basic health-care protocols, but she'll soon start to follow nurses who have more duties. The apprenticeship process in the Harbor requires all who are interested in this line of work to learn under the tutelage of every person on the clinic staff, so that each person is well-rounded. Then, after they've learned from everyone, they are able to choose a specialty. This way, they all have a basic understanding of various needs, and they can help out in other ways when their special areas of expertise are not needed.

When I arrived at the office, Terrah was sitting at one of the tables close to the receptionist's desk at the side of the room. She was looking over some documents, probably studying since she plans to follow someone new within the next few months.

"Hi Terrah," I said, walking over to the table. "Are you still able to talk?" she nodded her head and gestured for me to sit down in the chair across from her. As soon as I sat down, she put the papers aside and smiled in my direction. It felt as though she was waiting until the last possible minute to put her readings away. She is dedicated to realizing her dream of becoming a doctor, and I admire her for staying true to her goals.

"Basically, I just want to learn more about you before I hear your story since I'm new here, and you've already formed bonds with the other girls. Is it okay for me to ask you some questions?" I know she probably already knows what I'll ask based on conversations with the other girls, but I thought it would be polite to explain myself.

"Of course," she said.

"Okay, so can you tell me a little bit about you?"

"Hmmm … I have really curly brown hair, and it's like a weird texture because it's between like white people hair and like African American hair, so it's this really weird texture, and it's difficult to take care of." She pulled at her hair to show me the texture. "So, normally I'll have it in a braid or something. I have medium–tone skin and dark brown eyes that are almost black. My closet is so weird. I wear graphic t-shirts, and I'll pair them with jeans or leggings. I bite my nails a lot, so I have really short nails."

She paused for a moment, and then she continued. "I'm really just an understanding person, and I am good at like sympathizing with people and not judging them because of who they are or decide to be. I'm also really sensitive, and I know this because I'm easy to offend even if I try not to be easy to offend. I am really defensive over stuff I believe in. I think I'm a really clumsy person, so like I'll trip over my own feet or something like that. I'm also really jumpy and kind of explosive in a way. I'm also not afraid to just be my weird self. I don't know how to explain weird. I'm just not afraid, so I don't need to try and hide myself and my personality."

I waited a moment to see if she had more to say. After I shifted a bit in my seat, she continued. "I want to be successful," she said softly. "I want a good job. I want a family … a big family. I want to live my life as much as possible. If I can't have that I'll probably end up being really upset because I try to work really hard for the stuff I want, but I tend to feel that if I don't get it, I'll end up pretty upset, angry, or sad. I just need people to be by my side. I need people who I can trust. Because if I'm surrounded by people who I trust and love, I tend to stay like levelheaded."

A lot of what Terrah said in our meeting tied into what she said during our group conversation. She used her personal characteristics and dreams as the foundation for her speculative character. She made her character shy and nerdy, just like she is. The other day, she told us she put herself into the story because the issues the character faces are issues she's also concerned with. It seems like speculative writing is one method she uses to talk about things in her world. It seems like a method of writing they all use.

"My best talent is probably writing," Terrah continued, bringing me back to our discussion. "I like writing fantasy mostly because I've always liked reading about things that aren't true, things made up in somebody's head. I want to know how that happened. And it's fun to learn about things that aren't particularly true, especially when you're trying to get away from things that are. So, in the back of my mind, I was like, 'I think it'd be fun to create books like these. I'm going to start writing stories now.'"

What fascinated me about Terrah's story was how she said she liked fantasy because it allowed her to get away from things that weren't true. But in the fantasy story she told us about, she put parts of her life into the unrealistic landscape. I'm not sure what to make of it, but it brings me back to my first reading of Butler. Whether consciously or unconsciously, it seems fiction stories are ways to create ourselves, but they are also ways to create maps that will tell us which directions to go and which to avoid. I'm wondering where the girls' maps are leading me.

As I thought through the details of Terrah's story, someone called her to the back. They probably had a patient to tend to, and although our conversation was important to me, I know Terrah's life as a future doctor is important to her. She gave me a look that said, "I'll stay if you have more questions, but I'd really like to go now," and I laughed.

"Go ahead," I chuckled. "I'll see you on Saturday!"

"K. Bye!" Terrah said, as she pushed her papers together, put them in a folder, and placed them under her arm. I tried to get a glimpse of what was happening, and I saw a pregnant person being wheeled into a small room. Seeing the person was a weird experience. For some reason, I thought all the children had come here from within GC. I didn't think about the possibility of babies being born here, babies who will never have the dream extraction before they are brought into this world. Babies who have a chance to thrive in a place of love that dreams with them.

December 15, 2085

Following in the other girls' footsteps, Terrah gave us a little more information before she began her story. "For the ideal or perfect side, I chose Greek because Greece is in Europe, and so I had the idea that side would be predominantly white. The word I picked is Greek for, I believe, perfect or something similar to that. It's either perfect or ideal, I think. So, when choosing a name for this new country, they would probably choose something from a European language or something. And then for the other side, the invisible side, it was a Japanese word because it's a different race. They would be predominantly Black, or Asian, or you know. And they would probably have chosen something that comes from a different race than just something European."

That was helpful information to have. When we met last Sunday, she talked a little about why she chose the name Miaeni for the underrepresented side, but she didn't talk about what the other side would be called. I just assumed it would be called the United States based on everything happening in GC. I'm glad she let us in on her thought process because naming, once again, has proven to be an important aspect of the story.

"I'm Fine"

> "Oh, come on Lissa," I whined. "This is a once in a lifetime opportunity."
> "I just don't know," she responded.
> Why was she so against me leaving? This was a good thing, or so I thought. Yeah, I'd miss everyone, but this school is better than any other on this side of the wall.
> "Hey, just think about it, Ella. You have two days, she told me. I nodded, and we went our opposite ways.
> When I got home that afternoon, I started on some homework, but I couldn't focus. I've always wanted two things: to go to a better college and to make my family happy. What if having both those things was unrealistic?
> Two days had passed, and I'd come to a final decision. "I'm going to miss you, Zorie, "Kyan mumbled. I put my final shirt in my bag and turned around.
> "I know, Ky. I'm going to miss you, too. I'll be back soon. I promise."
> "Okay," he said. I walked over to my doorway and pulled him into a hug.
> "I love you."
> "I love you, too." He responded.
> "Zorella, are you packed? It's time to go," my mother yelled from downstairs.

"Coming," I yelled back. I grabbed my suitcase and backpack and walked out to the car.

"So what made you want to go across, Zorella?" My mom asked.

"It's better than any of the schools here. Very few people here were accepted. I need to go," I explained. I watched my dad nod and silently sigh. I knew they didn't want to force me not to go.

We arrived at the train station not long after. We all got out and I gave hugs to my family.

"Take care of yourself, Zorella. Call us when you get there," my mom said.

"Yes, Mama," I responded. And with one last hug to each of my family members, I boarded the train through the wall.

Long ago, due to racism, sexism, and homophobia, the country that used to be called the United States of America split into Miaeni and Idonikoes. If you were oppressed you lived in Miaeni, and those who were in control lived in Idonikoes.

I'd stayed in Miaeni since the day I was born. It never really felt like home, so that's why I left. It meant I could go to an amazing college and escape the cage I was in.

After a few hours, we made it to the other station. We all got off and loaded onto the buses that would take us to campus.

As I sat in a window seat, a girl around my age crawled in next to me.

"Hello," she exclaimed. I was slightly shocked by her enthusiasm.

"Hey," I responded.

"I'm Theo—I mean Thea," she said.

"I'm Zorella."

"Are you from Miaeni?"

"I am. Are you?"

"Yes. I'm studying animation. How about you?"

"Animation. That means we could be in the same dorm."

"Wouldn't that be cool?"

I continued chatting with Thea, and I felt myself getting really close with her. She was so sweet and innocent.

"Yeah. My mom didn't want me to come either. My dad thought it was a good idea, though," Thea explained. "He said it was good they were thinking of people other than themselves."

"I can see sense in that. Hey, random question: Why do you guys live in Miaeni? I don't mean to be offensive, but you seem so normal," I asked.

"It's okay. It's an interesting story actually. My mom used to live in Idonikoes, and so did my dad. My mom is Asian. She came out as demisexual to her parents, and they got really upset. She lived out on the streets for a while before meeting my dad. He worked as a waiter, and she was starving. He bought her dinner then brought her to his apartment. She lived with him for a while, and they fell in love and decided to move to Miaeni. A year after, their trans baby—me—was born!" Thea explained. The last comment was immediately brought to my attention.

"Wait, you're trans?" I asked shocked.

"Yeah. Is that a problem?"

"No. I just remember when you were telling me your name and you almost called yourself Theo." I had brushed it off then.

"Oh. That. I kept the fact that I felt like a girl away from my parents for a long time. A month or two ago, I told them, and they didn't care. I didn't know what I wanted to be called because I liked my name so much, so I chose the female version like a week ago."

"Well Thea, you live quite the life," I said.

"Tis true," she responded. "Hey, were you going to have a roommate?"

"I don't know. I didn't know anyone going, so ..."

"Well, you know me now. I was looking for a roommate, but I also didn't know anyone."

"Well hello roommate, I guess," I joked. We laughed and continued chatting.

When I received a letter for the University of Chicago, I was stunned and extremely hesitant to go. I didn't know anyone going, and I thought my friends and family would never want me to come back, but I received a call that night that changed everything.

I finally finished my unpacking and sat on the couch in the living room. Thea went to the welcome party, but I decided to stay home. I just sat there and examined the room until I heard my phone vibrating.

I picked it up to see Alissa FaceTiming me. I quickly picked up.

"Zorella!" was the chorus that came from my phone.

"Mom! Dad! Kyan! Alissa!" I called.

"How's Chicago?" my mom asked.

"It's good. It's a nice city," I replied.

"Have you met anyone new?" Alissa questioned.

"Yeah! I met this girl named Thea on the bus from the train station. Did you know that you can't take a train from Miaeni into Idonikoes? Only to border towns. From there, you either get onto a bus or on an Idonikonian train," I explained.

"Interesting," my mom said.

"Have you tried any Chicago style foods?" Kyan asked.

"Actually, yes," I answered. "I had a Chicago dog. It was great. I'll take you to get some if you visit.

"Well, it seems like everything is going well," my dad chimed.

"It is. I miss you guys, though."

"We miss you, too," Alissa stated.

"Enjoy yourself," my mom ordered.

"Okay!" I responded with a salute.

"We have to go, sweetie. We'll talk later," my dad told me.

"Okay. Bye," I said.

"Bye!" they all yelled at once.

I put my phone down and smiled. I got ready for bed and before falling asleep, I thought, I'm going to like it here. It's all going to be fine.

The girls clapped and cheered once Terrah finished. They loved her story, and so did I. Her characters brought up so many important conversations about GC— about our divided world, about oppression based on race and sexuality, about how GC makes us move away from our families and our homes. I also see the Othermothers' teachings influencing her story, too. I see the communitarian foundation growing in the friendship between Thea and Ella, the resistance against homophobia through her characters' identities, and the anti-oppressionist stance of the overall story. Once again, the speculative was guided by reality.

"I noticed some changes ..." I started.

"Yes!" Terrah said before I could tell her about the changes I saw. "I thought I needed somebody who could help Zorrella become more comfortable with that area. Since her best friend wasn't coming, I thought I needed somebody who kept her level-headed instead of wishing she could go back. So, she had a good friend. If she had a good friend, I thought it would make sense for her character to be able to stay there instead of leaving."

"I also kind of thought, after thinking about her character more," She stretched her arms toward the ceiling and lengthened her legs underneath the table. "Even though the party would have been a fun choice for her, she wasn't really that kind of person. She wants to adjust to what's going to become her home space before exploring around and finding other places to visit. So, if she went to that party, it wouldn't give her time to become closer with the area she was in."

Based on the smiles of approval, I could tell we all loved her story additions. She pointed out an important part of the GC world I never thought about until moving here: how some Dreamers don't think the way GC tells them to; how some Dreamers are co-conspirators even though there aren't enough of them; how some Dreamers also believe everyone should be included. That's what I see when I think about Thea's parents and where they came from. That's what I'm thinking about Cody, the man I saw in the fellowship hall almost two months ago. Maybe that's also a way of seeing the unseen, finding our accomplices in unfamiliar places and faces. Like Gholdy said and like Terrah showed, the commonweal needs everyone to be included, and finding community amongst all groups is required for oppression to end. I wonder ... are there accomplices in Altered Truth?

10

RESEARCH PARTNER STORIES

Avenae'J

December 16, 2085

When the girls and I arrived at the library, there was an air of excitement and sadness. This will be our last week together, and although the girls aren't leaving the Harbor, I'm pretty sure I am. Within the next week or so, I need to send Charles my next correspondence, and I have to decide what to include. Will I say that I've found nothing, and I need to go back to Altered Truth? Will I send another vague message and stay for a full six months in the Harbor? Will I stop corresponding and live out my days in the underground?

I can stay in the Harbor, knowing Charles and the rest of the staff will never find me, but something about working with these girls made me feel like I needed to go back, like I needed to continue doing this work outside of this safe space so other Endarkened youth can find their way to the Harbor too. I don't think I can be like Harriet-2, but I know I can be Lauren Jane, helping Endarkened people find the maps, escape GC, and access their dreams. Of course, I still have time to change my mind.

"Okay. So, my story title, it's called Dystopia," Avenae'J began as she sat in her seat. "The name of my main character is Avenae'J. Its time is 2020, and the place is Alaska, but like, Alaska is not part of the US."

"Is it a part of Canada?" Talyn interrupted turning her chair so she could face Avenae'J.

"It's not a part of anything. It's by itself," Avenae'J replied. "Um, this is probably very vague, but my story is about a young woman who falls in love and because of this, she wants everyone else to feel happiness and love. She comes up with a plan to start an uprising to bombard and overthrow the enforcers, but she wants to do it in a peaceful manner, like overpower them to where they get scared and stop. There are more people than there are enforcers, but the enforcers

DOI: 10.4324/9781003159285-10

have guns, so that's why they don't do anything. The characters are Merino, Purdue, Felipe, Moretti, and Officer Carabinieri."

The girls sit quietly as Avenae'J finds her place on the page. "I also want to talk about my character, Avenae'J. She has a golden–bronze skin tone, and she's a chemical engineer. She's one of the most unique people, but they don't know her natural hair color is dark black because she dyed the tips of her hair dark blue. She made that dye herself. She has jet black irises with pure white eyes. She feels a need for a change in the world, and she has sadness for the ones who aren't able to feel because of the Change Room. She is shy, but when she talks about her passions, she is very outgoing and likes to speak loudly about them. She's happy, and she likes to let people know that she is happy. She is intelligent, curious, brave, honest—these all will come into play later on—and then mischievous, but for the good. She's a thief, but she uses her thievery to help."

In the corner of the room, I saw Edi giving a pile of books to a community member. I don't know if they're new, or if giving people 20 books is just how Edi makes sure we have enough information. It looked like the person wouldn't be able to hold too much more, but Edi had several more books in her arms. Bailey saw what was happening, got up from her seat, and grabbed some books from the overburdened resident. They looked extremely grateful.

"I took a lot of things from myself," Avenae'J paused for a moment and looked at the ceiling. "She's a mixed female. I'm about to list off the things she's from: She's African American, Caucasian, Irish, Swedish, Southeast Asian, Puerto Rican, and Northwest African. That's what I'm mixed with. She has a sort of deeper feminine voice with a mixture of two accents, a country accent and then sort of a Latin American accent."

"She lives in a world where everyone is the same," Avenae'J said, her brown eyes still gazing intently on something I couldn't see. "Everyone is on the same level. There is no president or leading body; everyone rules. With an oligarchy, it's just a small group of people, but everyone is ruling in this type of oligarchy. Everyone lives alone in their own house with the same amount of pay and the same amount of land. Everyone and everything is the same. They all wear large black cloths over their heads with openings where the eyes are supposed to be. They wear black flowy materials so no one can tell what color, ethnicity, or gender anyone is. Every single time they put clothes on, they have to pin it because all clothes have to be a size too big for them so no one can tell what size everyone actually is. This has been the law for around 10–15 years. They all wake up at exactly five o'clock, and if they don't, they'll be taken to this place, the Change Room, where they get genetically modified so they do what they're supposed to do."

As I listened to Avenae'J tell us about the details of her story, I got chills. So much of what she said reminded me of the world above. There is no president because GC and its buddies rule us all. It's an oligarchy run by business corporations. We all live alone except during the harvesting. We definitely don't make the same amount of money, but all Endarkened people are paid minimal wages. We aren't required to wear the same clothing, but we do have uniforms that match our company colors to let everyone know who we work for. We also have the Change Room although I've never been forced to go there. There are so many similarities between the world above and Avenae'J's story.

"She dreams that everyone was being themselves," Avenae'J continued. "She dreams that she could live in a world where everyone can be themselves and enjoy themselves, where they don't have to talk a certain way or act a certain way. But she's okay with the fact that she's not allowed to be who she can be because she doesn't want there to be a third civil war."

"Third?!" Talyn and Terrah shouted simultaneously before they both looked at Amber.

"Yeah," Avenae'J said.

"So, an alternate reality? That's a very interesting concept," Talyn mentioned.

"So, in this world, there was a civil war between ethnicity groups," Avenae'J replied. "So, yeah. Um, she loves how she has a mixture of everything in herself. I haven't thought of anything else, like I haven't thought of what she needs."

"She may just need someone she can talk to," Talyn suggested.

"Yeah, she probably needs people because she is so lonely," Avenae'J said, a slight frown forming on her face. "But she can't have that because in this world, you're not allowed to have feelings. They're not allowed to express themselves whatsoever."

"It sounds like something from ..." Talyn began.

"The Giver!" Amber interjected.

"That 19-something," Talyn commented, finishing her sentence.

"1984?" I asked.

"Yeah, with like the thought police," Talyn answered.

"So, the reason why she does what she's told to do is because she's seen so many people who were beaten and taken away. She didn't want that to happen to her, so she is traumatized." Avenae'J paused again and then said, "I guess I just need someone to tell me what I should take out because I feel like it's too long already. But the stuff I've put in it helps for the end. I'm putting too much in it, but at the same time, I'm putting just the right amount for stuff that's going to be in it later."

As Avenae'J went back and forth on how much information to include, the girls sat there in silence. It seemed they didn't have anything else to add, but I think there was more to their reticence. The story Avenae'J wrote, although it had some speculative elements, was our history. 2020 was the year dream extraction experiments began, and 2030 was when the first successful extraction occurred. It was the year GC came to power. 2045 is when the abortion laws went into effect, and it was the year Trence ended presidential term limits. It was also the year Change Rooms were created. To begin a story using our history and our current reality must have hit the girls harder than Avenae'J anticipated. All the stories included harsh realities, but no one gave a historical account grounded in an alternate, but similar reality.

"Well, at least what do y'all think about my names: Avenae'J, Purdue, and Felipe?" Avenae'J asked, disrupting the silence.

The girls laughed, and Victoria said, "Perdue sounds like a farm ... like that chicken farm that used to exist."

"The what?" Terrah giggled.

"Like the chicken farm where chicken used to come from. Do y'all not eat chicken?" Victoria joked.

"I do!" Talyn answered, "I can eat like three pieces!"

The girls settled into an easy laughter as they moved into discussions about chicken. It's funny to me how little things like chicken hold so much context. We used to eat chicken, but ever since the companies started deregulating meat, Endarkened chicken comes with an asterisk—*contains 10% meat. A conversation about Perdue, about real chicken, is a conversation about history.

I don't think Avenae'J got much help on what to remove, but the girls did seem to be more at ease. Maybe there is nothing to take out because it's important to see our history, even the painful parts. Our history and our present are important, even if we don't want to hear about it. I think that's what Octavia Butler was trying to say. She wanted to show us who we are and who we were. I would've never found this place if she chose to remove the rough parts. I think what I'm learning from the girls is that history is just as important as the present and the future. To see the unseen, we have to know who we are and who we used to be.

December 19, 2085

The plan was to meet Avenae'J in the Harbor's science wing. I laughed when I heard about it because I didn't know there were "wings" in this place. Within the wing, there were several branches of scientific study, including math, zoology, engineering, ethnography, astronomy, and linguistics. They have their specialties, but they all work together in the same area, finding ways to connect their disciplines in meaningful ways in hopes of one day fixing the world GC further corrupted.

The science wing begins with a circular meeting place with tables and chairs grouped in ovals around the room. The meeting place branches off into several hallways with eight rooms in each, and each hall is dedicated to a specific science focus. The halls seem to have an open-door concept, so although they have their own sections, it's easy for them to collaborate. They respect each other's individual projects, but they know collaboration is one open-door away. It's interesting to see because I'm so used to the separation of the sciences.

Avenae'J often chose to go to the science wing during the day, learning various skills so she could become an engineer. She is the president of the Harbor's astronautics club, and she is always helping the mathematicians and historians as she hones her other science skills. I admire the dedication to her future craft.

I found Avenae'J sitting in the meeting area at a table to the left. She smiled, and her raised cheeks lifted her glasses about an inch off her face. "Welcome!" she said enthusiastically.

"Hey there!" I said. "Are you ready to give me the story of your life?" Avenae'J laughed, but then she nodded.

"What do you want to know?" she asked.

"Whatever you want to tell me about yourself would be great. I'm just trying to learn more about you before you tell your story on Saturday," I explained. "I guess you can start by just telling me about your writing?"

"Well, I've been writing since I was in second year," Avenae'J settled down in her chair. "From like second year to fourth, it was more non-fiction/fiction writing. I remember this book I wrote in second year with one of my best friends. We wrote about things we had done, and then put a fiction twist. The book I wrote with my best friend was the first piece of writing I was really, really into. I'm pretty sure I was doing something before that, but that was my first major piece of writing. I was really deep into that book. I wanted to publish it."

"That's awesome you began writing books so young. I can just see the way you light up when you talk about it. What else do you like to do, or what else makes you happy?"

"Well, one of my happiest memories was graduating from eighth year because it's a bridging ceremony, and I was going into SecondHOME." Avenae'J looked deep in thought, as if she were creating a mental picture of the event. "I wore a dress going to my knees, and it had this train on it, and it was black. Our uniform was black and white, so we had to wear all or either. I had on these really nice shoes, and I loved them so much. I don't know why, but I just felt so beautiful. I felt like the spotlight was on that day. I don't normally feel very pretty or like the prettiest."

"I have been bullied on a lot of occasions in my life," Avenae'J looked behind her to watch the bustling group of scientists that passed. "I've never been bullied by Endarkened people. I've been bullied by Dreamers. I was just put down by them, and it's probably not for the reason I'm saying it is, but it's just what it seems like to me. The old school heritage in my state would cause them to bully a lot of Endarkened people. A lot of us were bullied by Dreamers."

"I see," I said somberly. I wasn't surprised, but she shouldn't have had to experience that.

"I like coding," Avenae'J said, abruptly changing the subject. "I remember this one time, I was talking to this observer, and I remember him saying he was really surprised and proud I was actually coding because he'd never seen anything like it. He never thought we could do that. I think he didn't think a lot of Endarkened girls code. But they do it, and they make it known, so, I'm pretty sure he was just not paying attention."

I hate that the Dreamer made that comment, as if he could not fathom a young Endarkened girl excelling in her coding abilities, but, once again, I was not surprised. "It seems like you do a lot of research on Endarkened people because you know about people who do what the observer said you couldn't do," I said it as a statement, but I meant for it to be a question.

"I like to read. I like to read the news and research stuff based on what I see in the news. I also like just researching. What's this? What's that?" She pointed to a few objects around the room.

"What types of things do you research?"

"Um, how people aren't being represented," Avenae'J said. "How there are some crimes that aren't being spoken out about in the world, and they're ones that really matter, but nothing's being said about them. They tell people about it, and the people just don't care. The only way the crimes are being spoken about is through social media. Not even the news is speaking about it! But what's really annoying is how they used to talk so much about 45, but they couldn't talk about the kidnappings of children, the beatings of children, the beatings of children on buses, how kids are being bullied and beaten up and being beaten to death and being killed."

She had a point. During Trence's reign, there was so much talk about the buffoonery of the office without much information on the damage he was doing. Of course, there was some outrage and media attention for a few weeks on the issues, like Avenae'J mentioned, but then Trence would do something else, and the media would shift to a new, more popular story. If that didn't happen, Altered Truth was there to save the day. The only time those news stories were brought up again was when someone would remind the world every so often to "Never forget." The thing is, no one had forgotten, there was just too much to worry about. Too much going wrong. So much happening that it was hard to focus on any one thing. And when someone did decide to focus on a specific issue, they were bombarded with questions about why they weren't centering the whole of every other problem. It was a mess.

I noticed Avenae'J had a lot of thoughts about the world, and based on her call to research, I thought she would have some ideas about changes we should make. Maybe, she'll have ideas about changes I should make. So, I asked her, "Who do you think was responsible for making sure there was social justice in the world of 2020, and why do you think that?" I figured this question could give me more insight into what she was thinking, and based on her story, I thought I could learn more about how she was connecting her personal world to her fictional one.

"I mean, it's pretty obvious," Avenae'J replied. "It was 45s ... well, it was him and other people. There were people who thought there were more important issues, and that may have been true, but that's true with other things, not with murder cases and kidnappings. Talking about 45 was not more important than an Endarkened mom who was killed, who was literally beaten to death in the front yard of a Dreamer household. Sometimes, it just seemed like Trence didn't want issues to be talked about, and that's why he did all that stupid stuff. He also made the world more racist because he was obviously racist, so his being racist made it look like ... well ... the president kind of put this force on the world. Not everyone was racist, but a lot more people were."

"Yeah," I affirmed. There were racist people before Trence took power, but he emboldened many of them to come out of hiding. He gave them permission to be direct in ways that were previously shamed. The energizing of his racist base helped our current future gain momentum.

"People were being racist all because of 45," she paused for a moment before saying, "I guess, not necessarily because of him, but him being president put a force onto America. Some people in America were being racists even if they weren't just because 45 was."

Hearing her talk about our history saddened me. I don't believe Trence was the catalyst for racist thinking. It's existed in this country since this country existed. Still, I can understand the need to blame someone, to put a face on a nebulous term, to attribute the horror of the country onto one person so you can believe the rest of the people are so much better than that. But blaming one person lets so many others off the hook. It lets them cower under the label of follower, as if they have no part in it, as if they are incapable of making decisions on their own.

"So, I know these issues are important to you. It shows in what you say and what you write. I kind of see you as an activist in the way that you speak out about these issues. Do you consider yourself to be one?"

"I like to speak my mind, but I've never actually gone out and done anything about it," Avenae'J tapped her fingers on the table. "I want to, but I just ... I don't know how. I can't. I don't consider myself an activist, but I do like to talk to people. I like to talk to them about what's going on, so maybe they'll understand and maybe they'll do something about it. I don't know if I consider myself one. I don't think I am, but I would like to be. It's not enough to just dream about it and talk about it. It's more so actually going out and doing it."

I'm not sure she realizes this, but writing and telling her story is going out and doing it. She's sharing her thoughts on our present and historical issues. I think activists use their writing and other methods to do just that. We all can't be Harriet-2, but we all can tell our stories.

December 22, 2085

On our last day of storytelling, I told the girls of my plan. This space is so uplifting and filled with love, and although I love it here, I know I can do more above. I can help other Endarkened children find the Harbors. Maybe, I can help the Harbor find new Dreamer accomplices. I'm already in a good position to do that. The girls understood my point, but they were not happy about my choice. While we sat at the table, waiting for Avenae'J to begin, the girls' heads were down and most didn't say a word. It was eerily quiet even for a library. Luckily, Avenae'J announced that she was ready to begin. I was glad for a break in the silence.

"Dystopia"

Aljaska is a supposedly Utopian society where everyone is supposedly equal, and no one looks or sounds different outside of their home. No one and no thing is different. Everyone wears all black, the clothing is all loose and long so no one can tell the body shape of another or the race of anyone. They wear black scarves tied around their faces so that no one can tell their race or see their beauty, and lastly they have monotone voice machines attached to them so when they talk an accent cannot be heard. Everyone has the same amount of income, the same amount of living space, equal opportunities at education and life, and there is only one known type of flower and tree. Myosotis, commonly known as Forget-Me-Nots, are used in medicines to erase the minds and suck out the souls of all who put it in their bodies. The white spruce tree is used to keep the people in the town, and its bark and sticks are used to deprive people of their personality. They are only used for the ones who start uprisings and show their faces and bodies to people.

January 14, 2090: Avenae'J's House

Her alarm bell rings, and Avenae'J Marino turns over to turn it off, but in the midst of turning, falls off the bed, hits her arm on her bedside table knocking her alarm clock on the floor, and lands face first into her carpet floor groaning out of pain and tiredness. With the alarm bell still ringing her ears off, she contemplates getting up, and then remembers her important exam that tests to see what colleges she should and could get into. Standing up and walking to the bathroom, she realizes how much this test means to her and could mean for her future in chemical engineering.

She straightens up, and places a stud in her nose, and pulls her medium length jet black hair with dyed blue ends into a low ponytail tucking it into her long-sleeved black blouse. As she did this, she daydreamed about a world where everyone could be themselves without any officers attacking them for doing so.

Front of High School

She arrives at her school, and right before she walks through the archway, she notices a man being beaten for his scarf coming off. He sits there with his arms crossed over his face and covered in slash marks from the whip of the enforcer. Then the enforcer stops whipping and without the guy noticing, pulls out his club, and when the guy removes his arms, they hit him so hard in the head that he was knocked out, and the enforcer drags him over to a long black car with a golden emblem in the front resembling that of a tiger. The head of the enforcers, Enforcer Carabinieri, steps out of the car and throws the guy into the car and climbs back in, yelling at everyone to mind their business and go to school. She walks away and

walks through the high Roman archway and walks along the path behind
it to large wooden doors that mark the entrance to an even larger white
stone brick building with vines and moss growing all over it that shows
how long it's been there.

Lobby of High School

Walking inside the building, she is trampled by people and falls face first
with her books sliding across the slick tile. She hurries up, and while picking them up, a guy offers to help her up, and she doesn't realize until she
bumps into his legs. When she grabs his hand, and gets up, he hands her
a book, and he looks like he's just seen a ghost, and says, "Your scarf." He
is so mesmerized by what he believes to be the most beautiful person he
has ever seen that he almost does not realize that Avenae'J starts to walk
quickly away. He immediately starts to follow her until she reaches the
women's bathroom, and he waits outside for her.

Women's Bathroom

In the bathroom, Avenae'J stares into her reflection, and starts to cry out of
anger (at herself for allowing her scarf to fall off), terror (at the fact that an
enforcer could have seen her), stress (at college registration and exams), and
tiredness (from lack of sleep). To calm herself down, she takes a deep breath
and then punches her hand. She repeats this combination three more times
to make it four times, and this relieves her. The deep breaths calm her terror and stress, and punching her hand relieves her anger. She then splashes
her face with cold water, to relieve her tiredness, and she looks into the
mirror again staring into her eyes and telling herself that she will ace this
exam, and with that, she wraps her scarf around her face making sure
it's tight enough. She then grabs her belongings and exits the bathroom,
walking face first into the chest of the guy who saw her without her scarf.

June 14, 2090: Avenae'J's House

"Okay, okay, on a more serious note, there is something else we want to
tell you," Avenae'J says looking at him directly in the eyes. "We have
found a sort of feeling/attraction towards one another, and we believe it to
be love, and we want other people to feel this way as well."

"Not only romantic love, but family love and friendly love," Phillipé
says finishing her statement.

"What exactly are you guys thinking," Perdue says with a concerned
but excited facial expression. "Because I want to make sure that we are on
the same page."

"Yes, Perdue we want to start an uprising," Avenae'J says causing
Perdue's eyes to pop out of his head with excitement. Avenae'J and Perdue
have been wanting to start an uprising for a long time now, but never had
any motivation/evidence to cause them to do it.

June 21, 2090: Outside the Change Room

Crouched behind bushes, they notice a familiar golden emblem, telling them they are in the right place, and they see Carabinieri step out of the car dragging a numb body behind her leaving a bloody trail in their wake. Then they also notice an unfamiliar woman step out of the car, wearing a pencil skirt and blouse, which makes Avenae'J a little suspicious and angry because that is not how Aljaskians dress, and it makes her punch her hand four times to calm down. She is a very pale woman with bright red hair and bright red eyes covered by a pair of red aviators. Carabinieri and the woman walk over to a large steel door and the woman puts a number into the keypad without gloves.

The woman walks in first and Carabinieri walks in second dragging the body with her and the door shuts. After a few minutes, the black car leaves, and Avenae'J motions to Perdue and Phillipé to follow her, and she pulls out a weird flashlight. When she turns it on, instead of it being a bright white or yellow light, it is a black light which emits ultraviolet light. She flashes it on the keypad, and it shows fingerprints on the numbers 2, 4, 0, and 5.

"There are 24 combinations that could be the key to this keypad," Avenae'J says thinking aloud. "Phillipé type in 2045."

The Elevator

He does that and the steel door automatically opens into an elevator, and they all walk in and the door closes.

"How'd you know that was the combination?" Perdue asks.

"It's the year Alaska became Aljaska," Avenae'J answers suddenly being jerked back by the force of the elevator.

The Change Room

The elevator opens to reveal a dimly lit passageway with doors running down each side of it, and they all immediately get chills, letting them know they are in The Change Room. As they walked through the halls, there was the constant sound of water drip dropping into puddles formed on the floor, and an occasional scream that would go on for minutes. Lights flickered on and off giving the place a very dreary look and the dimness of the lights gave the place an even more dark look than the steel walls do. The enforcer's boots could be heard alongside the click clacking of the mysterious woman's heels and the dragging of the body. Drops of blood can also be slightly seen, and then it gets quiet. A grunt is heard after the thud.

"Get in there," Carabinieri says and slams the door with the sound of screaming following it. They start to speed up walking and check each door until they get to one that is locked. Avenae'J nods to Phillipé, and he pulls a lock picker out of his book bag and puts it into the lock. He presses a button, and almost instantly the lock clicks and the door opens, revealing a traumatized young man sitting in the corner with his head in his arms, and slash marks across his arms and forehead. They walk in and over to the man cautiously trying not to frighten him, and Avenae'J pulls out a first aid kit and Perdue pulls out a camera.

"What's that for," Phillipé questions.

"For evidence," Perdue replies. "If you want to start an uprising, you have to make sure you have photographic evidence that shows the people why they should rise against the powerful. Don't clean him up yet Avenae'J, I've got to get good and genuine photos." He takes a couple shots, and half-way through the guy wakes up and seems very frightened and confused to be surrounded by three unknown people.

"Hey, it's okay we're here to help. My brother's taking pictures of your scars to show what's happened," Avenae'J calmly states.

"Oh okay," the man says. "I'm Bishmal."

"Okay Bishmal, could you remove your arms from your face so I can get the scars," Perdue asks politely.

"You should take pictures of the entire facility. I bet that would scare the heck out of people," Bishmal suggests.

"I have been, I even took pictures of how you were brought here," Perdue replies.

"How come we didn't hear you?" Phillipé asks.

"My camera has a setting where I can turn the noise off," Perdue answers.

Footsteps are soon heard coming down the corridor, and Bishmal motions for them to go hide in the corner behind the door, but right before, Avenae'J places a pill into Bishmal's mouth. When the door opens, a man in a doctor's coat walks in with a large wagon of medical supplies that makes the corner behind the door a perfect hiding place because the wagon makes it difficult to close the door. Perdue crawls over a bit so he can get a good shot and starts to record, and when he does, Bishmal screams as the doctor scrapes off a piece of his skin and puts it into a vial, then he sticks a needle into him and takes out a syringe full of blood and divides it into four different colored glasses, he then cuts some hair off and puts in a vial as well, and he continues to remove things from Bishmal, and then he leaves. As soon as it was safe enough Avenae'J, Perdue, and Phillipé step out of the corner and over to Bishmal.

"Hey dude, are you okay," Perdue asks.

"Yeah I'm good, whatever she gave me, worked really fast and I felt absolutely nothing," he replies. "I was acting the entire time."

"Welp, you could've fooled me," Perdue says laughing as Avenae'J and Phillipé clean Bishmal up. Perdue stands up and just as he does the door opens up to reveal Carabinieri. Perdue pulls out a club and smacks him across the face, and just as he does, he calls out, "Enforcers, we have a breach."

"RUN!!!!" Perdue yells to everyone. They run in the opposite direction in which they came, and come up to a crossroads, Avenae'J and Phillipé go right and Bishmal and Perdue take a left. As they take a right, Bishmal screams a loud ear shredding scream, and it echoes through the halls and rings through Avenae'J and Phillipé's ears as they run to a near door and hide inside of it. It turns out to be a closet, and it has many vials and test tubes containing chemicals and ingredients used to make medicines, in particular the mind erasing and the personality/soul depriving medicine. When they start to look around and see what they can find, a gun is shot, and a loud thud follows it. Then, a man groans.

"Please, don't," he says. Then a final gunshot is fired, and it goes dead silent. Avenae'J goes and sits back against the door and starts to silently cry in her knees. Phillipé walks over and sits beside her allowing her to place her head onto his shoulder. He rubs her shoulder and gives her comfort.

"I bet you that it was not your brother," he says. "Let's look at the signs, it was Bishmal that screamed, he had no shoes on, he has lost quite a bit of blood, has not eaten, and he's drugged from the medicine you gave him. Perdue has none of those symptoms, and he has a perfect bill of health with a pretty good football coach."

"Yeah, I guess you're right," she says. "I just feel so bad that Bishmal died that way, he did not deserve that."

"This is why we're on this suicide mission, to help the people remember who they are, to celebrate the past ones who died because of these people, and to give our descendants a future that they will want and appreciate," Phillipé reminds her.

"Yeah, I guess you're right, let's get off this floor and get something useful," Avenae'J says standing up and turning on her white light flashlight, handing one to Phillipé as well. They notice that one wall is lined with vials that have a label on each. The labels say what it contains, the date it was collected, and a name.

"Grab them all, we'll figure out where to take them when we get back to town. I'll also grab a few of each of the ingredients," Avenae'J says stuffing as much as she can into her bag. They finish getting everything they need and start out the door as cautiously as possible, peeking out the door making sure no one is out there before they go. Once they are out, they walk quickly toward the end of the hallway, where they find Perdue taking pictures of blood on the walls. When they find each other, they celebrate in silence and make their way to the elevator conveniently located a door down from where they are. When they get inside, they press the up button surprised as to why this one has buttons, but the other elevator didn't, and when they reach the top, they run out.

Outside the Change Room

When they turn around, they see a familiar white stone brick building with an archway and vines and moss growing all over it. The Change Room is beneath their high school, meaning that Area 140 is beneath the town.

"Oh my freakin' gosh," Avenae'J exclaims with her jaw dropped.

"The Change Room and Area 140 were beneath us this entire time," Perdue says looking as if he was about to pass out.

"I need more than a physical shower, I need a mental shower, because I legit need to clear my mind of everything that just happened," Phillipé says jokingly but means it in a serious way.

"For real," Avenae'J agreed. "But first we need to make copies of the SD card in your camera, Perdue."

June 22, 2090: Phillipé's House

They sit there in his house for hours researching people/addresses, hacking into private/personal servers, clearing up photos, copying SD cards, and making antidotes. After 73 hours, they make a list of the people on the vials, where they live, and their status being if they are alive or deceased, and they have clear photographic evidence to start an uprising.

The Letter

Dear everyone,

If you are receiving this letter, that means you have been asked to join an uprising. This is the year everything changes. It has gone on this way for too long. People want to express themselves again, like they did 50 years ago. We want to be able to have relationships with the people we love. We have witnessed The Change Room ourselves, and what is there is horrendous. There are people constantly screaming out of terror and pain, blood is all over the walls, and the people there get pieces of them taken so that they can be tested, not only hair and urine, but pieces of skin. If you do not believe us, we've attached the pictures to an email that has been sent out. On that email, there are simple blueprints to making a gun and a drawing of the things needed to make the gunpowder inside of the guns. You can simply find these things at the store, just do not make it noticeable. As Barack Obama once said, "We are the change that we seek." The uprising will take place July 4, 2090 at 12:00 pm, the uprising will not start unless we feel that we have enough people, so we hope all of you join, because we cannot do this by ourselves, we need everyone.

Signed,

Avenae'J Marino, Perdue Marino, and Phillipé Moretti

Avenae'J was met with thunderous applause. She smiled widely, waiting for the clapping to lessen before giving us a little more insight into her story.

"The end was an epic plot twist because I wanted Area 140 to be underneath," Avenae'J began. "Everyone thought it was so far away in the country somewhere, so I wanted it to be underneath everything, right underneath places where they were. The Change Room is underneath HOME, and it's also in other parts of Area 140, like the hospital. No one knows it's underneath anything because *they* don't want anyone to know. They already have to beat people; they don't want to have to go anywhere to take care of people."

When she said, "take care of people," she meant to torture and possibly kill them. Essentially, the government in her story was too lazy to take their villainous tactics elsewhere; instead, they tortured people underneath buildings meant to protect and educate. There's something especially evil about placing the torture chambers right under the hospital and the school, but it made so much sense. From the very beginning, the girls talked about their negative experiences in FirstHOME. During our sessions, we've also had long conversations about how hospitals help to oppress Endarkened people. I mean, without their aid, the Dream Extraction wouldn't happen, and the Harvesting wouldn't succeed. I see how Avenae'J, like the rest of the girls, was analyzing our world, and although the Harbor needs to hear these stories, I feel like the people above ground need to hear them, too.

11

CONCLUSION

Going back, dreaming again

December 24, 2085

We ended the last story session on a somber note, so I asked the girls to join me one last time before I told Layli of my decision to return to GC. We met at our oval table, and the girls sat together. I noticed Victoria and Amber didn't sit as close to me as they normally do, and I wondered if they were upset because they knew I planned to go back, to help more Endarkened people find the Harbor. I was going to help others, but it also meant choosing to go back to GC's world, choosing to leave the girls. I'm sure this work will continue with Trinity and Kenny once I leave, and I hope the girls will continue teaching through their writing, but I won't be here to learn with them, at least, not in the same way. Even if I'm not present within the Harbor, I will always carry their stories with me.

I brought us together to have a talk about how much we'd grown since we started writing and sharing together. I hoped we could talk about why we stayed and why it's important for us to continue our writing even beyond this space. I hoped this conversation would be the last one I needed to strengthen my resolve.

"A few weeks ago, I asked if I could learn with you. Now, we're at the end of my time in the Harbor, so I wanted to know what you thought about it. I want to take this experience and use it to teach some of the Dreamer accomplices. I want to use my position to broaden the Harbor network." I looked at each girl as I spoke.

Bailey replied first. "I feel like we got more comfortable with each other. Since we got used to each other, we could just talk about random stuff at random times and just go on forever."

"Um," Talyn said. "It was better than HOME. I mean, it was better than my social life at HOME which was little to none because I stayed in the same friend group for three years … variety is important."

DOI: 10.4324/9781003159285-11

"I feel like it was a warm environment," Terrah tugged at her sleeve. "We were all just laughing. It's free. There's nothing like strict schedules or anything, and I like all the learning we were doing. It was a lot of fun. I'd make it longer, though, so we could spend more time together. I know it's four hours each time, but it was not enough."

Victoria turned her chair toward me. "It was actually really fun. Like I've gotten to know y'all more, and we have a lot in common. If we were at HOME, we probably wouldn't talk to each other so much because we're all so different from each other."

The girls knew each other from their frequent conversations, but after hearing Victoria's response, I realized that our learning sessions created space for them to learn about each other's stories beyond their public conversations. They came together for their chats, but those weren't sustained communities. This learning group was different, though. A beloved community was formed.

"You said you have a lot in common even though you're so different," I said, returning to the group conversation. "What do you have in common? What are the differences?"

"We're all geeks, first of all," Victoria's shoulders moved up and down as she laughed. "We love a lot of stuff people would say are uncool. Like, we all love watching *Harry Potter* and *Star Wars*, and we love anime. Normally, we'd have to hide that or embrace it and be weird. We come here and talk about it and be normal. I'd say we're probably the same because we're all still kids, but we see things from a different perspective than others. Like, we'd rather read the book before we watch the movie because we want to know what the difference between the book and the movie is, and we want to see how they compare, how there's a total difference, and how they make mistakes and stuff like that. I'm not saying being smart is not cool because it is cool, but I guess people would rather be like the person who has the latest shoes or who has the latest hairdo or nails or whatever."

I thought about her answer, and I wondered why we couldn't do both. Why can't we want the latest trends and still enjoy speculative films? I understood her point, though. The genres they liked to read and watch were disconnected from Black girls. It wasn't considered "normal" for Black girls to enjoy speculative genres. It wasn't "normal" for Black girls to want to write speculative fiction. To embrace a love of things considered abnormal for Endarkened people places the label of "weird" on the girls.

"I think it was amazing because everyone is so nice, and we understand each other," Amber's voice elevated as she spoke. "It was really fun, and I'm understanding a lot of things I hadn't before, like the way we were writing and how we were … not necessarily getting stuff from each other, but … I don't know the word for it. Like, at HOME, the observers, they didn't really want us … like, when we were doing individual things, they didn't want us talking to each other, but when we talk to each other, we know what we're doing, and it's more social. I didn't like the silence."

She pulled on her hair as she continued, "Also, in the group, some people knew about what I read, so I had more people to talk about it with. That is the best feeling ever, not having to explain the whole thing. I don't know what it is, but when you're with people who understand it, you just feel like you can talk more about it. I get bored having to explain things over and over. This was a lot different."

"I think everyone is hilarious!" Avenae'J laughed. "There was such an amazing atmosphere. We were here for four hours every day, and it felt like 30 minutes because we were just having so much fun. I never wanted to leave because I don't really have friends like that. I'm able to be here and be in this atmosphere of everyone knowing what everyone's talking about, and that matters. Being in a group where people know what's going on ... that's what it feels like."

They continued to come to this oval table because they formed a subcommunity of "weird" girls who didn't fit the norm of Endarkened identity they were used to seeing. They created a place that honored their hobbies and allowed them to be around others who had been considered "outcasts" because of what they enjoy. In so many ways, the learning sessions were communal spaces where they could rejoice in the weirdness and define themselves and their hobbies. They formed a community that welcomed whoever they chose to be.

After our meeting, I sat in my bed, thinking about everything that's happened over the last few months. I left my job at Altered Truth in an attempt to find Acorn after reading Butler's book. I was invited into the Harbor, made a member, and invited to unlearn with Endarkened girls who already had a grasp on the elusive concept of Endarkened dreams. Now, after all of this, I've made my decision. I'm going back to Altered Truth. I have to. I have to help other Endarkened children reach this place, and I'm in a position to do something. I may not be an activist like Harriet–2, but I can use my words to do something. I can be Lauren Jane.

I never thought I'd go back. In fact, the Lauren Jane of 2 months ago would've scoffed at the idea. But now? I'm realizing there's so much work to be done outside the Harbor, where Endarkened girls still aren't allowed to dream; where Endarkened people are still surveilled and killed by enforcers; where enforcers use the fear codes to exonerate themselves from our murders; where GC and its brethren control and dispose of Endarkened bodies at will. In the Harbor, we have an enclave of safety, a place where we all can learn and grow together. It has its problems, but many come from our socialization in GC's system. We are taught GC norms, so we are all in a process of unlearning, just like the Othermothers said.

I did some unlearning by talking with Ebony and Gholdy, but I unlearned the most in the learning session. In the beginning, I wanted to see what they would write, to learn how they might critique GC, and to better understand the barriers in their way. Working with them helped me find answers and see where I need to go from here. The girls were unapologetic in their critiques of GC, and hearing their stories showed me how much their narratives aligned with each other and with my own story. I know their personal stories can help whoever is willing to listen and learn about the horrors of the current HOME structure. Most importantly, though, I know their stories are critical for the future of our world.

The girls critiqued the supremacist values of GC by openly talking about how racism, sexism, and homophobia are embedded in GC's foundation, a foundation that led us to this moment in our collective future. Unafraid, they spoke and wrote, in spite of the silencing often imposed above. They refused to be muzzled any longer now that they weren't in the clutches of GC or their HOME observers. Something about being in the Harbor, being able to rejoice and find community in their perceived weirdness, provided a space to nerd out and collectively imagine a new world for Endarkened girls who don't fit the rigid mold of Blackness GC prescribes as the only option. I can only imagine what we could do if this type of unlearning was brought to the surface, rather than being forced to the underground. I can only imagine what the girls' stories will do for the people above.

They gave GC some attention because it exists, but they never dwelled on it, turning their attention to each other and to themselves. They talked about their love of old speculative fiction texts and spoke of how they found solace in these Dreamer-centric stories even if they didn't see themselves within them. In the realms of magic and wonder, anything can be possible, so they used the genre to create visions of themselves within stories that consistently ignored or erased them. They shouldn't have to create themselves in these stories, but Black girls are magic in so many ways, using their Endarkened powers to center themselves in imaginative landscapes even when some people don't want them there. I wonder what would happen if Dreamers were decentered for once, if the dreams of Endarkened girls were set free.

I also can't help but notice how all of the girls included Endarkened characters based on themselves. Bailey was the sister who saved the main character from harm in the virtual reality game. Talyn was the main character who believed in the power of the mind, the power to choose her own destiny even when a traitor comes to thwart her plans. Amber and Victoria shared personality traits and physical characteristics with their protagonists and included their family members as major characters. Avenae'J and Terrah included aspects of their identities, and used their characters to think through their ideas about social issues in the world. They each found a way to write themselves and their stories into a future existence, into a reality where they win; where they get to be the princess, the savior, or the activist … where they get to embrace the full spectrum of their identities.

In so many ways, they used these stories to metaphorically write about their lives, to symbolically think through their existence in a world where GC rules and Endarkened people lose. GC's rule book was written to ensure Dreamers win. The girls critiqued this idea, disrupting the altered truth that says Dreamers are the only ones to hold knowledge, that Dreamers are the only ones allowed to dream.

In writing about their lives, critiquing GC and its followers, and dreaming of new worlds, they imagined possibilities beyond our reality. They imagined a world aligned with the Harbor's ideals, one where all people are free, where all people exist in community. They showed me a world I must help to create.

December 27, 2085

Charles,

Seeing the unseen and engaging in unlearning are essential components of the operation. To unlearn, you must learn.

—Jane

Once again, it's not a lie per se, but Charles will never get it. My goal is to tell him the truth by giving him the most convoluted pieces of information I've gotten in this place. If I read this when I first arrived, I'd have no idea what it meant. It's not common phrasing, and it definitely wouldn't make sense to Endarkened people who have yet to make it to the Harbor. I wonder if that's why the Othermothers speak that way. It's a code that keeps unwanted ears from understanding what's being said even when we speak right in front of them. I kind of wish I could see Charles' face when he reads this note. I wish I could've seen his face when he read the last one. I'll see him soon enough, though.

Once written, I took the letter to the Harbor hub. There's a courier there who smuggles our letters into GC's mail system without getting caught. I guess when mail is completely automated, it's easier to hack the system. The hub was a bustle of energy as always, and I know I'm going to miss this feeling of joy and community. It's awfully lonely in GC, and even lonelier when you work for one of the specialized divisions. But even though I'm still wary, I know the work I plan to do will help Endarkened people find the Harbor. I know my spirit guided me to this place to hear the Harbor's testimony, witness its stories, and do something with this knowledge. Even though I'm still sad to go, today I chose to bask in the joy of Endarkened people.

I saw Layli at a small table on the left side of the hub working with a group of residents. She was dressed in the Harbor's colorful garb, but the others were dressed in gray, blue, black, and brown jumpsuits. The pale blue one looked quite similar to the one I kept in the corner of my room. I never thought I'd see someone wearing the uniform in here, at least not someone who's been here for a while. Maybe they were new and hadn't gotten a chest of altered clothing yet. Maybe they were heading back out like I am.

As I got closer, I saw they were creating a list of some sort. Each of them was huddled over narrow slips of paper writing words so small I'd need a microscope to decipher the letters. There were more slips in the middle of the table, and as one person finished a slip, they grabbed another and started writing again. It looked like grueling and monotonous work, but it must have been important because they were all concentrating on the task at hand, refusing to let the bustle of the Harbor get in their way. I kind of wondered why they chose to do it here instead of going to a quieter place.

"Um, excuse me, Layli?" It was supposed to come out as a declarative statement, but it definitely sounded more like a question.

"Hello, Sister! It's been a while," she said with a large grin. "How are you liking it here?"

"That's kind of what I came to talk to you about," I said, shifting my glance away from her for a moment. "I really love it here, and I've learned so much in the few months I've been in community with you all, but … um … I want to go back. No, that's not what I mean. I need to go back. I learned things, and I can be useful to the Harbor by helping others get here, and I think I'd be really good at it because I worked in a high office, and they trust me as much as they trust any Endarkened, and I think …" Layli put her hand on my arm, signaling for me to calm down.

"It's okay. We all have roles to play in the commonweal. Sometimes that role is to stay in the Harbor, and sometimes it's to go back to GC and make change in different ways. We need people like you out there. In all honesty, we can't do it without that help. It's a network for a reason. Actually, if you want to help, we're doing some of that work now."

"Of course, I'll help!" I said a little too enthusiastically. I was just happy to have something to do with myself other than standing there awkwardly. "What exactly are you doing?"

"Well, when you were in FirstHOME, you heard an observer repeat a list of names," Layli began. "These names eventually led you to a map. Now, not every observer is a part of our cause, but we do have many who want to do more, who want to help Endarkened people find the Harbors, who want to do the work of being co-conspirators. Some are at a point where they feel comfortable just giving names to the children in hopes they will find the maps on their own. Some are at a point where they are willing to teach Endarkened children to access dreams on their own. It's a greater risk than naming, and they often get found out and reprimanded, but they are doing the work for the benefit of the kids who are under their care. Then, there are some who do the work of stealing books from GC's clutches, disrupting the GC regime, leading people to the Harbors, and putting those maps directly in kids' hands. Each of these requires risk in a society that refuses to center our stories, but we need their help. We can't do it alone."

"We call them dream facilitators." Layli finished writing on one slip and moved to the next. "These facilitators are often on the front lines, and we appreciate their efforts to undermine the system keeping Endarkened dreams at bay. These slips of paper contain lists of names and books. We get these to the facilitators, and they share the information with other co-conspirators at and around their HOMEs. We wish there were more, but you know how that goes. Some of them are scared. They don't want to lose their jobs or have the lead observer reprimand them. We get that, but sometimes, we wish they'd put the Endarkened children first. Either way, these slips are necessary to send out every so often because GC sometimes finds out about the books and orders them to be destroyed. It's good for us because we get a copy of the book before it's incinerated, but it's bad for those above because that book is no longer there and no longer in print."

If I hadn't fully fixed my feet to go back before, I'd definitely made the decision now. "I'd like to help if that's okay?"

"Of course," she moved over so I could sit next to her.

"Would you mind talking with me later this week? I have an idea," I said as I wrote names on the tiny slip of paper.

"Yes. Let's meet on Saturday. We can meet in the library since that's where you've spent a lot of your time."

"That would be great!" I exclaimed. Then, for the next few hours, I continued writing names on slips of paper—Clayton, Onyebuchi, Ireland, Older, Davis, Clark, Hamilton, Elliott, Callender, and Barron. I wrote until I could write no more.

December 29, 2085

I arrived at the library before Layli in hopes of seeing Edi. She's always been so kind and supportive, and I wanted to let her know my plan. She wasn't in there, though, so I sat at the oval table that now symbolized the hopescape the girls and I created. Sitting alone was awkward because I was so used to hearing the girls' voices. I was used to listening to their stories about FirstHOME, about GC, about themselves, and about their Harbor families. Now, there was only silence. I took out the girls' stories and reread them. The girls weren't with me, but I could still hear their voices. I could still hear their collective and individual histories through their words.

Layli walked in, and her rainbow-colored kaftan shimmered. Somehow, the Othermothers always seemed to bring sunshine with them, as if the sun couldn't stand for them to be away from it. Layli sat down next to me and smiled. I think she was waiting for me to speak first, so I did.

"Good morning, Layli. Thank you so much for meeting me."

"Of course, Sister. So, what's this idea you had?"

"Well … I need to go back to Altered Truth. I love it here. I really do. I just know I can do good elsewhere. If it's okay with you and the Othermothers, I want to be a Harbor spy. I can get information to you, but I can also help others find the Harbor."

"I had a feeling this is what our conversation would be about," she affirmed and placed her hand on mine. "Tell me. What did you learn from working with the girls? I'm guessing they are the catalysts for this new state of events."

I took a deep breath and thought carefully about what I planned to say. "Gholdy told me the dream extraction doesn't remove our dreams because GC doesn't have that power even if they try to make it seem like they do. They just use the surgery to block our dreams, asphyxiating them before we have the chance to let them breathe. But, for those who read, see, or hear the dreams of other Endarkened people, the block is gradually removed. So, like you said, the best way to combat the extraction is to experience the work of others. Many of the speculative maps are written by Endarkened adults, but I know Endarkened youth also have important stories to share. They also have maps to give us. We just need to learn to listen to them."

She didn't say anything, so I kept talking. "I just reread the girls' stories, and I see how they embrace the ideals of Afrofuturism. They reclaim and recover aspects of the past GC has stolen from them by writing stories that show themselves as the heroes, the princesses, the chosen ones, and the saviors. They counter negative GC ideals and uplift positive Endarkened narratives by refusing to adhere to the stereotypical roles that GC tries to box them into. Instead, they tell stories about communal, individual, and familial identities that differ from GC's prescribed norm. They embrace the weird. They imagine new possibilities for their future and the futures of all Endarkened people. Their stories are activism."

"If you could've seen them in here each meeting, you'd also see they exhibit the ideals of womanism, too!" My hands were flying as I talked. "I mean, they truly loved the people around them and embraced each other's identities. They openly talked about their sexuality, their racial identities, their scholar identities, and even their nerd identities. Through their discussions, I saw how they were committed to the survival of all people even though they are particularly concerned with the survival of Endarkened people. Through their writing and in our learning sessions, I saw them using their lived experiences as sources of knowledge, engaging in communal dialogue as a way to create new knowledge, and using emotion and care as essential to their existence. I learned so much from being in community with them, and I must share this knowledge with Endarkened people above."

Layli sat there looking into the distance for a moment. I wasn't sure she followed my ramblings, but I had to tell her what had been going through my mind since my last meeting with the girls. I wanted to show her why I must go back.

"I'd like to find a way to get their stories out into the world. I want to help make sure people can see and hear the stories of Endarkened girls. They have important things to say. They have important dreams that may lead other youth to the Harbor, so they don't have to wait until they're my age to find it."

I lowered my voice and looked Layli in the eyes. "The learning sessions were amazing because of the ideals holding this place together. There's a community of people who welcome each other's interests. There's reverence for the commonweal, respect for youth voices, actions toward anti–oppression, and a deference to the everyday knowledge held by Endarkened people. The Harbor honors our stories—past, present, and future. That's not how it is up there. The HOMEs stifle the imagination. Their regulations and arbitrary rules inhibit innovative thinking. When I leave this place, the girls can start their own learning sessions or continue to work in community with people who are already willing to listen to their stories. In GC's America, no one listens to us. They don't want us to dream. But there's freedom in writing our futures. There's liberation in spaces like the Harbor even though that same liberation doesn't exist everywhere because so many Dreamers refuse to let it. I want to fight against that. I want to make sure Endarkened people not only learn to access their dreams, but they also learn how to use those dreams as maps." I finally stopped talking and waited for Layli to respond.

She must have been waiting for me to make my point because she smiled and finally spoke. "Then, you must go. As we said before, everyone is allowed to follow their own spiritual and individual evolutions. We do not force anyone to stay here. But to protect the Harbor, you must undergo another dream extraction procedure. It's so we can protect you. To ensure you don't completely lose your will or your memories, we can provide you with an extraction blocker called the Denman Chip if you'd like. With the blocker, it will take you approximately one week to get your will and memories back."

"So, the Denman Chip blocks the dream extraction from fully taking over but the dream extraction will still work for a few days? And I'll lose my memories of this place, but they'll come back?" I dreaded the aftereffects of the surgery but knowing I wouldn't completely forget everything made me happy. I was also excited because I'm sure the Denman Chip was probably how Harriet–2 was able to keep passing the release tests after getting the extraction surgery so many times. I didn't get it at first, but her ability to come back was because the Harbor was with her at all times. If I get the chip, too, in many ways, I'll be like her, working within the confines of GC, but relying on the Harbor and the stories of Endarkened people to guide me back to the work I need to be doing.

"Essentially," Layli said, interrupting my thoughts, "the Denman Chip will allow for the dream extraction and memory serum to work for one week before it counters them both. This will give you time to pass their exit tests, and it will ensure that when you get home, there will be no changes to alert them of a failed process. Once you have the chip, its ability to help you overcome the extraction is unlimited, so no matter how many times they try, within one week, your will to dream will return. Most of our operatives get them, but most of the Dreamers don't need them because GC doesn't surveil them the same way. They just use their privilege as a way to undermine the regime in ways we can't. But like I said, it's not mandatory."

"I'll get the chip." I'd already made up my mind to get it when she first mentioned it. "When does all of this happen?"

"I guess it can happen whenever you'd like it to."

"Now?"

"Soon," she laughed.

I could wait because I had another 2 months before my Altered Truth reconnaissance mission was over, but I also knew the longer I waited, the more time I'd have to think of reasons to not go back. I didn't want to talk myself out of it in the months I had left. Plus, if I went back now, I could spend the next few months thinking of a plan and learning more about how Harriet–2 was able to survive so long doing this work. There's got to be a way. She did it, and so can I, even if we'll be doing things a little differently.

"I'd like to leave as soon as possible, then. The sooner I leave, the sooner I can get information out to the Endarkened people above."

"Have you spoken to the girls about this yet?"

"I have. I actually told them about it during our last meeting."

"Well, I'm sure you'll be able to keep in touch. Once you have been to the Harbor and learned from the people who live and move within it, it never leaves you, and you never leave it. You and your spirit are a part of the commonweal. You may have chosen to leave this place, but you will still be a part of this community. I don't know if you remember, but Ebony once told you we are not restrictive, and we mean that. We may not want to go above because we feel there is more work to do here, to heal ourselves and to heal others like us, but we respect and honor your choice to do as you must."

"I still don't get the non-restrictive thing, but I'm working on it," I said. "I was honestly waiting for someone to be mad at me."

"Definitely not. There are multiple ways to exist in community. You are choosing your way. I'll need to check the schedule over in the science wing, but I'll let you know when you can schedule your surgery later today." She got up to leave, but I put my hand on hers before she moved away from the table.

"Thank you, sister," I said. "I needed this."

"I know. We all need the space to heal. We all need the chance to figure out our role in the commonweal," she said as she walked out of the library.

December 31, 2085

I write this entry as I sit in the doctor's office. I guess it'll be the last one before I forget everything … for a week, at least. I'm glad this is the writing I'll see when I wake up, though, because something really important happened last night. I had my first dream.

Initially, my mind was filled with blinding whiteness, a silent white backdrop, with no pictures or sounds. I'm used to this. It's the same thing I've been seeing since I was brought into this world. But then, the darkness came, a space of dreams, a place where imagination could grow. It was beautiful. There was blackness, then various shades of brown, and then rainbow colors. When the colors settled, I saw … them. In the distance, there were six stars lighting the night sky. They danced around, moving from space to space, and then they started to come together, forming an oval shape around the moon. The girls were my dream. They were the stars. Our table was the moon. I guess Octavia was right. She said all that you touch, you change, and all that you change, changes you. Butler's book, Elonnie's help, Harriet–2's words, the girls' stories—each of these has touched me in some way, and I am forever changed because of it.

I am Lauren Jane, a writer and a dreamer, and GC will never be able to take that from me. I found Acorn, my homeplace, and it was located in an enclave of Endarkened people. I found Earthseed, my people, and it was situated in a dreaming community with six Black girls. There are many Harbors around this country, but there are so many Endarkened people who can't find them because GC has continually attempted to steal our dreams from us, to steal our future from us. I will fight against this. I will share the maps the girls created. I will help other Endarkened children access the maps they already have written down inside of them. I have so much work to do, and I'll need help to do it. I'll need people within the commonweal to aid me on my quest for imaginative justice. I'll need people who know Endarkened people have something to say, people who know that Black girls dreams are critical to our future. This will not be an easy fight, but it is a necessary one. It is battle worth pursuing.

So, I must ask this question: Will you join me?

COMPANION 1
EXPLORING THE INTRODUCTION

S. R. Toliver

As a general rule, introduction chapters should provide preliminary information that can put the research in context. It helps to provide focus, and it allows the researcher to bring the reader into the study. Within this section, the reader should understand the social and political context in which the study takes place, and they should also understand the background that led to the creation of the study. Moreover, the introduction provides the why. Why is this study relevant? Why did the researcher choose to highlight this specific area of scholarship? What is the value of this work? Within *Endarkened storywork*, these questions are still answered, but they take on a different form, one that still brings the reader into the topic, but allows space for creativity in hopes that the author will not need to explicitly name important points.

To be a story listener is to find meaning in the story through synergy, but I also understand certain codes may be difficult to decipher for some readers. Although I do not detail every single component that went into the creation of each chapter, I include elements of the empirical data, the real world, and the research literature, alongside my personal experiences to show how each was essential to creating the storied whole. Hopefully, these details will assist readers in better understanding the work embedded within the story and the effort needed to engage in *Endarkened storywork*.

The research

The Introduction did not focus on the research literature but it was represented. For example, a major part of the introduction is Jane's reading of Octavia Butler. I felt that it was important to include a critical content analysis (Short & Worlds of Words Community, 2017) of O. Butler's work because T. Butler (2018) argued that although it is important to examine themes in literature, it is also important to note how books can "signal as to where Black girls are most prevalent or at least can thrive in the literary imaginations of writers and readers" (p. 39). In the story, O. Butler's novel is used as a map to locate a space where Endarkened women can thrive. Further, Butler's novel is the catalyst for Jane's journey to "Acorn." Kynard (2010) discussed Black women's use and creation of hush harbors, where the "current work of maintaining, rescripting, and reauthorizing African American challenges to white hegemony" are centered instead of "merely providing utopian safe havens or survival strategies" (p. 35). O. Butler's (1993) book is a map to a place of maintaining, rescripting, and reauthorizing Endarkened life in the midst of the GC state.

The literature also shows up in Jane's work life. Collins (2000) suggested that Black women are often rendered invisible in various spaces, and Jane and the other Endarkened workers are often rendered invisible in Altered Truth. They use that invisibility to gather information and give themselves an advantage, a form of trickster technology. Further, there is a lot of conversation about being a "good one" that I connect to Higginbotham's (1993) concept of the politics of respectability. Respectability politics is a specific form of resistance where some Black women believed it necessary to implement dominant values, ones that would allow them to avoid negativity from white people. However, Stafford (2015) noted that "the reason why being 'respectable' doesn't work is because no matter how respectable you may be acting, your performance isn't undoing the very real systematic ways in which our world operates" (par. 10). I show Jane using respectability as a weapon against dominance, but I also show how respectability often isn't enough because even though Jane is considered a respectable Endarkened employee, she is still treated poorly. I chose to include these aspects because my research partners often talked about being in the "good" classes because they did their schoolwork, but even though they were placed in the upper level courses, they still dealt with racism via teachers and administrators.

Lastly, the literature guides the creation of FirstHOME. Black girls are growing up in an age of systemic violence that affects their chances for academic and social success. They are less likely than all of their female peers to graduate on time or to obtain a postsecondary degree (Baxley & Boston, 2010; George, 2015). They are 5.5 times more likely to be suspended than their white female peers, and they also receive more suspensions than any other racial group (Joseph et al., 2016; Onyeka-Crawford et al., 2017). They are forced to modify their culturally sanctioned ways of being and adopt standards of "racelessness" (Evans-Winters, 2005; Fordham, 1988; Ricks, 2014), or assimilation into white culture while distancing themselves from Blackness, to avoid ostracization in secondary classrooms. When they do achieve academic success, their accomplishments are belittled as some educators focus more on their social decorum, rather than their academic triumphs (Carter, 2006; Fordham, 1993; Morris, 2007). These data position Black girls as corporeal sites of struggle, where their very being stands in opposition to the discourses of diversity, equity, and inclusion touted by various educational stakeholders. I include this information because it is important in the description of Black girls' schooling experiences, but I also used the story to extrapolate the ways some people use that data to keep Black girls confined within these violent schooling spaces.

The workshop

Even though the girls from the research study are not directly mentioned in the introduction, their presence is felt. For example, a major aspect of the story revolves around the Endarkened people's blue eyes. In the third workshop, the girls and I had a conversation about character eye color. When Terrah mentioned that she gives her characters "rare eye colors … green eyes or blue eyes or purple eyes," I asked the other girls if they do the same. They all agreed, and Talyn added that having a character with rare eyes is "obviously setting them up to be different." She also stated that characters with "regular" eye colors suggest that "they're invested in their community" and that they "actually care about those around them." I wanted to include this concept because each of the girls highlighted eye color as an important aspect of the character's personality, but I also wanted to take Talyn's comment into account, that regular-eyed people are invested in their community. To do this, I created a society where Endarkened people have unnatural blue eyes, as they are cut off from their current and historical community. The dreamers have regular eye colors, and they are invested in their community, although it is often to the detriment of the Endarkened community.

Another way the girls' writing shows up is through worldbuilding. In later chapters, when reading the girls' short stories, you'll notice a dark tone undergirds their fictional work. In Terrah, Avenae'J, and Amber's short stories, the world is dystopic. Terrah's story speaks to a literal division, where the United States is vertically split in half with predominately white residents on one side and people of color predominately on the other side. Avenae'J's story revolves around a world so oppressive that people are forced to hide their race, gender, ethnicity, sexuality, etc. Those who refuse to comply are taken to the Change Room and tortured until they are shells of their former selves. Amber's storied world is filled with violence and chaos. It's so violent that even peaceful protestors are shot in the streets. Victoria's story comments on patriarchy and includes aspects of the "chosen one" trope. Talyn's story includes commentary on racism and deceit. Bailey's story is based in the horror genre, where the main character cannot find a way out of a confined space.

Although the reader has not yet arrived at their stories, aspects of their narratives guide the larger one. I explicitly use the Change Room in the larger story to suggest that the story Avenae'J tells mirrors the world of the story. Jane, in many ways, is the "chosen one" aligning her character with the one Victoria creates. Just like the people in Terrah's story, the Endarkened are separated from the Dreamers. Just like Amber's world filled with violence, the world I created is also imbued with physical and mental violence. Borrowing from Bailey and

Talyn, I create a horrific landscape that centralizes conversations around racism, deceit, and confinement. Borrowing from conversations with all of the girls, I create a world where Endarkened people's names are removed since the naming of characters was important in the girls' storied creations. Ultimately, although the girls are not physically present as characters in the introduction, their ideas were essential to the overall construction of the narrative.

The real world

I begin the introduction section with social, political, and educational background information that examines and responds to the current world. It was important to provide context for how this dystopian world came to exist, so I considered the social issues consistently mentioned within the workshop, and I asked myself what would happen if the problems were not fixed within the next 50 years. In this way, I ground the futuristic world in the current one, finding ways to show how the past—our current societal moment in the case of the story—can and will impact the future.

For instance, the girls often talked about surveillance and police brutality, so I came up with the enforcers. Pipkins (2017) used critical discourse analysis to discuss the discursive strategies used by police officers to justify the murder of unarmed citizens who are predominately Black. The statements used by the enforcers, called fear codes in the book, mirror the statements used by current law enforcement in murder trials. The officers listed in the Altered Truth meeting are the last names of officers who have been charged in the murders of Black people. In most cases, the officers were acquitted of the crime (Crenshaw et al., 2015; Hafner, 2018). Further, Charles is praised for getting an enforcer acquitted, this enforcer is based on Officer Betty Shelby, who murdered Terence Crutcher in 2016 and was acquitted of all charges. In 2017, a district judge expunged her record, effectively sealing the court case (Hamlin, 2017). Lastly, since 2014, The Marshall Project, a nonpartisan and nonprofit news organization, has kept track of news articles showcasing police officers planting evidence on civilians, so I included this as a tactic of the enforcers and also connected it to the work of Octavia Butler (1993). Essentially, I took the girls' concerns and placed those concerns in the context of the futuristic story.

As an Afrofuturistic story, it was also important to include information about Black life. I included references to Black maternal mortality since the CDC (2019) reports that Black, American Indian, and Alaska Native women are "two to three times more likely to die from a pregnancy-related causes as White women – and this disparity increases with age" (par. 1). I extended this reality and connected it to the process of dream extraction. I also alluded to the violent anti-literacy laws in which enslaved people who dared to read and write "often suffered severe punishment for the crime of literacy, from savage beatings to the amputation of fingers and toes" (Division of Rare Manuscript Collections, 2002, par. 1). This information was included as a rumor about what happens to Endarkened people if they attempt to steal a restricted book. In addition, I included commentary on the Tulsa Massacre that occurred in 1921 and resulted in major losses for Black families (Astor, 2020). Messer and Bell (2010) contended that media framing prevented Black survivors from receiving justice, and stories like this created the foundation for the Altered Truth Division. Lastly, Girey Cuviems is a portmanteau. It is a combination of George Gey, Julien-Joseph Virey, Georges Cuvier, and J. Marion Sims, white male scientists who gained fame by mutilating or taking from Black women's bodies.

The inclusion of Black history couldn't solely rest on Black pain; therefore, I made sure to include Black joy, too. Elonnie Junius Josey was the founder of the Black Caucus of the American Library Association and the ALA's second Black president (American Libraries, 2009), and he is the librarian who helps Jane get the book. Claudette Colvin was the first Black girl to challenge bus segregation in 1955 (Adler, 2009); Tarika Lewis, a 16-year-old high school student, became the first young woman to gain entrance into the Black Panther Party in 1967 (Robertson, 2016); and Naomi Wadler is an 11-year-old activist who provoked a strong reaction from listeners when she spoke out against gun violence at the March for Our Lives rally (Beckett, 2018). Each was alluded to in the conversation between Jane and the director of Altered Truth. Additionally, Harriet Tubman escaped enslavement and became a leading abolitionist and political activist who helped other Black people attain freedom. Upon her death, she told friends and family, "I go to prepare a place for you" (Public Broadcasting Service, 2019, para. 11). Thus, even after dying of pneumonia, she was still working to ensure Black freedom. As I included information about Black oppression, it was also essential to talk about Black liberation and rebellion. It was critical to include the ways we used various technologies toward the process of freedom.

The personal

I do not include much of my personal story in this section, but there are elements of my lived experiences that I do include. The only deeply personal reference is to my 11th grade English teacher, Lori Jackson. I'm not sure if she knows how much of an impact she had on my life, but as I say in the story, she was the first teacher who really saw me. I felt comfortable and safe in her classroom. I felt like she wanted me to do something great and believed that I could do so. I include her in the story because it's my way of showing just how special she was to me. The other aspect of my life included in this section is based on schooling experiences. I was considered one of the "good ones" in school, and I could never figure out if that was a compliment or not. I also remember that the only Black literature we read and the only Black movies we watched were centered on Black pain and struggle. We were never presented with stories about Black joy, Black freedom, and Black liberation. I wanted to talk about what that felt like for me in school, and that was the basis of the physical tests for FirstHOME.

The last major element of my life included in the first chapter is my love for Octavia Butler. I first read Octavia Butler's *Parable of the Sower* (1993) when I was in college. I did not read it as a map at that time, but when I was imagining the best way to get Jane to the Harbor, Butler's novel was the first thing that came to mind. I reread it for the creation of that section of the story, highlighting aspects of the book that could be interpreted as a map to Acorn. It was a fascinating experiment in critical content analysis, and it made me wonder how many other books could be read through the same lens. Myers (2014) acknowledged that readers often view books as maps as they search for their place in the world and make decisions about where they want to go. He noted that books carry cartographies that can show readers all the places they can go with no blind spots. It made me wonder how books had been maps for me, how books led me to what I'm doing right now.

References

Adler, M. (2009). *Before Rosa Parks there was Claudette Colvin*. NPR. https://www.npr.org/2009/03/15/101719889/before-rosa-parks-there-was-claudette-colvin.

American Libraries. (2009). *Civil rights pioneer, librarian E. J. Josey dies at 85*. American Libraries. https://americanlibrariesmagazine.org/blogs/the-scoop/civil-rights-pioneer-librarian-e-j-josey-dies-at-85/.

Astor, M. (2020). What to know about the Tulsa Greenwood massacre. *The New York Times*. https://www.nytimes.com/2020/06/20/us/tulsa-greenwood-massacre.html.

Baxley, T. P., & Boston, G. H. (2010). Classroom inequity and the literacy experiences of black adolescent girls. In J. Zajda (Ed.), *Globalization, education and social justice* (pp. 145–159). Springer.

Beckett, L. (2018). 'Never again': How 11-year old Naomi Wadler became a rallying voice of Black protest. *The Guardian*. https://www.theguardian.com/us-news/2018/mar/31/naomi-wadler-the-11-year-old-helping-lead-a-protest-movement.

Butler, O. (1993). *Parable of the sower*. Grand Central Publishing.

Butler, T. T. (2018). Black girl cartography: Black girlhood and place-making in education research. *Review of Research in Education, 42*(1), 28–45.

Carter, S. P. (2006). "She would've still made that face expression": The use of multiple literacies by two African American young women. *Theory into Practice, 45*(4), 352–358.

CDC. (2019). *Racial and ethnic disparities continue in pregnancy related deaths. Black, American Indian/Alaska Native women most affected*. https://www.cdc.gov/media/releases/2019/p0905-racial-ethnic-disparities-pregnancy-deaths.html.

Collins, P. H. (2000). *Black feminist thought: Knowledge, consciousness, and the politics of empowerment*. Routledge.

Crenshaw, K., Ritchie, A., Anspach, R., Gilmer, R., & Harris, L. (2015). *Say her name: Resisting police brutality against black women*. [Policy brief]. African American Policy Forum. http://static1.squarespace.com/static/53f20d90e4b0b80451158d8c/t/560c068ee-4b0af26f72741df/1443628686535/AAPF_SMN_Brief_Full_singles-min.pdf.

Division of Rare Manuscript Collections. (2002). *In their own words: Slave narratives*. https://rmc.library.cornell.edu/abolitionism/narratives.htm#:~:text=In%20Their%20Own%20Words%3A%20Slave%20Narratives&text=In%20most%20southern%20states%2C%20anyone,amputation%20of%20fingers%20and%20toes.

Evans-Winters, V. (2005). *Teaching black girls: Resiliency in urban classrooms*. Peter Lang.

Fordham, S. (1988). Racelessness as a factor in black students' school success: Pragmatic strategy or pyrrhic victory? *Harvard Educational Review, 58*(1), 54–84.

Fordham, S. (1993). "Those loud black girls": (Black) women, silence, and gender "passing" in the academy. *Anthropology & Education Quarterly, 24*(1), 3–32.

George, J. A. (2015). Stereotype and school pushout: Race, gender, and discipline disparities. *Arkansas Law Review, 68*(1), 101–129.

Hafner, J. (2018). *Police killings of Black men in the U.S. and what happened to the officers*. USA Today. https://www.usatoday.com/story/news/nation-now/2018/03/29/police-killings-black-men-us-and-what-happened-officers/469467002/.

Hamlin, C. (2017). *Fatal shooting of unarmed Black man will be removed from ex-cop's record*. NewsOne. https://newsone.com/3755586/betty-shelby-terence-crutcher-shooting-update-tulsa-police-record-expunged-tulsa/.

Higginbotham, E. B. (1993). *Righteous discontent: The women's movement in the Black Baptist Church, 1880–1920*. Harvard University Press.

Joseph, N., Viesca, K. M., & Bianco, M. (2016). Black female adolescents and racism in schools: Experiences in a colorblind society. *The High School Journal, 18*(3), 396–418.

Kynard, C. (2010). From Candy Girls to Cyber Sista-Cipher: Narrating Black female's color consciousness and counterstories in and out of school. *Harvard Educational Review, 80*(1), 30–52.

Messer, C., & Bell, P. (2010). Mass media and governmental framing of riots: The case of Tulsa, 1921. *Journal of Black Studies, 40*(5), 851–870.

Morris, E. (2007). "Ladies" or "loudies"?: Perceptions and experiences of black girls in classrooms. *Youth and Society, 38*(4), 490–515.

Myers, C. (2014). *The apartheid of children's literature*. The New York Times. https://www.nytimes.com/2014/03/16/opinion/sunday/the-apartheid-of-childrens-literature.html.

Onyeka-Crawford, A., Patrick, K., & Chaudhry, N. (2017). *Let her learn: Stopping school pushout for girls of color*. National Women's Law Center.

Pipkins, M. (2017). "I feared for my life": Law enforcement's appeal to murderous empathy. *Race and Justice, 9*(2), 180–196.

Public Broadcasting Service. (2019). *Explore Harriet Tubman*. PBS. https://www.pbs.org/black-culture/explore/harriet-tubman/.

Ricks, S. A. (2014). Falling through the cracks: Black girls and education. *Interdisciplinary Journal of Teaching & Learning, 4*(1), 10–21.

Robertson, D. (2016). *A look back at black panther women amid the party's 50th anniversary*. Vibe. https://www.vibe.com/2016/11/impact-of-black-panther-women/.

Short, K. G., & Worlds of Words Community. (2017). Critical content analysis as a research methodology. In H. Johnson, J. Mathis, & K. G. Short (Eds.), *Critical content analysis of children's and young adult literature: Reframing perspective* (pp. 1–15). Routledge.

Stafford, Z. (2015). *Respectability won't save Black Americans*. The Guardian. https://www.theguardian.com/commentisfree/2015/oct/12/respectability-politics-wont-save-black-americans.

COMPANION 2
THEORY IN THE WORD

S. R. Toliver

Theories help us to explain, anticipate, interpret, critique, and broaden our worldview. They provide us with a blueprint for understanding a specific phenomenon and encourage us to investigate various elements that influence our studies. Theory is integral to Endarkened storywork. Endarkened feminist epistemologies (EFE) and indigenous storywork (ISW) broadened my worldview and helped me to access alternative truths I had learned to forget. They helped me to explain my need to engage in the work of story and critique traditional qualitative research methods that asked me to leave story outside of my academic work. Before I found Endarkened storywork; however, my study was informed by a combination of womanism and Black feminism.

In communicating her journey toward EFE, Dillard (2000, 2006) stated that she first examined themes and patterns she noticed in her data and placed that information in the context of Black womanist and feminist thought. She then asked questions of the data that helped her to theoretically ground her work and clarify EFE to the broader research community. Thus, womanism and Black feminism helped her to articulate EFE. In the same way, womanism and Black feminism grounded me on my journey toward Endarkened storywork. The chapter is titled "Womanism in Action" because womanism greatly influenced my thinking, but even though womanism was my guiding theory, I am still heavily influenced by Black feminist scholarship. Womanism pushed me to consider the everyday realities of Black girls and reflect on the relationship between the girls, social justice, and freedom technologies. Black feminism helped me to think through the oppositional knowledge the girls used to dismantle oppressive structures and create spaces of freedom. Thinking of the girls' work with these theories in mind led me to question my own positionality as a researcher and convinced me to dream otherwise about my scholarship.

This section showcases many of the womanist and Black feminist ideas that were integral to the thought processes that lead me to Endarkened storywork. To create it, I reviewed readings on womanism and tried to figure out a way to represent my theoretical underpinnings without regurgitating the information gleaned from reading these works. I could have had the characters verbally list the characteristics of womanism, but I wanted to show these ideals through the character's thoughts and actions in the same way that my ancestors condensed their theoretical observations about life into Anansi stories. I wanted theory to be embodied within the story's plot, characters, and settings in ways that extend beyond traditional research writing. Through this chapter, I showcase how I used my imagination to make theory come to life. I explain theory through the alternative site of storytelling.

The research

Walker (1983) coined the term, womanism, and stated that it is a word based on the Black colloquial term, womanish, which refers to the courageous, knowledge-seeking, and willful behavior of young Black women. Phillips (2006) expanded the term, defining womanism as a social change perspective that is rooted in the everyday experiences and everyday problem-solving methods of Black women and other women of color. Additionally, she argued that this perspective can be used to end "all forms of oppression for all people, restoring the balance between people and the environment/nature, and reconciling human life with the spiritual dimension" (p. xx). That is, womanism, although centering the experiences of Black women, focuses on a wider commitment to social justice, a commitment that centers Black women, but extends beyond them to ensure the betterment of humanity and the world we inhabit. It is a critically situated theory that centers social justice, community, and sisterhood in an effort to eliminate oppressions for all people.

One of the major ways I include womanism is through the presence of the Othermothers. Although I borrow the term 'Othermother' from Collins (2000), I used Phillips' (2006) discussion of mothering and motherhood to create the characters in the story. Phillips argues that motherhood is a "set of behaviors based on caretaking, management, nurturance, education, spiritual mediation, and dispute resolution" (p. xxix). It is not purely associated with biology or restricted by gender labels, as anyone, no matter their gender or sexuality can mother other people. The Othermothers in this text embody these behaviors by taking care of the Endarkened people in the Harbor, no matter their individual needs. They ensure that new arrivals are given a chance to unlearn the ways of GC, and they make space for people to come as they are and learn as they would like. This ensures that each person can feel cared for, and that each person feels as though they are welcomed in the Harbor.

I based the other mothers on scholars who have greatly influenced my work: Layli Phillips Maparyan, Alice Walker, Patricia Hill Collins, Venus

Evans-Winters, Ytasha Womack, Gholdy Muhammad, Ebony Elizabeth Thomas, and Maisha Winn. Layli Jane Walker represents womanism, and Venus Jill Collins represents Black feminism. Gholdy Jill Winn represents Black women scholars whose work centralizes Black people, Black writing, and Black genius. Ebony Jane Womack represents Black women scholars who focus upon the speculative, specifically centering their work on Black people and their consumption and production of speculative fiction. Naming is important in womanist scholarship, and as I was writing a story that hinged upon the works of brilliant Black women scholars, I wanted to make sure that I honored them in some way.

Other characteristics of womanism are also displayed throughout this chapter. For instance, Phillips (2006) discussed that womanism views the commonweal as the goal of social change. She stated that the commonweal includes humanity, the Earth, the Universe, as well as the spiritual and transcendental. When the relationship between all aspects is balanced, a commonweal is reached. I represent this by showing how Jane is not yet a part of the commonweal. She is not one with the Earth and the universe, so she cannot see Savannah for how it wants to be seen. Furthermore, I show the womanist characteristic of hospitality by showcasing how the Harbor residents create positive encounters for newcomers by refusing to let any Endarkened community member feel ostracized for their clothing, opting for a vibrance of color and humanity. I include the nonideological aspect of womanism by ensuring that the Harbor makes space for people to explore themselves and their identities without forcing anyone to adhere to a certain belief system. This was critical to me because a womanist space of caring is drastically different from GC's restrictive society. Ultimately, rather than list the characteristics of womanism, I infused them within the Othermothers and the innerworkings of the Harbor.

As the study also centers Black girls, I included research on Black girl literacies. I acknowledge how literacy enables us to make sense of our lives (Muhammad, 2012) while also helping us to seek, restore, and create justice in this world (Winn, 2013). I include the ways in which Black women and girls have created hush harbors, unauthorized spaces of resistance that create possibilities for imaginative disruption (Kynard, 2010; Price-Dennis, 2016). Once again, I include Butler's (2018) concept of Black girl cartography, but in this chapter, I recognize how many Black women writers have engaged "in an ongoing dialogue with past, present, and future Black girls and women," and I metaphorically represent how some of the writings could materialize "as testaments, letters, and entries to younger selves and future selves, to women and girls that we have grown with and some whom we may never meet" (p. 33). I take this information literally, thinking about what it would mean for future Black people to use speculative literature as letters of freedom to future generations of Black folks. I consider how speculative fiction writing could act as a literacy technology and how decoding the meanings within these works could require linguistic technologies.

The workshop

For reasons of confidentiality, researchers often use pseudonyms to denote the physical locations of our studies; however, place is essential in womanism. If we are to truly understand everyday people and everyday life, we must attend to the everyday locations of Black people. This study took place in Savannah, GA, and the girls who participated in the study had different ideas about Savannah. Talyn said that it was the most haunted city in America, but it was also a very important place because of its historical value to Georgia. Terrah stated that it was an old and pretty city, but Victoria said that it was a place of violence because many people had gotten shot or hurt. In the story, I used the girls' descriptions to create a picture of Savannah. The ash and eerie quiet are meant to provide a haunting feeling; the lack of care for a burning city represents violence and people hurting; and the description of the buildings is meant to represent a once beautiful and historic city.

The real world

The inclusion of real-world elements is also tied to place. For instance, Savannah's first great fire occurred in 1796, destroying 229 buildings, and the second great fire occurred in 1820, destroying 463 buildings (Savannah Fire Rescue). I use these historical events to show precedence for large fires in Savannah's history. In the story, I add a third great fire, and I use the year 2063 to pay homage to the reintegration of Savannah's fire department that happened after the NAACP and the city reached an agreement for the fire department to hire six Black firefighters in 1963 (Savannah Fire Rescue). Another aspect of Savannah's history that I included was the tunnel system. There are numerous tunnels beneath Savannah, but many of them are closed off. They cover a wide area underneath the city, although the reason behind the tunnels' construction is unclear. Most rumors, however, report of slave and liquor transport and the housing of dead bodies (Savannah Magazine, 2017). I wanted to acknowledge the history behind the tunnel system while also imagining the tunnels as sites of resistance. I wanted to imagine a womanist-informed space of solace underneath the oppressive world above.

Another major influence from the real world is the conversations around the lack of diversity in children's books. Literature is the means by which people find the Harbors, but Endarkened children's access to diverse speculative texts hinders them from finding the maps (Myers, 2014). I arrived at this idea by considering the limited texts written by and about Black, Indigenous, Asian, Latinx, and multiracial authors (Cooperative Children's Book Center, 2020). This, alongside Thomas' (2019) argument that "in the Anglo-American fantastic tradition, the Dark Other is the spectacle, the monstrous Thing that is the root cause of hesitation, ambivalence, and the uncanny" (p. 23), caused me to think about the Endarkened's place in GC. Specifically, Jane was never able to read speculative books by Black authors when she was in school. Instead, she mostly saw Dreamer depictions of her existence. The lack of access to speculative texts and the monstrous representations of self within the texts she was given made it difficult for her to dream her way out of GC's clutches. The imagination gap (Thomas, 2019) is not just caused by GC's scientific procedure, it is also caused "by the lack of diversity in childhood and teen life depicted in books, television, and films" (p. 6) and by the stereotypical depiction of existence in youth media and literature. However, one look into Butler's (1993) novel, and she had the imaginative tools necessary to set herself free.

The personal

There are several connections between my personal story and the chapter. For example, during my study, I consistently reserved hotels in Pooler, GA because they were less expensive than hotels in Savannah, and I went home to Atlanta in between my site visits. At the beginning of the chapter, I had Jane stay in Pooler and travel to Savannah each day. I included this information to represent my own traveling in and outside of the area. I also included it to talk about how I felt about traveling back and forth between research location and home. Although I had worked with the writing program for several years, I still felt like an outsider because I would come in, do some workshops, and travel back to my home four hours away. For me to truly do this work, I needed and wanted to be immersed in the area, but it was not financially feasible. Instead, I started immersing myself in Savannah's history and the girls' experiences of Savannah, and that helped me become more connected with the land.

Although it is not explicitly stated in the text, my positionality is also represented in this chapter, specifically through Jane's musings of who she is. I had the Othermothers ask Jane who she was because I, too, needed to answer that question for myself. It was not an easy task because self-work is difficult work, but it was necessary if I planned to move this story forward. I consider myself to be a dreamer, a writer, and maybe even a storyteller. I know the importance of my name because my mother ensured that I knew who I was. Stephanie means crown or victorious, and I've had to grapple with that meaning in the same way that Jane had to contend with her own naming. Like Jane, I have often wondered how my life would be different if I knew authors like Octavia Butler, Samuel Delaney, Nalo Hopkinson, or George Schuyler existed when I was younger. Like Jane, I kept my interests in the fantastic, in dreaming, a secret for fear of retaliation. Like Jane, I'm still working on understanding my purpose in this world and in this work. In so many ways, I am Jane and Jane is me. Imarisha (2015) stated that Octavia Butler handed down a responsibility to dream as ourselves. With this responsibility, she asked, "are we brave enough to imagine beyond the boundaries of 'the real' and then do the hard work of sculpting reality from our dreams?" (loc. 167). With this story, and this chapter specifically, I had to be brave enough to imagine beyond my reality and use the text to sculpt reality to form my dreams.

References

Butler, O. (1993). *Parable of the sower*. Grand Central Publishing.

Butler, T. T. (2018). Black girl cartography: Black girlhood and place-making in education research. *Review of Research in Education, 42*(1), 28–45.

Collins, P. H. (2000). *Black feminist thought: Knowledge, consciousness, and the politics of empowerment*. Routledge.

Cooperative Children's Book Center. (2020). Books by and/or about Black, Indigenous, and people of color (All Years). https://ccbc.education.wisc.edu/literature-resources/ccbc-diversity-statistics/books-by-about-poc-fnn/

Dillard, C. B. (2000). The substance of things hoped for, the evidence of things not seen: Examining an endarkened feminist epistemology in educational research and leadership. *International Journal of Qualitative Studies in Education, 13*(6), 661–681.

Dillard, C. B. (2006). *On spiritual strivings: Transforming an African American woman's academic life*. State University of New York Press.

Imarisha, W. (2015). Introduction. In A. Brown & W. Imarisha (Eds.), *Octavia's brood: Science fiction stories from social justice movements* (pp. 3–6). AK Press.

Kynard, C. (2010). From candy girls to cyber sista-cipher: Narrating Black female's color consciousness and counterstories in and out of school. *Harvard Educational Review, 80*(1), pp. 30–52.

Muhammad, G. (2012). Creating spaces for Black girls to "write it out." *Journal of Adolescent & Adult Literacy, 56*(3), 203–211.

Myers, C. (2014). *The apartheid of children's literature*. The New York Times. https://www.nytimes.com/2014/03/16/opinion/sunday/the-apartheid-of-childrens-literature.html

Phillips, L. (2006). *The womanist reader*. Taylor & Francis.

Price-Dennis, D. (2016). Developing curriculum to support Black girls' literacies in digital spaces. *English Education, 48*(4), 337–362.

Savannah Fire Rescue. (n.d.). *Savannah fire rescue history*. Savannah Fire Rescue. https://www.savannahga.gov/2618/Savannah-Fire-History

Savannah Magazine. (2017). *Beneath the surface*. Savannah Magazine.

Thomas, E. E. (2019). *The dark fantastic: Race and the imagination from Harry Potter to The Hunger Games*. NYU Press.

Walker, A. (1983). *In search of our mother's gardens*. Harcourt.

Winn, M. T. (2013). Toward a restorative English education. *Research in the Teaching of English, 48*(1), 126–135.

COMPANION 3
FICTIONALIZING THE
RESEARCH LITERATURE

S. R. Toliver

It took me a while to decide on a title for this chapter. The introduction chapter included aspects of my research findings, but it still introduced the reader to the world located within the text. The second chapter included information about the research context as well as my positionality, but it predominantly focused on the theoretical underpinnings guiding this work. This chapter, however, was much more convoluted because it expands the theory, incorporates the literature review, and includes the methods. It covers a lot, and because of this, I didn't feel comfortable just calling the chapter a literature review. Because it expands much of the work, however, I thought "Expanding the Literature" would be appropriate. I highlight this point to reiterate that all aspects of the research—the theoretical or conceptual framework, the literature review, the analytic process, the findings—work together to create the story. Said another way, all parts of the research endeavor exist as a part of the commonweal; they cannot be severed from one another because doing so would disrupt the balance. To dream otherwise in qualitative research means to consider how alternative sites of research require alternative methods of thinking about the divisions created in traditional research documents.

The research

Info–dumping is a technique used by many science fiction writers, as there must be some way for writers to condense scientific subject matter into the world of the fictional text. It often fits uneasily into a science fiction work, but it's necessary to ensure that the reader knows the information and facts behind a character, setting, or plot choice. One way to dump info on the reader is to include an uninformed newcomer who must learn how something works and have that character talk to a more knowledgeable character. In many ways, I consider an info–dump to be a form of literature review, as the researcher attempts to analyze and synthesize relevant literature in hopes to explain the information and facts behind the creation of a study. From this line of thinking, Chapter 3 can be classified as an info-dump chapter, as Jane consistently asks questions about the Harbor and a more knowledgeable character is readily available to respond to her queries. Of course, there are many critiques of info-dumping, as some creative writers will argue that it stilts the progression of the story. What I appreciate, though, is that many science fiction authors info-dump anyway.

In the chapter, Jane first asks questions about Afrofuturism—what it is and how it guides the Harbor. As I mention in the preface, I define Afrofuturism as a cultural aesthetic in which Black authors create speculative texts that center Black characters in an effort to reclaim and recover the past, counter negative, and elevate positive realities that exist in the present and create new possibilities for the future. I created this definition after conducting a literature review (Toliver, 2021) on how public and academic scholars defined Afrofuturism. I published this literature review on my site, ReadingBlackFutures.com, for those who are interested, but I'll briefly summarize the findings. Public scholars argued that Afrofuturism reclaims the past to imagine a future (Fitzpatrick, 2018; Giles, 2018), combats oppression (Latief, 2018; Staples, 2018), and envisions new, utopic worlds (Dozier, 2018; McKnight-Abrams, 2018). Academic scholars contended that Afrofuturism combats dystopic realities (Allen, 2017; Lavender, 2007), reclaims and recovers lost histories (Faucheux & Lavender, 2018; Yaszek, 2013), and addresses diverse issues (Davis, 2018; Morris, 2016). I represent my definition and the literature review in a short conversation between Jane and Erin.

After learning from Erin, Jane comes in contact with the head librarian of the Harbor, Edi.

She asks Edi to help her figure out the ideals that guide the Harbor, and she specifically asks for more information about how the Harbor honors everyday people, centralizes collective well-being, and allows an unencumbered way of thinking. Thus, she wants to learn more about womanism. Rather than exclusively giving Jane information about womanism, however, Edi also includes scholarship on Black feminism. I did this because I see womanism and Black feminism as sisters (Phillips, 2006), and I thought it was important for Jane to have an understanding of both.

As Jane walks through the Harbor, she notices these theories in action. Following Walker's (1983) definition of womanism, Jane sees Endarkened people who truly love the women around them; who appreciate women's culture, emotional flexibility, and strength; who are committed to the survival of all who inhabit the space and all who do not; and who are dedicated to nurturing a connectivity between humanity and spirituality. Following Black feminist thought (Collins, 2000), Jane sees Black women using their lived experiences as credible sources of knowledge, engaging in communal dialogue as a way to create new knowledge, and utilizing emotion and care as essential to their existence. As she wanders around the Harbor, Jane witnesses what "the optimization of well-being for all members of a community" (Phillips, 2006, xxv) might look like.

As womanism begins with Black women and girls and other women of color and then branches out to other minoritized groups, Edi also tells Jane about the importance of centering Black girls in the Harbor. Edi acknowledges that Black women have been marginalized in social justice discussions, but she states that their status as adults has granted them more prominence in social discourse, specifically in writing. Award-winning Black female authors like Octavia Butler, Toni Morrison, and Alice Walker "use[d] their knowledge production to reshape the Black body...in social discourse and to create new ideological and social terrain in which Black bodies (and the Black people inhabiting them) could safely exist" (Cooper, 2017, unpaged). They used their political, social, and economic experiences to create literature that enabled them to inscribe themselves as subjects, rather than objects, naming themselves in a world determined to confine them to a "fungible existence" (Cherry-McFaniel, 2017, p. 42; Smith, 1978). Thus, by writing about their lives, their experiences, their hopes, and their dreams, Black women have been able to critique social oppression and challenge dominant discourses that attempt to silence or misrepresent them (Muhammad, 2015a; Rooks, 1989). Black girls, however, are not often afforded that privilege. Instead, Black girls' stories and dreams are often voiced by others. Adults are the authors of stories and research on Black girls, and although Black girls are included, their voices are often muted behind the words of others.

After Jane reads the texts Edi gives her, she starts to see Black girl literacies research in action. Specifically, she notices that some Endarkened people explore who they are and connect their lived realities to larger oppressions in the world (see Haas Dyson, 1995; Henry, 1998; Muhammad & McArthur, 2015; Stornaiuolo & Whitney, 2018), while others center their unique identity positions (see Edwards, 2005; Henry, 2001; Wissman, 2011). She learns how Endarkened people have historically challenged stereotypes (see Brooks et al., 2008; Fordham, 1993; Jacobs, 2016; Richardson, 2013). She observes how other Endarkened people work to define themselves (see Brooks et al., 2010; Ellison & Kirkland, 2014; Hall, 2011; Hinton-Johnson, 2004). She sees Endarkened people using their writing to make societal change (see Brown et al., 2018; Fisher et al., 2016; Muhammad & Womack, 2015). Just like womanism, Jane sees Black girl literacies research at the forefront of the Harbor's daily operations.

The last major question Jane asks concerns how Black girls have used writing to combat GC and how Jane can help. Gholdy answers her first question by starting with the history. In her conversation, she notes that Endarkened women have always engaged in numerous tactics to create a socially just world. She mentions Othermother ancestors to show the robustness of the Harbor network. These Othermothers are based on Chicana writers, like Moraga (2011), Anzaldúa (1987), and Castillo (1994) who provided a combination of nonfiction essays, fictional prose, and poetry to address the ways in which Chicana scholars eviscerate boundaries in an effort to further understand their fluid and complex identities.

The Othermothers are also based on Indigenous scholars, like LaDuke (2005) and Tuck (Tuck & Yang, 2012) who challenged settler colonialism and used their writing to promote Indigenous knowledge and theorizing in education (Tuck, 2009). Further, she includes Asian Othermothers, like Fujiwara (2018) and Yamada (2015) who wrote against the erasure of Asian people in the United States and in feminist research. Lastly, she includes Black Othermothers, like Assata Shakur (1987), Moya Bailey and Trudy (2018), and Audre Lorde (1984), to showcase how they refused to focalize one aspect of their identity, refused to accept gendered violence against Black women and girls, and refused to submit to societal surveillance. With this history given, Gholdy notes that there is little information about how or if Black girls mimic or differ from Black women's writing practices (Muhammad, 2015b), but she knows it is important to consider them because Black girls are committing brave acts of self-empowerment, and readers are empowered every time they listen.

After these conversations, Jane is able to expand her thinking. She realizes that Endarkened people communicate through story, silence and speech manipulation, signifying, singing, dancing, acting, stepping, styling, crafting, and creating (Richardson, 2002). She understands how Black women have consistently been silenced and how our knowledge is constantly ignored or erased, but still we push on and strive to ensure that our voices are heard. The most important realization she has, however, resides in the fact that she and all the Endarkened people are dreamers. Imarisha (2015) stated that "whenever we try to envision a world without war, without violence, without prisons, without capitalism, we are engaging in speculative fiction" (p. 3). Gholdy references this idea and tells Jane that she has always been a dreamer, and no amount of extraction, erasure, or silencing can completely remove her dreams. From this, Jane realizes that every time an Endarkened person fights for their future, they are engaging in dreaming. Jane has been dreaming all along.

The workshop

The writing workshop took place at Deep Center, a nonprofit writing program in the southeastern United States. Deep Center was founded in 2008 as a program that uses creative writing, cultural production, and art to assist Savannah's young people to flourish as community leaders, learners, and change agents (Deep Center, 2021). I chose this site because of the relationship I had established with the center and because the Black girls who agreed to participate in the study would already be a part of Deep Center's extended writing community. Having a Black communal space is essential for Black women and girls' self-affirmation and growth (Muhammad & Haddix, 2016) and for developing strategies of resistance (Collins, 2000). So, it was vital to have a space where the girls could feel comfortable enough to have important, but possibly difficult discussions, and it was important for the girls to have a space where they felt safe enough to share their dreams. I wanted to include information about the context for the study, so I represented Deep Center's programs through the inclusion of Kenny and Trinity's writing groups in the Harbor's library.

The real world

In this chapter, the real world seems to fall away, as Jane is in the Harbor, an underground world that is intentionally different from the real world. However, to create a world that is drastically different from the real one, I had to look into the everyday realities of this world. I had to think about the capitalist structures that confine our existence, the racism that continuously results in violence against Endarkened people, and the disruption of Endarkened healing spaces by well-meaning allies. Analyzing these aspects of the world helped me to imagine something different. What would it be like if capitalism was erased from society? What would it be like if Endarkened people had a safe place to exist, free from the surveillance of our bodies? What would it be like if we were given space to heal before being forced to work with others? I considered these questions as I created the Harbor.

In looking into the everyday realities of this world, I began to think more about muted group theory (MGT) (Ardener, 2006; Kramarae, 2009; Orbe, 1998). A discussion of MGT could be included in the research section of this companion chapter, but I want to acknowledge how people with minoritized identities *are* silenced in the real world. In coining the theory, Ardener (2006) articulated that a society defined by dominant groups—including white, male, and adult—mutes or erases the experiences of nondominant groups by silencing their voices, overlooking their realities, and positing the group as "mere black holes in someone else's universe" (p. 63). Muted groups exist in any society that includes unbalanced power relationships (Orbe, 1998), and it is a theory that attempts to highlight oppressive communication structures. Specifically, MGT suggests that people assigned to minoritized groups,

> may have a lot to say, but in mixed situations they may have little power to say it without getting into trouble. Their words (and interests and work), unless presented in a form acceptable to those in dominant groups … The speech of those in subordinate groups is often disrespected, and their knowledge often not considered sufficient for decision or policy making. Their experiences are often reinterpreted for them by others, and they are encouraged to see themselves as represented by the words and concepts in the dominant discourse (Kramarae, 2009, p. 669).

Black girls' voices have often been muted in our society (Fordham, 1993), but Boylorn (2013) noted that Black women and girls use communication and language to make themselves relevant and to build connections to people with shared life experiences despite numerous attempts to silence them. In this way, she acknowledged that the goal of the theory is not only to address how popular discourse silences nondominant groups but also to examine how muted groups use verbal and nonverbal communication to make their voices heard.

In the real world, dominant groups attempt to control the methods of communication, which allows them to control and often create the structures that confine our beliefs, values, and norms. Those whose voices dominate society are always able to present their ideas, but Endarkened people are often muted. I represent MGT through GC's controlling mechanisms, showcasing how GC silences Endarkened voices, overlooks their realities, and positions them as unimportant bodies who take up space in their dreamer-centric universe (Ardener, 2006). To create the Harbor, I wanted to resist this muting. I had to consider what it would be like for Endarkened people to have the freedom to speak out against oppression without fear that they will experience violence.

The personal

The methods section of any research study is supposed to describe what was done, justify the research, and explain how the data were analyzed. I describe my analytic process at the beginning of this book, but in this chapter, I demonstrate what I was thinking when I created the workshop upon which this story is based. I wanted to provide a clearer connection between the creation of the workshop and the womanist influences that undergirded its creation. I also wanted to acknowledge my thoughts about working with young Black girls as an adult Black woman because I was situated in an insider–outsider position (Merriam et al., 2001). Yes, I am a Black woman who loves speculative fiction, but my identity as an adult and my positionality as a researcher and observer differed from the girls' identities, and I had to contend with that difference. Through Jane's thoughts about the construction of an Afrofuturistic workshop for Black girls, the reader is offered a glimpse into my thoughts behind the actual workshop.

There are a few other personal touches in this chapter. My sister's name is Erin, and although she is not a speculative fiction nerd like me, I can always count on her to extend my thinking. She is brilliant, and when she is asked about a subject that really interests her, she can talk for quite a while. I wanted to show this relationship by having her explain Afrofuturism to Jane. Edi is a character based on real-life scholar Edith Campbell who is an associate education librarian in the Cunningham Memorial Library at Indiana State University. I admire her work on Black children's literature, and I learn so much from her articles, so I wanted to include her as someone who is consistently teaching me. Lastly, although I could have had Jane learn from any Othermother, I wanted her to do some unlearning with Ebony, who is based on real-life scholar and educator, Ebony Elizabeth Thomas. I admire Ebony's work, and I am forever indebted to her mentorship. Every time I read one of her articles or engage her in conversation, I realize I have so much more unlearning to do. Including these amazing Black women in the chapter was a way for me to pay homage to them for always pushing me to think more deeply about the world, about speculative fiction, and about myself.

References

Allen, M. D. (2017). Kindred spirits: The speculative fictions of Pauline E. Hopkins, Octavia E. Butler, and Tananarive Due. *CLA Journal, 61*(1–2), 95–108.

Anzaldúa, G. (1987). *Borderlands/la frontera: The new mestiza.* Aunt Lute Books.

Ardener, E. (2006). Belief and the problem of women and the 'problem' revisited. In E. Lewin (Ed.), *Feminist anthropology: A reader* (pp. 47–65). Blackwell Publishing.

Bailey, M., & Trudy. (2018). On misogynoir: Citation, erasure, and plagiarism. *Feminist Media Studies, 18*(4), 762–768. https://doi.org/10.1080/14680777.2018.1447395.

Boylorn, R. (2013). *Sweetwater: Black women and narratives of resistance.* Peter Lang.

Brooks, W., Browne, S., & Hampton, G. (2008). "There ain't no accounting for what folks see in their own mirrors": Considering colorism within a Sharon Flake narrative. *Journal of Adolescent & Adult Literacy, 51*(8), 660–669.

Brooks, W., Sekayi, D., Savage, L., Waller, E., & Picot, I. (2010). Narrative significations of contemporary Black girlhood. *Research in the Teaching of English, 45*(1), 7–35.

Brown, R. N., Smith, B. E., Robinson, J. L., & Garner, P. R. (2018). Doing digital wrongly. *American Quarterly, 70*(3), 395–416.

Castillo, A. (1994). *Massacre of the dreamers: Essays on Xicanisma.* University of New Mexico Press.

Cherry-McFaniel, M. (2017). #WOKE: Employing Black textualities to create critically conscious classrooms. *English Journal, 106*(4), 41–46.

Collins, P. H. (2000). *Black feminist thought: Knowledge, consciousness, and the politics of empowerment.* Routledge.

Cooper, B. (2017). *Beyond respectability: The intellectual thought of race women.* University of Illinois Press.

Davis, J. A. (2018). Power and vulnerability: BlackGirlMagic in Black women's science fiction. *Journal of Science Fiction, 2*(2), 13–30.

Deep Center. (2021). *Our Story.* https://www.deepcenter.org/about/our-mission/.

Dozier, R. (2018). *Four thoughts on the future of Afrofuturism.* The Outline. https://theoutline.com/post/4978/what-is-the-future-of-afrofuturism?zd=1&zi=culensa5.

Edwards, D. (2005). "Doing hair" and literacy in an afterschool reading and writing workshop for African-American adolescent girls. *Afterschool Matters,* (4), 42–50.

Ellison, T. L., & Kirkland, D. E. (2014). Motherboards, microphones and metaphors: Re-examining new literacies and Black feminist thought through technologies of self. *E-Learning and Digital Media, 11*(4), 390–405.

Faucheux, A., & Lavender, I. (2018). Tricknology: Theorizing the trickster in Afrofuturism. *Journal of Science Fiction, 2*(2), 31–46.

Fisher, M. T., Purcell, S. S., & May, R. (2016). Process, product, and playmaking. *English Education, 41*(4), 337–355.

Fitzpatrick, A. (2018). *It's not just black panther. Afrofuturism is having a moment.* Time. http://time.com/5246675/black-panther-afrofuturism/.

Fordham, S. (1993). "Those loud Black girls": (Black) women, silence, and gender "passing" in the academy. *Anthropology & Education Quarterly, 24*(1), 3–32.

Fujiwara, L. (2018). Multiplicity, women of color politics, and Asian American feminist praxis. In L. Fujiwara, & S. Roshanravan (Eds.), *Asian American feminisms and women of color politics* (pp. 241–261). University of Washington Press.

Giles, C. (2018). *Afrofuturism: The genre that made black panther.* CNN. https://www.cnn.com/2018/02/12/africa/genre-behind-black-panther-afrofuturism/index.html.

Haas Dyson, A. (1995). The courage to write: Child meaning making in a contested world. *Language Arts, 72*(5), 324–333.

Hall, T. (2011). Designing from their own social worlds: The digital story of three African American young women. *English Teaching, 10*(1), 7–20.

Henry, A. (1998). "Invisible" and "Womanish": Black girls negotiating their lives in an African-centered school in the USA (a). *Race Ethnicity and Education, 1*(2), 151–170.

Henry, A. (2001). The politics of unpredictability in a reading/writing/discussion group with girls from the Caribbean. *Theory into Practice, 40*(3), 184–189.

Hinton-Johnson, K. M. (2004). African American mothers & daughters: Socialization, distance, & conflict. *The ALAN Review, 31*(3), 45–49.

Imarisha, W. (2015). Introduction. In A. Brown, & W. Imarisha (Eds.), *Octavia's brood: Science fiction stories from social justice movements* (pp. 3–6). AK Press.

Jacobs, C. E. (2016). Developing the "oppositional gaze": Using critical media pedagogy and Black feminist thought to promote Black girls' identity development. *The Journal of Negro Education, 85*(3), 225–238.

Kramarae, C. (2009). Muted group theory. In S. W. Littlejohn, & K. A. Foss (Eds.), *Encyclopedia of communication theory* (Vol. 1, pp. 668–669). SAGE Publications, Inc.

LaDuke, W. (2005). *Recovering the sacred: The power of naming and claiming.* South End Press.

Latief, J. (2018). *Looking to Afrofuturism 3.0.* Design Indaba. http://www.designindaba.com/articles/creative-work/looking-afrofuturism-30.

Lavender, I. (2007). Ethnoscapes: Environment and language in Ishmael Reed's Mumbo Jumbo, Colson Whitehead's The Intuitionist, and Samuel R. Delaney's Babel-17. *Science Fiction Studies, 34*(2), 187–200.

Lorde, A. (1984). Age, race, class, and sex: Women redefining difference. In *Sister outsider: Essays and speeches* (pp. 17–32). Crossing Press.

McKnight-Abrams, A. (2018). *The new Afrofuturism.* VICE. https://garage.vice.com/en_us/article/437wq3/the-new-afrofuturism.

Merriam, S. B., Johnson-Bailey, J., Lee, M., Kee, Y., Ntseane, G., & Muhamad, M. (2001). Power and positionality: Negotiating insider/outsider status within and across cultures. *International Journal of Lifelong Education, 20*(5), 405–416.

Moraga, C. (2011). *A Xicana codex of changing consciousness—Writings 2000–2010.* Duke University Press.

Morris, S. (2016). More than human: Black feminisms of the future in Jewelle Gomez's The Gilda Stories. *The Black Scholar, 46*(2), 33–45.

Muhammad, G. E. (2015a). The role of literary mentors in writing development: How African American women's literature supported the writings of adolescent girls. *Journal of Education, 195*(2), 5–14.

Muhammad, G. (2015b). Searching for full vision: Writing representations of African American adolescent girls. *Research in the Teaching of English, 49*(3), 224–247.

Muhammad, G. E., & Haddix, M. (2016). Centering Black girls' literacies: A review of literature on the multiple ways of knowing of Black girls. *English Education, 48*(4), 299–336.

Muhammad, G. E., & McArthur, S. A. (2015). "Styled by their perceptions": Black adolescent girls interpret representations of Black females in popular culture. *Multicultural Perspectives, 17*(3), 133–140.

Muhammad, G. E., & Womack, E. (2015). From pen to pin: The multimodality of Black girls (re)writing their lives. *Ubiquity: The Journal of Literature, Literacy, and the Arts, 2*(2), 6–45.

Orbe, M. (1998). From the standpoints of traditionally muted groups: Explicating a co-cultural communication theoretical method. *Communication Theory, 8*(1), 1–26.

Phillips, L. (2006). *The womanist reader.* Taylor & Francis.

Richardson, E. (2002). "To protect and serve": African American female literacies. *College Composition and Communication, 53*(4), 675–704.

Richardson, E. (2013). Developing critical hip hop feminist literacies: Centrality and subversion of sexuality in the lives of Black girls. *Equity and Excellence in Education, 46*(3), 327–341.

Rooks, N. (1989). Writing themselves into existence: The intersection of history and literature in writings on Black women. *Iowa Journal of Literary Studies, 10*(1), 51–63.

Shakur, A. (1987). *Assata: An autobiography*. Zed Books, Ltd.

Smith, B. (1978). Toward a Black feminist criticism. *The Radical Teacher*, (7), 20–27.

Staples, B. (2018). *The Afrofuturism behind 'black panther'*. The New York Times. https://www.nytimes.com/2018/02/24/opinion/afrofuturism-behind-black-panther.html.

Stornaiuolo, A., & Whitney, E. H. (2018). Writing as worldmaking. *Language Arts, 95*(4), 205–216.

Toliver, S. R. (2021). Defining Afrofuturism. In *Reading black futures*. https://readingblackfutures.com/defining-afrofuturism/.

Tuck, E. (2009). Suspending damages. *Harvard Educational Review, 79*(3), 409–428.

Tuck, E., & Yang, K. (2012). Decolonization is not a metaphor. *Decolonization: Indigeneity, Education & Society, 1*(1), 1–40.

Walker, A. (1983). *In search of our mother's gardens*. Harcourt.

Wissman, K. (2011). "Rise up!": Literacies, lived experiences, and identities within an in-school "other space." *Research in the Teaching of English, 45*(4), 405–438.

Yamada, M. (2015). Invisibility is an unnatural disaster: Reflections of an Asian American woman. In C. Moraga, & G. Anzaldua (Eds.), *This bridge called my back: Writings by radical women of color*. State University of New York Press.

Yaszek, L. (2013). Race in science fiction: The case of Afrofuturism and new Hollywood. In *A virtual introduction to science fiction*. http://virtual-sf.com/wp-content/uploads/2013/08/Yaszek.pdf.

COMPANION 4
THE RESEARCH PARTNERS

S. R. Tooliver

This companion chapter accompanies Chapters 4–10 because the collection of chapters most closely aligns with traditional findings sections. In conventional research, the findings present the results of the study in a supposedly objective way without interpretation. The discussion section follows and is the space in which the researcher interprets the findings, connects it to the theoretical framework and research literature, and describes the significance of the results. Endarkened storywork rejects the upliftment of objectivity. It is impossible to present information without interpretation because the researcher's analysis of the data is essential to the creation of the story's foundation. The researcher engages with the stories of their research partners by becoming a story listener, interpreting the stories for themselves, and finding synergy between the stories and their own personal stories. In this way, objectivity cannot exist.

To align with this idea, my voice is diminished within these chapters, although not completely. I needed to create ample narrative space for the girls' stories to be told. Because of this, there is a lot more dialogue in these chapters, where the girls are just conversing with each other and telling the collective stories of their lives. I add small details to denote movement and mannerisms, but I don't engage in the same form of reflection present in the other chapters. This may seem like a genre shift, especially because the previous chapters contain a lot more of Jane's thoughts, but I lessen my interpretation of the girls' stories within these chapters to make space for readers to become better story listeners, to ask readers to find connections between their own lives and the lives of the girls whose stories they are blessed to read in these chapters. By centering the girls' collective and individual talk as well as their speculative fiction stories, I ask readers to read their stories and make their own reflections, rather than relying on Jane/me to make reflections for them.

The research

Findings sections may include research, but the major focus of those sections is on the results. I model that in this chapter, as research is often used to support Jane's thinking around the girls' conversations. For instance, I noted how the girls' stories and conversations showcased a reading of the word and the world, alluding to Freire and Macedo's (1987) work. I also discussed the importance of centering the girls' genius, an idea that is integral to the work of Muhammad (2019). After the girls discuss their schooling experiences in Chapter 5, Jane thinks about her own experiences dealing with arbitrary dress code rules and surveillance. Specifically, I consider how teachers often focus on Black girls' social decorum rather than their academic triumphs by thinking about the work of Carter (2006), Fordham (1993), and Morris (2007). I also consider how Black girls are overpoliced and surveilled by considering the work of Wissman (2007) and Fisher et al. (2016). The works of these scholars were essential to my thinking, as I connected the girls' experiences to the larger experiences of Black girls in the United States. Another example is shown as I'm grappling with some of the girls' statements. For instance, when the girls talk about wanting to leave the United States for safe havens elsewhere, I thought about the fact that anti-Blackness is a worldly endeavor (Sexton & Copeland, 2003). Essentially, I considered research mentioned in the previous chapters to think through conversations represented within this chapter.

The workshop

There were several small touches I included to connect to the workshop and the girls' stories. For example, in the story, I noted the use of pen and paper for writing because we didn't have consistent access to computers in the library, as many Savannah residents used those computers throughout the day. I mention that the girls called themselves "the Alfredas," a name they chose based on a running joke that began on the second day of the workshop. I use pseudonyms the girls chose for themselves to represent the focus on naming exemplified in the girls' conversations with each other. In addition to the small touches, I made sure the words presented in quotation marks were almost exactly aligned with the words the girls said within the workshop. I only made changes to ensure clarity and continuity in the story. For example, if someone said teacher or principal, I changed it to observer or head observer. If they said police, I changed it to enforcer. I also changed the verb tense from present to past tense to portray the idea that their schooling experiences happened before they arrived in the Harbor. I made this choice because the girls often noted the distinctions between our workshop space and their experiences in traditional classrooms. Last, I changed some speech to more align with the storied format, so some of the interruptions and word choices were changed, so they could be smoothly incorporated into the story. These changes were necessary to align with the story while still ensuring that the meanings behind the girls' words were left whole.

It's also important to note that the stories included within these chapters did not come from one transcript or workshop meeting. Instead, I took various conversations from the whole of the workshop and found ways to meaningfully put them together. For example, in the girls' individual chapters (Chapters 5–11), there are conversations from the workshop, from interviews, and from writing. I interweave all of them to expand on the girls' backstories and help readers further understand the girls' speculative stories. Another example is shown in Chapter 5, where multiple conversations are presented that occurred between the girls and me. I took various conversations and entwined them to create a cohesive set of conversations that would give readers a glimpse into our everyday conversation practices. In this way, I ensured that the girls spoke for themselves. The main character adds small details of interpretation throughout, but Jane's voice is not important here. What's important is that readers hear the stories and listen to the experiences of Black girls in their own words without someone else attempting to consistently interpret what they say.

At points, the conversation jumps may feel disorienting to readers, but I made that stylistic choice to match the real-life flow of conversation in the workshop. We never stayed on one topic for long because something one girl said would cause another girl to make a connection to something completely different or tangentially similar. I wanted to preserve this conversation style because it was real. It was how we engaged in community building, and to take out this aspect of our conversations would be a disservice to the ways that everyday Black girls sometimes engage in dialogue. Another element I tried to preserve was the focus of many of our conversations. Specifically, the girls often discussed issues within the US schooling system, namely, testing, unfair punishment, and teachers or administrators who didn't listen to student needs. Ultimately, the conversations provide a look into the lives and experiences of Black girls, while also showing their ideas about social in/justice.

The real world

The real world seeps into the girls' conversations because they are talking about authentic experiences and grappling with real-life issues that were happening in the world around them. For example, the girls often discussed issues relevant to the queer community. In the story, I include a discussion we had about the straight pride flag in which the girls critiqued the flag and the people who think it is necessary for the flag to exist. As two of the girls identified as bisexual (Victoria and Terrah), one girl identified as pansexual (Talyn), and the other girls defined themselves as allies to the LGBTQ+ community; this was an important issue to include. Their conversations showcase how the real world was consistently on their minds and how they used the workshop space to openly have those conversations and voice their opinions.

In addition to real-world issues that affected their lives, they also included conversations about their interests, activities that could be considered weird, nerdy, or dorky. For instance, Bailey discussed her love of anime by talking about *Tokyo Ghoul* (Mikasano, 2014), *Attack on Titan* (Kobayashi & Seko, 2013–2021), *Fairy Tail* (Sogo, 2009–2019), *My Hero Academia* (Kuroda, 2016–present), and *Noragami* (Akao, 2014). She also mentioned that she drew inspiration for her horror story from the plot of *Sword Art Online* (Kawahara, 2012–present), a popular anime series where characters get stuck in a virtual reality game, and Five Nights at Freddy's, an indie video game set in a fictional pizza restaurant that is haunted by homicidal animatronic characters. Victoria mentioned a love for speculative fiction by discussing an interest in the *Harry Potter, Star Wars*, and *Hobbit* franchises. She also drew story inspiration from *The Princess Diaries* (Marshall, 2001), *Twitches* (Gillard, 2005), and *Grey's Anatomy* (Rhimes, 2005–present). Talyn drew inspiration from various texts. Although she didn't remember the name, based on her description, I identified that her story was inspired by *All Quiet on the Western Front* (Remarque, 1929). It was also created by thinking about the powers wielded by characters in *Avatar: The Last Airbender* (Ehasz, 2005–2008) and *Fairy Tail*. Furthermore, when she asks the girls for name recommendations, she describes the character as "plastic," which refers to a materialistic person and is a term made popular after the movie, *Mean Girls* (Waters, 2004), was released. Essentially real-world issues and pop culture references were essential to the creation of the girls' stories.

The personal

As I mentioned earlier, Jane's comments represent my thoughts about the girls' experiences, lives, and stories. There are instances where Jane talks about her writing with the girls to represent the fact that I wrote alongside them during the workshop, and there are several instances of Jane thinking about the girls' conversations. In this section, however, readers will notice that although Jane is still present, she takes a backseat in these chapters. I wanted Jane to take the same position that I took as the workshop progressed. Yes, I made plans for the workshop tasks and writing activities, but as I stated in the opening chapter, even with those plans in place, the girls often ruled that space. When we talked about character, plot, setting, and conflict, I didn't present myself as the be all and end all to knowledge. I asked them about their thoughts and ideas about those terms. When we wrote together, I didn't ask them to write silently until they were done. We talked while we wrote. I wanted to represent these processes within the story, but I also wanted to consider the idea that the researcher is not the definitive voice of interpretation. I do present some of my musings within the girl's individual chapters, but I wanted to ensure readers could also interpret the stories for themselves. The work of story requires readers to make their own connections, not just rely on specifics detailed by the storyteller.

References

Akao, D. (2014). *Noragami* [TV Series]. Bones.

Carter, S. P. (2006). "She would've still made that face expression": The use of multiple literacies by two African American young women. *Theory Into Practice, 45*(4), 352–358.

Ehasz, A. (Head Writer). (2005–2008). *Avatar: The Last Airbender [TV series]*. Nickelodeon Animation Studio.

Fisher, M. T., Purcell, S. S., & May, R. (2016). Process, product, and playmaking. *English Education,* 41(4), 337–355.

Fordham, S. (1993). "Those loud Black girls": (Black) women, silence, and gender "passing" in the academy. *Anthropology & Education Quarterly, 24*(1), 3–32.

Freire, P., & Macedo, D. (1987). *Literacy: Reading the word and the world.* Bergin.

Gillard, S. (Director). (2005). *Twitches [film]*. Buena Vista Television.

Kawahara, R. (2012–present). *Sword Art Online [TV series]*. A-1 Pictures.

Kobayashi, Y., & Seko, H. (2013–2021). *Attach on Titan [TV series]*. Wit Studio.

Kuroda, Y. (2016–present). *My Hero Academia [TV Series]*. Bones.

Marshall, G. (Director). (2001). *The Princess Diaries [film]*. Buena Vista Pictures.

Mikasano, C. (2014). *Tokyo Ghoul [TV series]*. Pierrot.

Morris, E. (2007). "Ladies" or "loudies"?: Perceptions and experiences of Black girls in classrooms. *Youth and Society, 38*(4), 490–515.

Muhammad, G. E. (2019). *Cultivating Genius: An Equity Framework for Culturally and Historically Responsive Literacy.* Scholastic.

Remarque, E. M. (1929). *All Quiet on the Western Front.* Dead Reckoning.

Rhimes, S. (Creator). (2005–present). *Grey's Anatomy [TV series]*. Buena Vista Television, Disney-ABC Domestic Television, Disney Platform Distribution.

Sexton, J., & Copeland, H. (2003). Raw life: An introduction. *Qui Parle, 13*(2), p. 53–62.

Sogo, M. (2009–2019). *Fairy Tail [TV series]*. A-1 Pictures.

Waters, M. (Director). (2004). *Mean Girls [film]*. Paramount Pictures.

Wissman, K. (2007). "Making a way": Young women using literacy and language to resist the politics of silencing. *Journal of Adolescent & Adult Literacy, 51*(4), 340–349.

COMPANION 5
CONCLUDING THE STORY

S. R. Toliver

Chapter 11 best aligns with the discussion and conclusion sections of traditional research studies. The discussion section is where the researcher describes the significance of the findings after considering what is already known about the research topic, and the conclusion section helps readers to understand why the research should matter to them after they have finished reading everything the researcher has written. Within the story, I attend to these ideas by showing how Jane is thinking through all she has learned from her experiences in the Harbor and by having her think about the next steps in her life. Rather than telling readers everything they should or could know about the findings, however, I interpret the parts that are essential for Jane's unlearning process. Of course, there is so much to unpack in the girls' oral and written stories, but I don't interpret them for readers because, as I've consistently stated, the goal of Endarkened storywork is not to interpret all aspects of the work for readers. Fiction allows for a connection that traditional research writing does not. If the researcher interprets everything for the reader, it presents the argument that there is nothing more to learn from the stories. Instead, Endarkened storywork ensures that readers have much to ponder long after the story ends.

The research

Although this chapter concludes the narrative, there is one research connection included. Specifically, as Jane is thinking about the girls' stories, she acknowledges that their interests in the speculative are those not normally attributed to Black girls. Various scholars have recognized that speculative fiction is primarily presented as a genre for white, middle class, heterosexual boys and men (Butler & Beal, 1986; Gatson & Reid, 2011; Toliver, 2018). Of course, just being primarily presented as such does not mean that it is an accurate portrayal of reality.

Florini (2019) stated that even though fandom is constructed as white, it assumes a significant role in Black communities as Black nerds, or Blerds, cultivate fan spaces that resist white nerdiness. In other words, even if speculative fiction is presented as white, there are numerous Black people and other folks of color resisting that narrowed construction. The girls are a part of that resisting group.

The workshop

I begin this chapter by combining responses to a question I asked in the final interview with each girl. I asked them what they thought about the workshop now that our time together was over. Their responses were gathered right after the workshop ended, before they read the completed fictional story that readers of this book are now experiencing. I included their responses to this question because although I think my interpretation of the workshop could be valuable to some readers, the girls' beliefs about the workshop are more important than my own.

The world

One real-world connection in this chapter is the creation of the Denman Chip. I used this term to pay homage to Mary Richards Denman, also known as Mary Elizabeth Bowser, who was a Union spy during the Civil War (Leveen, 2019). Denman's espionage was essential to the abolition of slavery, so I created the chip as a way to show that Endarkened people who are supported by Denman will be the ones who end GC's regime. Since Jane was going back to GC to be a spy for the Harbor network, I wanted to showcase the ways in which Black women have always engaged in tactics of subversion to ensure their freedom as well as the freedom of other Endarkened folks. Mary went by many names— Mary Bowser, Mary Denman, Mary Jane Richards, M.J.R. I chose one person with many names to represent the many real people who will be necessary in the fight against oppression. She was one woman, but the Endarkened and their co-conspirators are many.

As Jane thinks through her decision to be a spy, she has to grapple with the repercussions of her decision. Specifically, Jane must decide if it's worth it to return to the world of GC after spending time in a space of joy and freedom, especially since her return will inevitably be marred by the oppression that guides the day-to-day operations of GC. I have Jane ask this question because it is one that is important for people who work to create spaces of Endarkened joy. Does it make sense to leave a space of safety when Endarkened people are consistently surveilled and killed by those who are sworn to protect them? Should she eschew her security and protection to go out into a world where people are free to murder Endarkened people at will because their lives are rendered disposable? Jane is talking about leaving the Harbor, but many Endarkened researchers have to consider what it takes to truly do this work every single day. I wanted to put these questions out there because these are important questions to ask. Of course, Jane decides that it is most certainly worth it, but, as Layli notes, it's not for everyone. Everyone's journey is different, and that's okay.

The personal

In this chapter, I essentially write a discussion section that details how I am interpreting facets of the girls' stories. I write it as a conversation with the self, as Jane tries to interpret all she's (un)learned by working with the girls. Rather than spend too much time detailing these connections, however, I have Jane think about what she needs to do next. Her musings and conversations align with my own thoughts and discussions I've had with mentors. Specifically, where do I go from this research study? How do I create more Harbors throughout the United States? Do I want to go back to the world above and work in a GC-confined world, or do I keep creating spaces for Black girls to write their dreams in Endarkened enclaves? I use the metaphors from the book to describe my thinking because at the time of writing, I was thinking with these metaphors in mind.

Of course, Jane ultimately decides to return to GC because she knows that she can do good work up there, that she can be a Harbor spy and help Endarkened people throughout the United States. Endarkened scholars situated within the academy use their positions to assist Endarkened people both within and outside of the "ivory tower." I felt and feel like I could do the same, and I use Jane's narrative arc to portray that. I also know, however, that this work cannot be done alone because it's impossible to do so. This is why I break the fourth wall and ask readers if they will join Jane—join me—in creating dreaming spaces for Endarkened youth. In breaking this wall, my goal was to show readers that they have been engaging with a Black woman's diary the entire time. In the same way that Jane leaves her diary for the Othermothers, she has left this journal for other readers to learn, too. In a way, this is what so many books do, and my hope is that readers will engage with Black girls' stories as story listeners, learn from them, and create new Harbors so all Endarkened children can thrive and dream.

References

Butler, O., & Beal, F. (1986). Black women and the science fiction genre. *The Black Scholar*, *17*(2), 14–18.

Florini, S. (2019). Enclaving and cultural resonance in Black "Game of Thrones" fandom. *Transformative Works and Cultures*, *29*. https://doi.org/10.3983/twc.2019.1498

Gatson, S., & Reid, R. (2011). Race and ethnicity in fandom. *Transformative Works and Cultures*, *8*(1). https://doi.org/10.3983/twc.2011.0392.

Leveen, L. (2019, June 19). She was born into slavery, was a spy and is celebrated as a hero—but we're missing the point of the 'Mary Bowser' story. Time https://time.com/5609045/misremembering-mary-bowser/

Toliver, S. R. (2018). Imagining new hopescapes: Expanding Black girls' windows and mirrors. *Research on Diversity in Youth Literature 1*(3), 1–24.

AUTHOR'S NOTE

All stories are true.

   –John Edgar Wideman

   When I first read that statement by John Edgar Wideman, I couldn't figure out what he meant. In school, I learned there was fiction and nonfiction. Nonfiction was based on facts, real events, and real people. In other words, nonfiction was based on truth. Fiction, however, was not. It was based on imaginary events, fanciful dreams, and extraordinary tales. Those stories could not be true. How could they be? However, once I sat down and grappled with that statement, I figured out what Wideman meant. All stories contain elements of truth; that truth just shows up in different ways—in characters, in settings, in metaphorical renderings of the current times.

   The story that you read is true, as it includes details from the Afrofuturist workshop, theory and research from scholarly articles, events and people from the real world, and aspects of my personal life story. It is my way of embracing the communal connections cultivated by my foremothers, a way to remember what traditional schooling forced me to forget. It is a way to bring life back to my research and recover Anansi for future scholars who dare to dream.

   In the preface, I talk about the Eurocentricity of traditional qualitative methods and how I'd forgotten the work of story. Through this book, however, I refuse and remember. I refuse scholarship that uplifts research participants as bounded individuals. I remember Afrofuturist technologies and the intergenerational feedback loop that connects Black folx across past, present, and future. I refuse the valorization of objectivity. I remember my life and my ancestors and how they both influence my thinking and being. I refuse the centering of Eurocentric methods. I remember to center and uplift Black storytelling.

   Of course, I acknowledge that Endarkened storywork will not be accepted by everyone, that some will try to negate my refusal and block my remembrance.

Some will say this work isn't rigorous enough, and others will say it lacks the structure and rigidity of true scholarship. After years of believing I wasn't cut out for this academic world, however, I realize that I'm not bound by those ideals, by inflexible standards created before Black folx were welcome in academe. I realize that true scholarship doesn't have to yield to whiteness. My ancestors used Anansi stories to describe, analyze, and investigate the world around them. They used story as research method. They made space for broad research methodologies that weren't limited by the confines of contemporary qualitative research. In this way, they prepared space for me to thrive well before modern academia existed.

In all honesty, I have no idea where this work will go from here, as my story is still being written. What I do know is that Afrofuturity is qualitative futurity. Black stories, Black theories and methods, and Black people aren't going anywhere. Our Harbors already exist, pushing against forgetfulness. Our Othermothers and sibs are waiting for us to be willing to unlearn with them. In community, we will continue to remember the theories and methods we've been asked/forced to forget and make space for them to exist in higher education and beyond. In the commonweal, we'll create balance, so future scholars do not feel forced to cleave themselves from their histories in order to "make it" in academia.

To future scholars who wish to create anew—through story, through song, through dance, through speech, through qualitative method—know that I am rooting for you. Anansi brought stories to the world. He used his cunning to thwart those who were bigger and stronger than him. He faced gods and won. If he can do that, we can surely look academia square in the face and tell the stories Anansi fought for. I dream alongside you in the Afrofuture, where Black thought and Black people are thriving. I see the unseen of academia and hope for a future where all are willing to unlearn. I write this text to prepare a place for you, to create a speculative map that might lead you to the Harbors you seek. I tell this story, so we can continue to refuse, remember, and revolutionize until qualitative methods finally catch up to what our ancestors knew from the very beginning. Find your Octavia Butler. Find your maps. Follow your dreams. Tell your truths.

This is my story which I have related. If it be sweet, or if it be not sweet, take some elsewhere, and let some come back to me.